Dark Ideas

Dark Ideas

How Neo-Nazi and Violent Jihadi Ideologues Shaped Modern Terrorism

Travis Morris

LEXINGTON BOOKS
Lanham • Boulder • New York • London

Published by Lexington Books
An imprint of The Rowman & Littlefield Publishing Group, Inc.
4501 Forbes Boulevard, Suite 200, Lanham, Maryland 20706
www.rowman.com

Unit A, Whitacre Mews, 26-34 Stannary Street, London SE11 4AB

British Library Cataloguing in Publication Information Available

Library of Congress Cataloging-in-Publication Data Available
ISBN: 978-0-7391-9104-0 (cloth : alk. paper)

ISBN: 978-1-4985-4872-4 (pbk. : alk. paper)

ISBN: 978-1-4985-4872-4 (electronic)

♾™ The paper used in this publication meets the minimum requirements of American
National Standard for Information Sciences—Permanence of Paper for Printed Library
Materials, ANSI/NISO Z39.48-1992.

Printed in the United States of America

Contents

Introduction

There are two sides to every innovation. Innovation is a creative solution to a problem and is generally considered to be positive. However, innovation can also have another side. These types of innovations are perceived as "dark" because they are judged to be immoral, unjust, or counterculture. Human shields, female suicide bombers, and online recruitment of ISIS fighters are examples of "dark" innovations. A dismissive reaction to these and other actions can detract from labeling them as calculated innovations in asymmetric warfare. Classifying terrorism tactics and strategies as innovations in asymmetric warfare has nothing to do with moral assessment, but is rather a sterile diagnosis of what is occurring. Since terrorism is often defined as a tactic, it is critical to recognize tactical innovations, especially those that influence strategies. This perspective advances the way in which citizens, scholars, and government officials understand terrorism as they can diagnose when a "dark" innovation has altered the current modus operandi and solicit some form of prognosis that addresses both the action and idea.

Action and ideas are the two major components found in every act of terrorism. Actions involve physical characteristics and ideas are abstract. Despite the thousands upon thousands of violent actions that have occurred over the past one hundred years, the ideas that form the baseline for each incident are comparatively few. START's Global Terrorism Database[1] from the University of Maryland recorded some 16,818 terrorism incidents from around the globe in 2014.[2] The vast majority of these incidents are grounded in the same ideas and actions; only the variables differ. There are times when a new innovation enables something different to occur at a strategic or tactical level, though these are not common. An innovation is defined in this context as a new idea or transformation that alters the status quo. The phrase "dark idea" is used in this book to mark innovations used by violent extremists. Sometimes these innovations take the form of tactics, like using a suicide bomber instead of throwing grenades or the anarchists' assassinations of governmental leaders. Sometimes an innovation is strategic, such as the promotion of the neo-Nazi idea that one's race is also your religion or the adoption of a closed cell organizational structure. Although technological advances have transformed recruitment and radicalization practices and terrorism strategies have changed over time, terrorism doctrine, an act of violence or the threat of using violence for a cause greater than the incident has not changed from the Sicarii in Jerusalem during the first century to the anarchists in Barre, Vermont. What have evolved are the ideas that have taken terrorism down different strategic and tactical paths.

The purpose of this book is to provide an additional understanding of these paths. This book was written to address the following question: What are some of the most impactful terrorism innovations over the past sixty years? Albeit a comprehensive answer to this question is beyond the scope of this work, it is important to have a point from which to continue further examination. This is a critically important question to ask and answer because all social movements, both positive and negative, share moments of ingenuity and creativity. These moments are a response to the current context and intend to confront and resolve problems from an ideologue's point of view. Identifying and understanding these innovations advances terrorism studies beyond group or individual examination and into the realm of violent extremist doctrine that has been evolving for centuries. Additionally, the following questions about these "dark" innovations are equally significant because ideas, tactics, and strategies do not exist in a vacuum. Understanding the individuals and the context that surround each innovation asserts that both micro and macro-level views are to be treated with the same level of priority. Each chapter addresses each of these questions: (1) What is the origin of each innovation? (2) What is the context that surrounds each innovation? (3) How did they transition from idea to action?

Extremist ideologies differ on surface dimensions such as a group or individual's grievances, geographic location, organizational structures, or subcultural norms. However, despite surface differences, all violent extremists' objectives are organized around a single variable—a transition to power. How power is operationalized in a violent extremist's ideal world varies, but in the end, the goal is to have their ideology and way of seeing the world and living in it to have more impact than they do at the present time. Innovations are intended to advance the ideas and actions of an individual or group to power.

Ideas are the source from which all violent incidents originate. From this perspective violent incidents, propaganda, recruitment practices, and organizational structures are diagnostic tools to understand the ideas that fuel an individual or group. Ideologies, secular or religious, are designed to function as pathways to power. The longer an ideology endures, the more it requires innovations to remain relevant. Each innovation, across any group, aspires to advance an ideology and the people associated with it. Therefore, it is crucial to identify, examine, and understand which innovations have become normalized within violent extremist subcultures because those successful innovations reflect effectiveness.

This book supports the perspective that it is critical to understand violent extremist ideology, to realize that it is a rational way of interpreting the world to adherents, and to see that their worldview can become forceful enough that adherents will die to support it. When people are willing to die for their ideas, it should indicate the degree of the power behind it. In other words, minimizing or categorizing all violent extremists as psychologically delusional is not a useful approach if serious counterterrorism efforts are to be effective. This approach is often seen in the media and has at times found its way into the academic literature of the past, but is not productive, especially as educated recruits join violent extremist groups.

The following chapters highlight the importance of specific ideas, that they are the products of specific individuals (or groups) impacted by the culture and context. Understanding an idea and the person who created or advanced it affords the ability to observe how an idea emerged in its socio-ecological environment or "natural environment." This is imperative because violent extremist innovations originate from individuals who use their intellect to craft new pathways to lead others out of the current environment into more advantageous positions. Although a particular idea may take decades or hundreds of years to be fully implemented, innovations are evolutionary ideological work for they are the ideological response and adaptation to the current environment.

A comprehensive examination of all innovations within terrorism is beyond the scope of this text. A starting point begins with two ideological strains that are pressing social problems in 2016 and beyond. Innovations associated with neo-Nazism and violent jihadis are examined in order to understand how dark ideas have manifested themselves in the past five decades. Two ideologies that are selected as a comparative approach can demonstrate that despite differences, the goal of innovations across groups and time can be similar. Instead of looking at groups and ideologies in divergent pathways, innovations across movements can be used as a strategy to understand the conceptual and analytic tools that have been developed in the area of violent extremism.

Specific incidents are discussed in each chapter in order to provide examples of how ideas eventually morph into actions. The incident itself is not the focus, but rather it provides the opportunity to understand the relationship between an idea and action. The following two violent incidents illustrate how a group gains attention and publicizes itself and its ideology "effectively" by innovations in target selection. These two examples are labeled "effective" because their actions resulted in the president of the United States commenting on their actions and ideas.

EXECUTION STYLE VIOLENCE IN THE UNITED STATES AND LEVANT

On April 8, 2013, a violent jihadi group that had been carrying out military operations in Syria and Iraq proclaimed itself to be the Islamic State of Iraq and Syria (Levant).[3] The announcement did not produce much fanfare in the U.S. media at the time. Between April 2013 and August 2014 ISIS, IS, or Da'esh continued to carry out attacks, executions, and atrocities against civilians, specific religious ethnic sects, and captured militants across the Levant.[4] During this time, ISIS began to appear in the U.S. media because of their actions; the media attention, however, was disproportionate to the level of media attention given to the beheading of James Foley, a Wall Street journalist and freelance writer from New Hampshire captured in Syria.

Despite U.S. government negotiations, a failed military rescue, and pleas from his family and monetary reward for his freedom, Foley was executed on August 19, 2014. His execution was staged and filmed in a dramatic manner. Foley's statements before his death were directed specifically to President Obama, the U.S. Armed Forces, members of Foley's family, and the West. He stated that his death was the result of the U.S. air campaigns against ISIS forces.

The video was meant to expose the execution and make a statement that reached the highest levels of American government and that the public could not ignore. The video of the execution was intended to rise above all news stories and become the central story. Foley's execution went viral with global media outlets giving it prime air time and running it as the front line story. As an American hostage, Jim Foley represented the United States, but as a journalist, he also represented the media. Jim Foley was not the only hostage executed by ISIS, but he certainly was the one who obtained the most publicity. It can be argued that ISIS was aware that killing a journalist meant that their story would be picked up and broadcasted across America and the globe in a similar fashion to Daniel Pearl. ISIS wanted free international media exposure in order to legitimize and promote their group on a global scale. ISIS's execution of Foley made that happen.[5]

If this incident is examined from the perspective of asymmetric warfare, the cost of video production and execution method is miniscule. It is important to note that at this point thousands of lives had been lost at the hands of ISIS before Jim Foley's execution. What made this incident different was the fact that a specific victim was selected who belonged to a targeted nationality and profession. A brutal method of death was selected, and it was choreographed, staged, and professionally filmed as entertainment. In the days following the execution, Foley's execution remained the leading news story, and President Obama issued a statement denouncing Foley's death and recognized ISIS's brutality, their ideology, and their methodologies.[6] Less than a year after Foley's death, President Obama issued another statement denouncing an act of violence on American soil that originated from a different ideological strain.

On June 17, 2015, twenty-one-year-old Dylann Roof entered Emmanuel African Methodist Episcopal Church in downtown Charleston, South Carolina, with a loaded Glock handgun. After sitting through almost an hour of Bible study, he stood up and subsequently began shooting those in attendance, which included the senior pastor, state representative Clementa Pinckney, and eight other African Americans. Dylann Roof, a white male, reloaded five different times, and during a lull in the shooting he asked one of the victims if she was still alive. He wanted to know so that she would be able to give an account of the incident. She later stated that as Dylann fired, he used racial slurs and incendiary language.[7]

The incident was initially labeled a mass shooting. While the shooter's motive and background were unknown, nine out of the ten shot died. However, after Dylann's arrest, details emerged that indicated Roof's actions were motivated by hate and some ideological affiliation with white supremacy and neo-Nazism. Photographs of Roof advocating white supremacy and neo-Nazi symbols were broadcasted on the media. He also published a manifesto that outlined his beliefs toward nonwhites and stated:

> I have no choice, I am not in a position to, alone, go into the ghetto and fight. I chose Charleston because it is the most historic city in my state, and at one time had the highest ratio of blacks to Whites in the country. We have no skin heads, no real KKK, no one doing anything but talking on the Internet. Well someone has to have the bravery to take it to the real world, and I guess that has to be me.[8]

Dylann's objective was similar to that of Timothy McVeigh, the Oklahoma City bomber. Both wanted their act of violence to be the single incident that would initiate a larger conflict. Roof had hoped that the shootings in Charleston would instigate a race war. President Obama denounced the attack and offered condolences to the families of the victims and to the people of Charleston and South Carolina and personally gave the eulogy at Rev. Clementa Pickney's funeral.[9]

Although these two events differ logistically, geographically, and ideologically, they share many conceptual similarities in regard to target selection, media coverage, and a political response by U.S. president Obama. Each incident was carried out in such a way that it became the major news story in the United States. Each incident reflected careful selection of a target and also a method to disseminate what the act of violence meant symbolically. Each act of violence is connected to a larger ideology that gives meaning and "rationality" to those who adhere to a specific ideology. From a marketing standpoint, both events and actions were effective and successful. They were effective because of the media time and intensity granted to cover each incident. They were successful because the president of United States validated the seriousness of each incident and needed to contextualize what it communicated.

Although the variables differ from ISIS's execution of James Foley, Roof's actions in Charleston, South Carolina, were also characterized by target selection, brutality, and propaganda by the deed (the action generates the message). The Charleston Emmanuel African Methodist Episcopal Church was selected based on the historical importance of the church and the influence of the members who attended. In a similar fashion with ISIS, Dylann had given specific thought about the symbolism of his action, the purpose of the attack, and the need to disseminate the meaning of the violence. The incident in Charleston, South Carolina, also bears striking resemblance to a similar plan that did not unfold in July 1993. Skinheads, members of the White Aryan Resistance, and members of the Church of the Creator were implicated in a bomb plot that targeted Los Angeles pastor Cecil Murray of an African Methodist Church in California. Similar to Dylann, they planned to initiate a race war, and the catalyst was the assassination of well-known African Americans like Al Sharpton or Louis Farrakhan. After an eighteen-month FBI investigation, those involved in planning and carrying out the attack were arrested. At this point it is uncertain whether the attack in Charleston, South Carolina, is connected to the previous plot.[10]

Two other innovations are also visible in both violent incidents. The first innovation involves ISIS's targeting "the far enemy,"[11] the United States, represented by Jim Foley, and the second is Dylann Roof's conceptualization of a "race war."[12] The following chapters will address these two innovations in detail, but what is important to note at this juncture is that both the concepts of the "far enemy" and a "race war" have become normalized subcultural values. Normalized subcultural values can be defined as strategies or tactics that are no longer questioned, but are expected as common practice. Other innovations that are now perceived as common practices are the American neo-Nazi use of the Hitler salute accompanied with "sieg heil" which was introduced in the early 1960s and the so-called Islamic State's prolific use of social media since 2014 to publicize beheadings as standardized "state" justice.

The dark innovations described in this book form the foundation of the current war of ideas or information warfare. Information warfare and strategic communications are terms that have been frequently used since 9/11. Information warfare is currently being carried out by legitimate nation states and dissident groups across the globe. Sayyid Qutb, who is seen as one of the most influential ideologues to today's violent jihadis, argues about the importance of war of ideas.[13] Qutb's statement was made from his own text that aspired to win Muslim hearts and minds.

I argue that ideas, particularly those that resonate throughout the decades, are more dangerous than single incidents or many incidences of violence. The danger of an idea is defined as the degree that it has normalized within a subculture and the relationship between the idea and the number of fatalities or injuries associated with actions. Although this may have some resonance for a particular point in history, if an idea continues to have traction decade after decade or century upon century, the death toll, injury, and economic impact associated with that idea far surpasses the number of casualties or injuries in a single incident. Therefore, it is important to understand some of these ideas can be traced to neo-Nazism and violent jihadism since these two ideologies are currently social problems on a global scale.

It is also critical to understand the place for ideas and ideologues when discussing violent extremism. It is meaningful to understand how messages are disseminated, the network structure of particular groups, theoretical construction explaining why individuals engage in acts of violent extremism, historical context, cultural aspects, radicalization processes, the amassing of large databases that provide comprehensive understanding through frequencies and variables, and subcultural processes. All of the aforementioned aspects not only assist scholars and practitioners in understanding violent extremism, but also aid in the contemplation of ways to counter it. I take the position that innovations can have long-term effects but also have the potential to resonate with larger segments of the populace which then moves a violent extremist or revolutionary idea to normalcy. Therefore, it is important to isolate some of these ideas in order to analyze them and to examine the ideologues who advanced the particular idea.

It is often stated that one cannot kill an idea.[14] While this may be true, it is possible to counter, minimalize, and reduce the power associated with a particular idea. Before even transitioning to countering an idea, it is essential to understand what an idea is, the functionality of an idea, and why that idea has a certain degree of traction among audiences. If the goal is increased under-standing, I argue that it is important not to separate the idea from the individual or context in which it originated. All dark innovations fall into two categories. They are meant either to diagnose the social, political, and religious problems or to offer a prognosis in order to remedy that situation. All ideas flow from these two elementary streams. It also can be argued that how these ideas are marketed and how they are intended to motivate audiences is another com-ponent. While this is true, this dimension is more about how the diagnosis or prognosis is disseminated in order to win hearts and minds.

NEO-NAZISM AND VIOLENT JIHADISM

The objective of this book is not to understand all the facets of neo-Nazism and violent jihadism but rather to focus on the significant innovations and ideologues that impacted both ideologies. Both neo-Nazism and violent jihadism are significant social problems that affect governments, societies, and economies across the globe. Both ideologies manifest themselves in dif-ferent subcultures. Neo-Nazis, generally, are more diffusely organized on a subnational level, while violent jihadism has stronger networks and organiza-tions. It is important to note that the use of the terms neo-Nazism and violent jihadism serve as ideological umbrellas. Instead of representing individual groups or persons, their ideas function as franchises of violence bent on changing the existing governing and social order. Neither Neo-Nazism nor violent jihadism has a single manifest core organization. Both position their ideas in a way in which any individual or group can be inspired to promote their cause either through word or deed.[15]

Neo-Nazism is generally used as a term to describe the post–World War II white supremacist individuals and groups who are intent on establish-ing a new order based on the doctrines of Adolf Hitler and Nazi Germany. Each individual and group that can be branded as neo-Nazi displays their ideology with various symbols that range from the swastika, to the Judeo-Christian Bible, to Norse runes, and to pagan rites that are blended together based on the premise that the white race is supreme. White supremacy is built on the idea that the white race is the apex of evolutionary natural selection and has demonstrated this throughout history based on intellectual and cul-tural superiority. Neo-Nazis argue that all nonwhites, Jews, and homosexu-als are at war with the white race and, therefore, whites engage in overt and covert warfare to prevent racial extinction. There is also a spiritual dimension that parallels political and social ideology and emphasizes that the white race is the best union between forces of the universe, humanity, and in nature. This union has created a genetic code that exists in the white race, and this code is often deified. There are many groups and individuals that can be identified as being neo-Nazi, and some examples are the National Alliance, Aryan Nations, the National Socialist Movement, and the American Nazi Party. Some of the influential leaders within the neo-Nazi movement discussed in this book are George Lincoln Rockwell, William Pierce, Ben Klassen, David Duke, and Louis Beam.[16]

Violent jihadism is a term used to classify a minority of individuals and groups who insist that holy war is an obligation for all true Muslims. This is a highly contested argument within political Islam, and this perspective is rejected by traditional, moderate, and progressive versions of Islam. To infer that violent jihad is an obligation equates this form of jihad to the other five pillars of Islam: prayer, pilgrimage, profession of monotheism, fasting, and almsgiving. The declaration that jihad is a pillar of Islam reshapes its importance in the faith. Violent jihadists are against Western influences that manifest themselves in secularism or feminism and any other anti-Islamic-isms that have been imported from the West. Violent jihadists claim that these -isms are part of a subversive strategy to uproot Islamic culture and to destroy the family and society from within by attacking Muslim morality and encouraging passivity in Muslim males. Violent jihadists perceive that existing Muslim governments are apostates, are puppets to the West, and are ignorant of the true faith. Violent jihadists assert that it is their right to use violence against anything that attacks Islam or shames the prophet. They also argue that the vast majority of self-professing Muslims are in reality ignorant of the true tenets of their faith.[17] Groups that adhere to this ideological umbrella are Al Qaeda, ISIS, Egyptian Islamic Jihad, and al Shabaab. Some of the leading ideologues discussed in this text and their innovations are Sayyid Qutb, Abdullah Azzam, Osama bin Laden, Mohammed Maqdisi, and Anwar Awlaki.[18]

The innovations of five violent jihadis and five neo-Nazis are analyzed in context in order to understand how innovations were introduced into the movement and still resonate in the year 2016. Although ten ideologues are selected, this book is not intended to provide a comprehensive list of all the innovations associated within neo-Nazism or violent jihadism. These selections are more potent innovations that have not only received traction, but are also identified as best subcultural practices.

Certain innovations have had a global impact beyond the original group and have altered the way in which other individuals and groups think and act. Several different methods determined which innovations to include. The first method involved identifying whose work is considered influential from within each subculture. McCants and Brachman (2006), leading scholars at West Point's Combating Terrorism Centers (CTC), determined whose violent jihadi propaganda was being read and referenced. Using the frequency

Methodology

of downloads, citation analysis, and bibliometrics from Al Taweed, the Al Qaeda virtual library, McCants and Brachman documented which pieces of propaganda and which propagandists were influential among violent jihadis.[19] McCants and Brachman's analysis created a list of "who's who" among effective violent jihadi ideologues. Generating an effective list of neo-Nazi ideologues involved the same process. EBooks proved useful for this task. EBooks, "the world's leading publishers for the racially aware," records the highest frequency of neo-Nazi propaganda downloads.[20] In the same fashion, EBooks records the frequency of which effective neo-Nazi propagandists forms the population baseline.

Purposive sampling was also used to select the innovations and ideologues outlined in the subsequent chapters. Certain criteria influenced how a certain innovation was implemented as a new subcultural idea and then normalized over time. Innovations were found to have an increased likelihood of implementation if they originated from ideologues who had one or more of the following characteristics: (1) was a founder of a separate group in the neo-Nazi or violent jihadi movement; (2) was an influential leader in their movement; (3) was imprisoned or tortured for their ideology; (4) died as a martyr; (5) demonstrated unwavering commitment to the cause; (6) served as a role model to members in the group; or (7) was honored by other violent jihadists or neo-Nazis as making a significant tactical or ideological contribution. Finally, innovations were selected based on strategic or tactical implications over time.

Data for this book was derived from primary and secondary neo-Nazi and violent jihadi sources. This includes books, articles, essays, interviews, magazines, videos, websites, and music lyrics. The data was interpreted through a comparative case study approach. A comparative case study were used because the differences and similarities that exist between neo-Nazis and violent jihadis increase the ability to see if an innovation transcends the ideologue or group. The stronger the differences and similarities between a sample in a comparative research design the better. Parallels demonstrate that innovations exceed variable differences found in geography, history, language, religion, worldview, politics, and philosophy.

Frame analysis and network text analysis (NTA) were used to analyze the data. Frame analysis has grown drastically over the past six decades and draws from the work of Erving Goffman. Goffman describes frames as mechanisms to understand social organization, experience, and social expression. Frames can function to define problems, diagnose causes (diagnostic frames), assign moral judgments, and suggest solutions (prognostic frames). When a certain innovation is framed appropriately, it can function as a powerful communication agent that has the potential to impact significant segments of a social movement. The innovations selected for this book have been successfully framed to the point that they are no longer seen as innovations, but rather a normalized process within violent extremism.

NTA provides a method for researchers to quantitatively analyze frames. A particular strength of NTA is that extracted networks can be collected in a theoretical fashion. The theoretical and philosophical assumptions behind NTA are: (1) that a relationship exists between frames and language; (2) a relationship exists between words and their intended meaning; and (3) social knowledge or shared meaning exists between cultures and context. NTA is used to construct a network of linked words and concepts by identifying the relationship that exists between the words in text. NTA involves using an ontology (or coding scheme) that combines ethnographic knowledge with computer-assisted quantitative methods associated with network analysis.

The book is divided into five chapters and each is organized in a similar fashion. Each chapter has several violent jihadi and neo-Nazi examples that illustrate how dark ideas move from an innovation into concrete action. Each example highlights a subcultural problem and how a dark idea addressed the issue. Two biographical sketches, one violent jihadi and one neo-Nazi, provide the micro and macro-level context for each idea.

The first chapter examines how to create a class of divine traitors. If an ideology is perceived as divinely inspired, then every individual and group associated with that idea is morally right because they follow divine principles. If an ideologue correlates the needs and desires of a group to a deity, then any attack upon those rights is also an attack against God or a divine force. It then becomes equally important to distinguish those who adhere to the divine right and are "true" followers from those who may profess or have attributes of that group but are "impure." Those members of a faith or a race who are stigmatized as "impure" can also be classified as traitors or apostates. In other words, members of a group that self-identify as being divinely right can now look upon others as traitors or apostates. Sayyid Qutb and Ben Klassen are the two ideologues examined in this chapter. Sayyid Qutb is recognized as being one of the leading thinkers in modern violent jihadi circles. He advanced the idea of jahiliyyah, or the state of Islamic ignorance, in such a way that it eventually enabled Muslims to kill other self-professed Muslims and classify them as Islamic traitors. Ben Klassen was the founder of the Church of the Creator, author of the *White Man's Bible*, and created the idea of racial holy war. Ben Klassen coined the phrase, "My race is my religion," which now equates the white race with a divine concept. Furthermore, Klassen argues that Christianity is a Jewish invention and was created in order to pacify the white race and eventually lead them to extinction.

Chapter 2 addresses how ideas are weaponized into propaganda. The challenge of normalizing innovations is to disseminate them to the masses.

This chapter addresses how two ideologues used old and new media to weaponize their ideas to catalyze others. Two of the most successful ideologues for weaponized ideas are William Pierce and Anwar al-Awlaki. Anwar Awlaki was a leading violent jihadist propagandist and an Al Qaeda member before his death in 2011. William Pierce was the founder of the organization the National Alliance and wrote and published *The Turner Diaries*, a fictional account that inspired the Oklahoma City bomber, Timothy McVeigh, and other neo-Nazi groups.

Chapter 3 examines two innovations that offer different strategic conceptualizations of violence. The ideas of Abdullah Azzam and Louis Beam legitimized a different strategy for the use of violence. Abdullah Azzam had a charismatic personality and was known as the father of jihad and as a warrior cleric. He personally influenced countless mujahedeen, holy fighters, through his recruiting efforts in the Soviet-Afghan War. He is almost single-handedly responsible for reconceptualizing jihad to what it is today. Louis Beam is a self-declared white American nationalist and former Klu Klux Klan (KKK) member who was active in the Aryan Nations in the 1980s. He published a document outlining leaderless resistance. Leaderless resistance, also called the Lone Wolf Doctrine, is currently used as a strategy of individual acts of terrorism by multiple groups across the globe.

Chapter 4 analyzes how a targeting paradigm can be shifted to identify the most threatening enemy. Violent jihadists and neo-Nazis claim to have numerous enemies. Rather than focusing on all enemies at the same time, an effective strategy concentrates on the most threatening enemy first and then sequentially eradicates the others. The innovations of Osama bin Laden, Al Qaeda's founder and leader, and George Lincoln Rockwell, American Nazi Party founder and leader, are examined in this chapter. In 1998, Osama bin Laden declared war against the United States in a written document, *The Declaration of Jihad on the Americans Occupying the Country of the Two Sacred Places*,[21] where he argued that apostate Muslim governments and Israel would collapse after the United States is destroyed. In the midst of the American civil rights movement and a communist scare, George Lincoln Rockwell directed neo-Nazi efforts against the Jews and stated that if the Jews were attacked first, then blacks and other nonwhites would succumb to white power.

Chapter 5 examines the need to create a soft version of extremism. Soft extremism is defined as a more approachable and palatable form of extremism that uses messages that appeal to large segments of the population. For example, instead of inflammatory racial rhetoric, morality issues and assaults on one's faith are used to focus on common beliefs in order to unite groups. Abu Mohammed al-Maqdisi and David Duke's use of soft extremism is examined in this chapter. Mohammed Maqdisi is a Salafi violent jihadist who maintains a wide-read multilingual violent jihadist library and is one of the most widely read ideologues on the internet. He was the mentor of the Jordanian Abu Musab al-Zarqawi, the founder of Jamaat al-Tawhid wa-al-Jihad, which would later morph into ISIS. Maqdisi. David Duke, former Klansman and Louisiana politician, has constantly taken the strategy of running the appeal of white nationalism, white victimization, and white civil rights.

Finally, chapter 6 examines a way forward. This chapter is broken into three sections. The first highlights the importance of the context surrounding a particular ideologue, the second focuses on methods to understand and dissect extremist propaganda, and the last section examines the relationship between dark ideas and information warfare.

NOTES

1. Study of Terrorism and Responses to Terrorism (START).
2. "START.umd.edu," accessed August 29, 2015, http://www.start.umd.edu/.
3. "What We Have Learned Since ISIS Declared a Caliphate One Year Ago | TIME," accessed August 29, 2015, http://time.com/3933568/isis-caliphate-one-year/.
4. Lock, Helen. "Isis vs Isil vs Islamic State: What Do They Mean—and Why Does It Matter?" *The Independent*, accessed August 29, 2015, http://www.independent.co.uk/news/world/middle-east/isis-vs-isil-vs-islamic-state—what-is-in-a-name-9731894.html.
5. Callimachi, Rukmini. "Before Killing James Foley, ISIS Demanded Ransom From U.S.," *The New York Times*, August 20, 2014, http://www.nytimes.com/2014/08/21/world/middleeast/isis-pressed-for-ransom-before-killing-james-foley.html.
6. "Statement by the President," *Whitehouse.gov*, accessed August 29, 2015, https://www.whitehouse.gov/the-press-office/2014/08/20/statement-president.
7. "Charleston Shooting," *NPR.org*, accessed August 29, 2015, http://www.npr.org/tags/415878235/charleston-shooting.
8. "Dylann Storm Roof Manifesto." *Daily Stormer*, accessed July 11, 2016. http://www.dailystormer.com/dylann-storm-roof-manifesto/comment-page-1/.
9. "Statement by the President on the Shooting in Charleston, South Carolina," *Whitehouse.gov*, accessed August 29, 2015, https://www.whitehouse.gov/the-press-office/2015/06/18/statement-president-shooting-charleston-south-carolina.
10. Smith, Brent L. *Terrorism in America: Pipe Bombs and Pipe Dreams Albany.* SUNY Press, 1994.
11. Gerges, Fawaz A. *The Far Enemy: Why Jihad Went Global.* Cambridge; Cambridge University Press, 2005.
12. Simi, Pete and Robert Futrell. *American Swastika: Inside the White Power Movement's Hidden Spaces of Hate.* Lanham, MD: Rowman & Littlefield Publishers, 2010.
13. Qutb, Sayyid. *Milestones.* Islamic Book Service, 2006. Print.

14. "You Can't Kill an Idea," *The Huffington Post*, accessed August 29, 2015, http://www.huffingtonpost.com/robert-koehler/you-cant-kill-an-idea_b_830881.html.

15. Simi, Pete and Robert Futrell, "Neo-Nazi Movements in Europe and the United States," in *The Wiley-Blackwell Encyclopedia of Social and Political Movements*, Blackwell Publishing Ltd, 2013.

16. Caspi, David J., Joshua D. Freilich, and Steven M. Chermak. "Worst of the Bad: Violent White Supremacist Groups and Lethality," *Dynamics of Asymmetric Conflict* 5, no. 1 (March 1, 2012): 1–17, doi:10.1080/17467586.2012.679664.

17. Morris, Travis. "Networking Vehement Frames: Neo-Nazi and Violent Jihadi Demagoguery," *Behavioral Sciences of Terrorism and Political Aggression* 6, no. 3 (September 2, 2014): 163–82, doi:10.1080/19434472.2014.922602.

18. Sageman, Marc. *Leaderless Jihad: Terror Networks in the Twenty-First Century*. Philadelphia: University of Pennsylvania Press, 2008.

19. www.tawhed.ws accessed January 19, 2016.

20. http://wn-pdfs.tk/ accessed January 18, 2016.

21. "Osama Bin Laden—Fatwa—Background and Declaration of War against the Americans Occupying the Two Holy Places," accessed August 30, 2015, http://www.mideastweb.org/osamabinladen1.htm.

Chapter 1

Manufacturing Divine Traitors

Sayyid Qutb and Ben Klassen

This chapter examines two ideas that have created a new subcultural class within neo-Nazism and violent jihadis: divine traitors. The term "traitor" is defined as someone who betrays his or her country, a principal, a religion, or a friend. Although the term becomes convoluted depending on perspective, if someone stigmatizes others as traitors, they then ascribe to possess the higher moral ground. In Arabic, this concept is commonly translated as apostate.

Traitors are labeled as morally reprehensible and even more so if they betray a deity or divine concept. It is arguable that a traitor is more detestable than an enemy because in some way they have been exposed to the divine and yet have rejected it. The creation of a "traitor" class within Islam and the white race makes it possible for whites and Muslims to advance the belief that only a select few of their number belong to a pure Vanguard. Members of this Vanguard then frame other Muslims or whites guilty of treason because they do not conform to their worldview. Since treason is a detestable crime, they argue that death is justified.

Sayyid Qutb is one of the most influential thinkers on what has evolved into violent jihad.[1] His work, his life, and his death are inspirational to violent jihadists. Qutb's life is divided into two periods. In the first period, he was a secular educator and a literary critic until 1948 when he changed courses. It was after a visit to the United States from 1948 to 1950 that the second period began when he returned to Egypt to join the Muslim Brotherhood and renounced his secular ways.[2]

Sayyid Qutb was executed in 1966 by the Egyptian government soon after he published his last philosophical treaties, *Milestones* or *Sign Posts Along the Road*. He was executed in Cairo in 1966 on the charge of plotting to overthrow the Egyptian government. His execution turned him into a martyr and catalyzed his thoughts and beliefs throughout the Muslim world. *Milestones* was published in over 2000 editions, was banned in Egypt and other moderate Islamic states, and was illicitly circulated through the Middle East over the internet to millions.

His contributions to modern-day violent jihadism are understood when compared to the weight of ideological texts from other movements. It is fair to say that what *Milestones* is to violent jihadism, *Das Kapital* is to Communism and *Mein Kampf* is to Nazism. Qutb's ideological work influenced Egyptian president Anwar Sadat's assassins; the planner for 1993 World Trade Center bombings, Omar Abdul Rahman; Al Qaeda's current leader, Ayman Zawahiri; Osama bin Laden; and the current Islamic State of Iraq and Syria (ISIS) leader, al-Baghdadi. Qutb's brother, Professor Mohammed Qutb, later became an ideological mentor to a young Osama bin Laden during his university days in Saudi Arabia.[3]

One of Qutb's innovations was centered on the concept of jahiliyyah. Jahiliyyah can be defined as being ignorant of divine guidance or used to describe pre-Islamic Arabia.[4] Qutb did not invent the idea, nor was he the first to use it as a "purification" concept, but he contextualized the idea to modernity. It could be argued that Qutb's contextualization of jahiliyyah has been one of the most innovative dark ideas to appear among violent jihadi thinkers in the past century. In Qutb's mind, there was no solution for jahiliyyah except for a complete Islamic revolution. Muslims who lived in a state of jahiliyyah were in fact apostates to Islam. Qutb reasoned that it was impossible for true Muslims to be secular and accept man-made laws. For example, Muslims in the Egyptian government were not Muslims but were traitors to their faith, because they followed human interventions instead of Allah's commandments. Qutb is not the only ideologue to view members of their own group as traitors.

Across the Muslim world, Islam is accepted as a conventional religion that has been extremely wary of theological "innovations." Numerous Islamic scholars over the centuries have sought to endorse and uphold traditional beliefs while discouraging potential dogmatic and political challenges based on radical claims. However, many radical jihadis assert that all Muslims should endeavor to return to their version of the original sources of Islam and thus remove such innovations from their religion. The current version of Islam, according to their view, is riddled with humanistic innovations and is therefore tainted. Since Islam is not contested as a conventional religion across the Muslim world, violent jihadi ideologue efforts are focused on purification through ideas and actions, while neo-Nazis are working to legitimize that race should be a religion.

Neo-Nazi ideologues have been engaged in a spiritualizing process of correlating the white race to a religion. Over the past five decades, neo-Nazis have attempted to make the white race metaphorically equal to the prophet

Mohammad through racial superiority and have constructed a series of beliefs that resemble a religion. Neo-Nazism maintains that the white race is the pinnacle of evolution; the mere existence of whites and their achievements "recite" knowledge of a higher power to the rest of humanity. From this perspective, the white race is sacred. Although there is not a unified approach to deifying the white race, this idea sets the groundwork for creating a class of whites who do not subscribe to their worldview and therefore are labeled race traitors. While the term "race traitor" has been used since the 1800s, it was a secular derogatory term, not a spiritual one. If race is one's religion, then betraying the white race creates a class of divine race traitors similar to Islamic apostates. Ben Klassen, the founder of the Church of the Creator, the Creativity Movement, and author of the *White Man's Bible*, furthered this idea within neo-Nazism.[5]

Klassen argued that one's race should be one's religion and advanced the idea that the white race itself is a symbol of divine creativity. All members of the white race are divine genetic DNA carriers according to Klassen and need to be protected from extinction. However, when certain whites collaborate with nonwhites on policies like affirmative action, these whites now belong to a class of divine race traitors because they are working against nature and divine providence. These self-destructive whites are guilty of treason against what is sacred, and they will be held accountable in a future racial holy war. Klassen crafted the phrase "racial holy war," better known by its acronym, RAHOWA, which serves as a concise mission statement and call to action for the white race. His conceptualization of racial loyalty, also the title of his organization's publication, implies that any white who does not share loyalty to one's race, or even worse, betrays one's race is committing divine treason. Klassen argued that these whites are worse than nonwhites or Jews because the white race is sacred and traitors are destroying their own kind. "Holy" as used in RAHOWA, condenses the idea that the white race is sacred, akin to a religious doctrine and whites that blaspheme their "holy race" become divine race traitors.[6]

Klassen believed that religion is more strategic than a white political party and that focusing on class struggle weakened national solidarity. In line with Hitler, he believed that the *Protocols of Zion* were authentic, eugenics were necessary for strengthening the white race, and that whites faced extinction because of racial mixing as a passive white population was unwilling to fight for their race. He believed that creating a religion based on race would correlate ideas with action which would eventually lead to a complete revolution via a race war. Racial holy war is an innovation that transcends the Creativity Movement and is now widely used across neo-Nazi organizations and individuals.[7]

Since its formation in 1973, Church of the Creator members were few in number, but the ideas of racial holy war, racial loyalty, and the divine sacredness of the white race normalized across neo-Nazi groups worldwide.[8] It is also important to note that the idea that one's race is one's religion has moved beyond Klassen's Creativity Movement and into a variety of white religions devoted to the same premise. The idea that race is a religious concept in neo-Nazism has not had the incubation time frame of Qutb's jahiliyyah. However, if the concept of divine race traitors fully evolved, then hate crimes would include whites killing whites because of racial motives drawn along racial treason.

SAYYID QUTB

Our whole environment: people's beliefs and ideas, habits and art, rules and laws—is Jahiliyyah. Even if these beliefs and ideas are considered to be Islamic culture, sources, philosophy, and thought, they are still Jahiliyaah constructs.[9]

The Man

Sayyid Qutb was born in 1906 in Musha, Asyut district in southern Egypt, during the British colonial rule. He was born to devout Muslim parents who were well established and widely known in the area. During his childhood, he experienced part of the mass rural migration to Cairo in 1920 because of hard economic times and the need for additional educational opportunities. While in Cairo, Qutb had first-hand experience with extreme poverty, the impact of rapid urbanization on the quality of life and an exploding population accompanied by insufficient social and infrastructure policies. All of this existed in a political environment of extreme corruption and British colonialism. His time in Cairo gave him the experiences needed for him to realize that Egypt was a nation in the need of change.[10]

Qutb's elementary education began at a religious school near his village. After he reached the age of ten, he had committed the Quran to memory. He later transferred to a modern government school, graduated from primary school in 1918, and then graduated from a teacher's college in 1928. Qutb later enrolled in Dar al-Ulum, the Western-style university where he graduated in 1933. He became involved in Egypt's Ministry of Education and drafted many projects for a reform in the education system, though few were implemented.[11]

Qutb experienced hardship on many levels during the 1940s. In this decade he lost his mother with whom he maintained a close relationship, a serious romantic relationship ended, and his interest in revolutionary ideas increased. Because of these events it could be argued that he increasingly felt alienated from Egyptian literary society. Adnan Musallam describes it this way, "Qutb's emergence as a serious student of the Quran, 1939 through 1947, was accompanied by his emergence as a stern moralist, an anti-Western thinker, and an anti-political, anti-literary establishment intellectual. These mutually reinforcing developments were, like the Quranic teachings, crucially significant in their makeup of Qutb ideology in the late 1940s, 1950s, and 1960s."[12]

Qutb's writing in the 1940s was increasingly political and religious. In the late 1940s, his view of Islam took a central role in his writings which culminated in *Social Justice in Islam*, published in 1948. In 1948, he obtained a government grant to study American instructional methods, pedagogy, curricula, and primary education. His friends and superiors thought that if he was exposed to the American education system in its proper context, it would moderate his thinking. He traveled to the United States, missing the publication of his book, the 1948 Arab-Israeli War, and the formation of the Israeli state. He attended Wilson Teachers College on the East Coast and then later obtained a master of arts in education at the University of Northern Colorado in Greeley.[13]

Qutb was fully convinced that Islam and Egyptian culture was far superior to what he experienced in the United States. When he returned to Egypt he used his direct observations as evidence to convince others of the West's spiritual and moral decay. He published, *The America I Have Seen*, in which he applauds American innovation, advancement, and prosperity. At the same time he highlights decay of materialism, racism, moral, and social decay, decrepit human values, the primitiveness of the American conversation, the hunger for war, pragmatism, and all the other "isms" associated with Western philosophy. His experiences in the United States solidified his damnation of the West, and he experienced Western jahiliyyah personally.[14]

Before Qutb's stint in the United States, his political allegiances lay with his father's secular national political party, the Wafd. It is important to note that a colonial perspective framed Qutb's early sociocultural and social-political development while Egypt's postcolonial period under Muslim rule shaped his ideology. He later stated that he was reborn in 1951 after joining the Muslim Brotherhood and renouncing his earlier beliefs and publications.[15]

Sayyid Qutb shared some of the Muslim Brotherhood attitudes. Al Banna established the Muslim Brotherhood in late 1928 as a response to Western dominance, particularly through British colonialism over Egypt. Banna and the Brotherhood believed that the solution to the problems imported from the West was a complete holistic return to Islam. Because of the Brotherhood's mission and growing numbers, it posed a substantial threat to the Egyptian monarchy. In response, the Muslim Brotherhood was banned, and Banna was assassinated in 1948. Because of Qutb's experience as a writer and educator he assumed the role of editor of the Muslim Brotherhood's weekly paper,

Al Manar. This assignment provided him the opportunity to emerge as a powerful voice for their cause.[16]

Concurrent to the Muslim Brotherhood's work, Abdul Nasser's National Movement grew as a popular alternative to the Egyptian monarchy. Abdul Nasser's platform was based on pan-Arab nationalism, but because of the opposition from the Egyptian monarchy, members of the Muslim Brotherhood and Nasser's National Movement became allies. Qutb became a leading intellectual in the revolution and a vocal supporter of the Free Officers led by Gamal Abdel Nasser. Because of their earlier collaboration, when Nasser successfully overthrew the monarchy in 1952, Nasser offered Qutb numerous positions in the new regime's administration. However, as Nasser began to institute change and ideological decisions were made, Qutb and the Free Officers' vision of Egypt were not on parallel tracks. He resigned in 1953.[17] By the end of 1954, the majority of the Muslim Brotherhood leadership was arrested, the Muslim Brotherhood was dissolved, and Qutb was jailed.[18]

In October 1954, members of the Muslim Brotherhood attempted to assassinate President Nasser in Alexandria. Qutb was one of the dozen Muslim Brotherhood arrested. He was tortured, tried, and convicted for his part in alleged conspiracy to overthrow the regime and was sentenced to twenty-five years hard labor. He spent six months in Tura prison on the outskirts of Cairo, but his ill health, in addition to the intervention of the Iraqi president Abd al-Salam Arif, secured an early release. Although his first bout in prison was short-lived, he was rearrested and later spent ten years in prison. While incarcerated, he used the time to solidify his thoughts in writing and wrote an extensive commentary on the Quran, *In the Shade of the Quran.* The writing in this particular text reflects the physical and psychological torture experienced at the hands of the Nasser government. Qutb was released in 1964 and soon produced another book entitled *Milestones. Milestones* argued that all earthly sovereignty belongs to God alone which was a direct threat to Nasser's government. He was arrested yet again in 1965, sentenced to death, and was executed in 1966.[19]

After his death, Qutb's written work appealed to the Egyptian educated classes. This was partly due to the fact that they could relate to Qutb's experiences and transfer some of their own frustration onto Qutb. In a distant way, he represented a tangible sense of betrayal to which the masses could connect. His martyrdom even has a special word in Arabic, "Qutbiyyun," or in English, "Qutbists." His death caused his work to become increasingly popular not only in Egypt but also to other influential revolutionary leaders in Syria, Tunisia, Sudan, and Lebanon where ideological parallels aligned with the Muslim Brotherhood. Also noteworthy is that even though Qutb was a Sunni Muslim, his message of a politicized Islam also influenced Ayatollah Khomeini and the Shiite revolution in Iran.[20]

Qutb's message remains potent decades later because of his philosophical approach. His thoughts were against the West, America and Europe, and therefore his arguments are still relevant in 2016. Modern violent jihadis still resent the power the West holds both physically and ideologically in their nations. Because of this control from the West, specifically the United States, these violent jihadis view it a necessary requirement to be ideologically liberated from the West and its values. Qutb's writing not only provided Muslim leaders like Osama bin Laden and Ayman Zawahiri with the foundation for a philosophical defense to attack the United States, but they have also provided adequate arguments to those who want to purify their own lands of divine traitors.[21]

The Innovation: Jahiliyyah

The literal translation jahiliyyah is commonly known as "the age of ignorance" and is used to reference pre-Islamic Arabian society. The term jahiliyyah appears four times in the Quran, but never in the way Qutb uses it. In Qutb's writing, he references the intellectual work of others like Mawdudi and Nadwi that also commented on jahiliyyah. However, it is how Qutb advanced its application in a way that others have not done that makes his stamp on the idea unique. Qutb describes jahiliyyah this way:

> Jahiliyyah—as God describes it in his Quran defines it—is the rule of humans by humans because it involves making some humans servant of others, rebelling against service to God, rejecting God's divinity and in view of this rejection, ascribing divinity to some humans and serving them apart from God. Jahiliyyah—in light of this text—is not a period of time but a condition, a condition which existed yesterday, exists today, it will exist tomorrow. It takes the form of jahiliyyah, which stands over against Islam and contradicts it. People—in anytime and anyplace—are either governed by God's sharia—entirely, without any reservations—accepting it and submitting to it, in which case they are following God's religion, or they are governed by sharia invented by humans, in whatever form, and accepted. In that case they are in jahiliyyah and are following the religion of those who are governed by that sharia, and are by no means following the religion of God. Whoever does not desire the rule of God desires the rule of jahiliyyah whoever rejects the sharia of God accepts the sharia of jahiliyyah and lives in jahiliyyah.[22]

According to this definition, any society that does not submit to God or worship God according to sharia is limited to a state of ignorance. The defining characteristics of jahiliyyah are the rejection of divine authority and submission to human authority, a blasphemous action. It is important also to note that in his text, jahiliyyah is not limited to time or geographic location area;

it is a spiritual and social condition that can exist in any location during any time either in small or large quantities. In this text, Qutb draws a metaphorical line in the sand and states that all societies are either Islamic or are defined by jahiliyyah. He states that it is impossible for Muslims to live a true Islamic life in a land where Islam does not govern.[23]

Qutb also provides criteria to diagnose jahiliyyah societies. He states that jahiliyyah societies are intellectually and morally confused. They incorporate falsified opinions, myths, superstitions, and misconceptions. Passions and morality are uncontrolled, while doubt and worry are prevalent. Society experiences large degrees of alienation and insecurity witnessed by racial and class rifts in which governments are exploitative and place material concerns above all. Jahiliyyah societies are identified by the proliferation of uncontrolled sexual expression, the violation of sexual ethics, and women abandoning their families and children for jobs and materialism. Science is also used to deceive populations and is used as a tool to remove God's actions into secular actions. In this case he states that such societies are backward, and only Islamic societies can be civilized. Although some of the criteria are found in previous scholarship, Qutb's contextualization of jahiliyyah to an Egyptian society permeated by Western norms and beliefs was more sophisticated and integrated than earlier forms.[24]

Qutb argues that one of the most threatening aspects of jahiliyyah is its ability to be cloaked as Islam. Qutb states that all democratic and communist societies are jahili because they deny the existence of God and deify a political party or process. Pagan societies, those that exist in Asia and India are also jahili because they worship beings and ancestors instead of the one true God. Christians and Jews are jahili because they are wrong in their conceptualization of God and on the degree of authority granted to theocratic human governments. He states that secularism is just another version of religion and that some say they respect religion, but it has no authority in their life. Qutb puts it this way:

> The Muslim community has long ago vanished from existence. . . . We can say that the Muslim community has been extinct for a few centuries, for this Muslim community does not denote the name of a land in which Islam resides, nor is it a people whose forefathers lived under the Islamic system in some earlier time. His name of a group of people whose manners, ideas and concepts, rules and regulations, by using criteria, are all derived from the Islamic source Muslim community with these characteristics vanished at the moment the laws of God became suspended on earth.[25]

Qutb states that man was sent by God to establish authority on earth. He states that man has control of the material world, but is neither its master nor its slave. He argues that true acceptance of divine guidance can only come through <u>unconditional submission to God. Submission begins with</u> the confession of faith, but confession means nothing <u>unless it is followed by practical action.</u> Practical action should take the form of adhering to all Islamic regulations. Qutb squarely confronts the Muslims living in democratic societies.[26]

Under this definition of Islam it is <u>impossible to be truly Muslim in a Western country.</u> He states that it is not possible because the social order is not governed by Islamic law and supports human-made government laws over sharia. He argues that living in this type of environment is <u>a type of slavery,</u> and it is delusional for a true Muslim to believe <u>that they can live a full and true Muslim life in this context.</u> This environment not only destroys the individual, but also destroys society; if the government is separated from God, all of the society and its institutions will be as well. If religion is not the ideal, then all other institutions and ideologies are mockeries and half-truths.[27]

Qutb's use of jahiliyyah helps to explain why Pan Arabism and Arab socialism began to fail in the late 1960s. They failed because they are human interventions. In his arguments, he strengthens his claim for the return to true Islam rooted in the divine. In doing so, he highlights that tensions among Muslims is an indicator of jahiliyyah and is an affront to God. Qutb separates the world into two camps: those that are truly for Allah and those that are in the house of war. He argues that the separation between self-proclaiming apostate Muslims, which are the vast majority, and true Muslims should be complete.[28]

Because jahiliyyah is universal, prevalent, and complex, the only solution is a revolution that can be initiated by a Vanguard who has committed themselves to serve Allah and Allah alone in every aspect of life. Their creed must be "no God but God," and their only motive and entire message must not mix any man-made laws such as democracy, pragmatism, or social reform with sharia. They must absolutely separate themselves from a jahiliyyah society in order to escape its powerful hold over their intellectual and physical lives. This separation is required for purification. Someday, if the space allows, a new Muslim society must be created in order to reestablish an environment in which the entire context's focus and governing structure is Islamic. Examples of Qutb's ideas are evident in "Dirty Kuffar," a music video uploaded to YouTube in 2004 and again in full form as ISIS or the Islamic State where apostates are identified, "tried," and executed.

The song/video, "Dirty Kuffar," by the British-Pakistani hip-hop group Sheikh Terra and the Soul Salah Crew was widely distributed on YouTube and other video-sharing sites beginning in February 2004. Kuffar is an Arabic-Muslim term for a non-Muslim "unbeliever" or any type of traitor to Islam. The video identifies certain Muslims as Kuffars, specifically former Egyptian president Hosni Mubarak, former Pakistani president Pervez

Musharraf, and religious scholar Hamza Yusuf. The following screen shot is taken from the video and depicts the former president of Egypt, Hosni Mubarak (1981–2011), as an apostate or divine traitor.

The music video of "Dirty Kuffar" features ski-masked rappers toting both guns and the Quran. In an obvious attempt to inflame passions, the video includes CNN footage of American soldiers shooting Muslims in Iraq, Chechens killing Russians, and the Twin Towers exploding with laughter in the background. Toward the beginning of the video, the hybridized phrase "G-Had" flashes on screen, superimposed on a background of Al Qaeda's black flag. Meaningfully, bin Laden is shown in a favorable light, morphing into a great lion. In the video, the rappers encourage their fellow Muslims to "throw them (*kuffars*) in the fire where they will burn, burn, burn." One scene shows a roadside bomb blowing up an American tank, with the caption "kill the crusaders." The video effectively fuses radical jihadist imagery with hip-hop, thereby incorporating many American rap themes of hypermasculine rage, defiance, and gunplay. Thus, the video generates a hybridized black-inflected frame that is designed to appeal to Muslim young men living in the West.

The lyrics actively celebrate jihadi movements and demagogues, while promoting jihadi violence against Western targets and political figures. The video images and lyrics equate Muslim divine traitors to President George Bush and Prime Minister Tony Blair.

DIRTY KUFFAR PARTIAL LYRICS-SHEIKH TERRA FEAT SOUL SALAH CREW[29]

Heard around the world like the grand pooh-bah, we're gonna be taking over like we took over the Shah from Kandahar to Ramallah we comin', sah, peace to Hamas and the Hezbollah.

OBL crew be like a shining star, like the way we destroyed them two tower, ha-ha!

The so-called Islamic States places a total ban on music under their version of the caliphate, so the "Dirty Kuffar" video is not permitted in territory under their control. ISIS has taken the idea of divine traitors to an unprecedented level in modern history. The following example illustrates ISIS's method of dealing with Qutb's jahiliyyah.

Mutah Safi Yousef al-Kasasbeh was a member of the prominent Jordanian family of the influential Sunni Muslim Bararsheh tribe out of southern Jordan. His F-16 fighter crashed near Raqqa, Syria on December 24, 2014, during Jordan's military intervention against the ISIS. The Jordanian government negotiated exchange for Safida al-Rishawi, a woman sentenced to death for an attempted Jordanian suicide attack. However, negotiations failed, and the Jordanian government asserted that al-Kasasbeh was killed by immolation on January 3, indicating that the negotiating process was a publicity stunt.[30] He was convicted of treason by the self-declared Islamic State.

On February 3, 2015, ISIS released a video which depicted the execution of Mutah Safi Yousef al-Kasasbeh. The title of the video, *Healing the Believers' Chests*, which is taken from the Quran, reads: "Fight against them! And Allah will punish them with your hands, cover them with shame, help you (to win) over them, heal the chests of believers."[31] The film was credited to the Islamic State's official Al Furqan Media Foundation. The film was disseminated broadly across social media sites on the internet before being picked up by major news networks. From their perspective, since al-Kasasbeh is guilty of treason against "the true believers," the manner of his death must reflect lex talionis or "eye for eye."

The professionally edited video begins by showing the downed aircraft, the pilot's capture, and related media coverage. The film begins with King Abdullah of Jordan stating that all pilots that bomb targets on ISIS territory were all volunteers. King Abdullah's appearance at the beginning of the video is meant to make the point that each Jordanian pilot carried out attacks against ISIS on their own free will. The video also blends together images of Americans and "Jordanian Muslims" fighting against those who have been labeled violent jihadists in Afghanistan and Iraq. Essentially, the video frames the Jordanian military as a proxy ally to the United States against those who claim to be true defenders of the faith.[32]

Al-Kasasbeh is then shown wearing an orange prison jumpsuit similar to the orange prison garb worn by those at Guantánamo Bay. The video transitions to him essentially "confessing" the details of his mission, the other details of the aerial campaign, and targeting information. It is interesting to note that as he describes ISIS targets, al-Kasasbeh uses the term mujahedeen, which is translated as holy fighters for jihad. In the video, the United States, Canada, France, Great Britain, and New Zealand are classified as the Crusader coalition. Jordan, the Emirates, Saudi Arabia, Morocco, Bahrain, Kuwait, Turkey, and Qatar are listed as the apostate Muslim nations that provided the aircraft, the bases, the weapons, and logistics on behalf of the Crusaders.[33]

The purpose of the video is to articulate al-Kasasbeh's treason and illustrate the symbolic nature of his death. He is framed as being guilty of collaborating with Israelis, killing civilians and true holy fighters. The video makes the case that the Jordanians collaborated with the Israelis over air space against Islam's holy fighters. The air strikes resulted in civilian casualties and were depicted in the film by showing burned women and children covered in rubble. The method of execution by immolation and by later being crushed by a vehicle with rubble dumped upon his body was a symbolic gesture to depict the type of death experienced by air raid victims.

Al-Kasasbeh's execution is an example of how an ideological and religious problem was overcome by a dark innovation. The problem is this: How can one Muslim justify killing another Muslim? From a religious standpoint, how can two self-declared members of the same faith justify killing other members that profess the same faith? The answer is based in an innovation that frames Muslims like al-Kasasbeh as divine traitors.

Sayyid Qutb is attributed with advancing the idea that resulted in al-Kasasbeh's death.[34] Qutb, if alive today, would argue that the Jordanian pilot was really living in a state of Islamic ignorance or jahiliyyah. This innovation enables a Sunni Muslim to look down upon another Sunni Muslim as an apostate, despite his or her profession of faith, because he or she is really living in a state of deception. Though they profess to be Muslims, they are not living life fully submitted to sharia. Their actions are worse than Americans or Europeans because they identify themselves as faithful.

The ISIS video provides a high visibility example of how Qutb's form of jahiliyyah has evolved into action over time. In the final moments of the film, the photo IDs of Jordanian pilots are shown, and each is labeled as a crusader. Since ISIS considers Muslim pilots to belong to the crusading West, any profession of Islamic faith is ignored by ISIS. The final statement on the video is translated into the following:

> On this occasion, the Islamic state announces reward of 100 gold dinars to whoever kills a Crusader pilot. The Diwan for state security has released a list containing the names of Jordanian pilots who participated in the campaign. So good tidings to whoever supports his religion and achieves a kill that will liberate him from hellfire.[35]

CHURCH OF THE CREATOR FOUNDER AND LEADER, BEN KLASSEN

> I now know we are on the right track and that we can build a worldwide religious movement for the survival, expansion and advancement of the White Race such as our race has never ever even dreamed of before. I am now convinced that in CREATIVITY we have the Total Program, the Final Solution, the Ultimate Creed. The response from our White Racial Comrades has thoroughly confirmed my conviction that in the creed and program of CREATIVITY lies the road to the resurrection and redemption of the White Race.[36]

Ben Klassen was born February 20, 1918, in southern Ukraine, north of the Sea of Azov, in the Mennonite village of Rudnerweide. His parents were German-speaking Mennonites who belonged to a 450-year tradition that spoke both low and high German. His family experienced some of the violence and food shortages that occurred during the Bolshevik revolution, and in 1924, his family sold everything and departed for Mexico. After a brief stint in Mexico, his family moved to the Saskatchewan province in Canada. In Canada, Klassen worked on their 640-acre family farm, attended Herschel High School, and began a teaching career after graduation. He tired of teaching and was accepted in an engineering program at the University of Heidelberg in Germany in 1939. Because of the outbreak of World War II, he was not able to attend college there but graduated instead with an engineering degree in 1943 from the University of Saskatchewan. During the war, he was a member of the Canadian Officer Training Corps. Afterward he worked as a nickel miner and later would move to Montréal to work for Northern Electric before moving to Los Angeles.[37]

In the United States, Klassen was employed in a variety of occupations and endeavors. He worked as a technical sales rep for Bardwell McAllister and was a realtor for Beacoms United Realty Office before starting his own real estate business, Silver Springs Land Company. In 1946, Klassen married. He had his first child in 1951 and then moved his family to Florida in 1958, where they remained for 25 years. He invented one of the first electric can openers and traveled to Germany to obtain a patent and market it to Siemens Electric. Klassen secured a contract from Robbins and Myers to manufacture, promote, and sell the can opener. The appliance was called the Canoelectric, and by 1962 they had sold 50,000 units.[38]

Klassen traced his interest in politics back to 1938 as a twenty-year-old when he read *Mein Kampf*. He believed that Hitler was the greatest leader of the white race, but he criticized him as an ineffective philosopher. Klassen recounted following Hitler and German politics during World War II, but he did not pursue any political endeavors. In the United States, Klassen states that he was most influenced by Senator McCarthy's attack against communism, the use of 20,000 National Guard troops in Oxford, Mississippi, in 1961 to admit an African American student to the University of Mississippi, and the assassination of President John F. Kennedy on November 22, 1963. In his autobiography he states that these events catalyzed him into political activism. He soon joined the John Birch Society, sold Bircher literature, and became the chairman for the John Birch Society Speakers Bureau.[39]

In 1966, Ben Klassen ran for a state legislator position in Broward County, Florida. Klassen promised to fight big government, recover individual powers over state rights, and keep tax dollars local instead of sending it to Washington, D.C. On November 8, 1966, Klassen was elected by a vote count of 57,843 to 51,543. However, one year later, Broward County District was restructured, and he was forced to run again, this time losing. After losing the election, Klassen supported the presidential candidacy of George

Wallace, ran an official Birch Society bookstore, and managed a real estate business. He was active in real estate for 10 years and negotiated some 2,500 transactions.[40]

Klassen's anti-Semitic beliefs became more volatile. He argued that the John Birch Society ignored the "Jewish problem," which he considered the central problem in the United States. In 1967, he left the Republican Party to work for Governor George Wallace's 1968 presidential campaign. Klassen discovered that Wallace's campaign manager was Jewish, which caused him to reconsider his support. He realized that neither the Democratic or Republican parties had a solution for the white race, nor did the Wallace party or any independent party. He resigned from the Birch Society and began to look at other organizations such as the Ku Klux Klan, the American Nazi Party, and National States Rights. No organization or party met his criteria for a successful plan that targeted the Jews, and on November 5, 1969, Klassen renounced his membership from the John Birch Society.[41]

Disillusioned from the Birch Society and existing political parties, he identified the need for a specific religion devoted to the white race. The culmination of his experiences in politics and his search for a replacement to mainstream organizations led to the formation of Creativity. According to Klassen, "One's race is one's religion," and in order to advance the white race as a religion, Creativity needed a tangible church, its own Bible, and members. From February through March 1971, Klassen completed the group's logo, was involved in publishing literature, signed up members, and outlined fourteen ideological points. He leveraged his Birch Society and Wallace contacts and held Creativity meetings that started with about forty members. Klassen attempted to expand his followership to proselytize new followers. He reached out with limited success to William Pierce, Matt Koehl, James H Madole, Tom Metzger, Frank Colin, and Harold Covington who all were neo-Nazi leaders at the time.[42]

In 1973, Klassen founded the Church of the Creator and declared himself to be the Pontifex Maximus, a term adopted from the Romans to denote the supreme leadership position of the Creativity Movement.[43] Members who belonged to Klassen's church argued that it was race, not religion, that embodied absolute truth. Klassen argued that the white race is nature's highest expression of culture, civilization, and creativity. He considered Jews and nonwhites as subhuman, labeling them mud races whose sole purpose is to conquer and eradicate the white race. Although the Church of the Creator began in Lighthouse Point, Florida, in 1982, he moved it permanently to a twenty-two-acre property in Otto, North Carolina. On this property he built a house of worship, a warehouse to stockpile Creativity publications, a house for his family, and a school intended for white boys. He was granted tax exemption as a bona fide nonprofit religious organization from the North

Carolina Department of Revenue. However, the state's approval was contingent on the federal government ruling, and the IRS had no record of that exemption.[44]

During the twenty years that he led the Church of the Creator, he wrote more than fifteen books. Three of them are classics in neo-Nazi publications. He authored the *White Man's Bible, Nature's Eternal Religion*, and *Salubrious Living*. He argued that Creativity and his church are not related to neo-Nazism, nor was he a white supremacist because he believed there should be no interaction between whites and nonwhites. Creativity attracted very few followers by the late 1980s, but he justified this as normal because even Christianity and Islam had endured early persecution. Klassen published a monthly newsletter, *Racial Loyalty*, which at the height of Creativity, supposedly had a circulation of about 15,000. He pushed eugenics in *Racial Loyalty*, and in order to boost membership, he ran a section to promote correspondence between prospective couples. His school was intended for gifted white boys in order to indoctrinate youth with a Creativity program. He created a flag to symbolize the church's mission, and he organized his church around a model meant to prevent government agent infiltration.[45]

His strategy was to convert elements of the far right to Creativity. Klassen argued that only a powerful movement backed by a single ideology could safeguard the white race and ultimately win a racial revolution.[46] It appears that Klassen's strategy was to seek out far right intellectuals in order to convert them and persuade them about the merits of Creativity. In the 1980s, the Church the Creator also had a presence in Sweden and South Africa.[47]

In the 1990s Klassen faced several personal difficulties. In 1992, his wife died of cancer, and he sold most of his compound, for financial reasons, to the National Alliance. He was being personally attacked by other neo-Nazis, and he struggled to find suitable replacement to take over the organization. Over the years, he had attempted to vet several candidates, but no adequate replacement was found to take over the organization.[48]

Now 75 years old, he prepared to take his own life. He justified the ancient Roman's view of suicide as an honorable action rather than to live in shame, captivity, or humiliation. Klassen had been in a deep depression because of the loss of his wife as well as the failure of his church. On August 6, 1993, he overdosed on sleeping pills and was found by his daughter. Klassen's successor, Rick McCarty, notified members of the church in a letter dated August 12, 1993, that their leader had died. Klassen was buried on his North Carolina property in a spot that has been designated as the Ben Klassen Memorial Park. His tombstone reads, "He gave white people of the world a powerful racial religion of their own area." After Klassen committed suicide in 1993, the organization floundered and was overcome by financial problems, arrests, and inept leadership.[49] Matthew Hale was appointed "Pontifex

Maximus" in 1996, and renamed the organization The World Church of the Creator before changing it again to the Creativity Movement.[50] Matthew Hale was convicted of soliciting the murder of a federal judge in 2004 and is currently serving a forty-year prison term in a super Max state penitentiary in Florence, Colorado.[51] Although the Creativity Movement can be described as a weak organization in 2016, the innovations of Ben Klassen continue to influence neo-Nazism and white supremacy beyond his organization or membership.

Innovation: Your Race Is Your Religion

Klassen believed that religion is one of the most powerful forces in the world. It could capture hearts and minds, unify diverse nationalities, and channel them toward a common cause. He equated religion to a controlled fire, which could be used for either good or bad. He looked to existing religions for a model, and ironically, he looked to Judaism as an exemplary religion of identity preservation. It didn't matter that Judaism was a Jewish faith, only that it served the Jewish people well over the years. He considered Judaism the most powerful religion ever created and a model worth emulating. He saw Judaism as a mechanism that had maintained the Jewish identity for centuries throughout conflict, persecution, and geographic boundaries. Klassen observed that Judaism had been extremely effective for the Jewish people, and he wanted something similar for the white race. He repackaged some of the ideas from Judaism and tailored them toward whites.[52]

Klassen compelled whites to unite around a faith where racial solidarity would be more effective than white nationalism. Creativity would be the mechanism to unite whites despite national differences. He saw a religious movement as a far more powerful unifying mechanism than political movement. Klassen pointed out that Creativity Creed emphasized whites as a unified group whereas National Socialism championed German nationality, and he criticized Hitler for nationalizing race.[53]

Klassen theorized that Christianity was a Jewish invention to win a race war. He argued that all Jews and nonwhites are the eternal enemy of the white race. According to Klassen, this conflict has existed for millennia, and his central argument was that Christianity was created by Jews in order to pacify whites. Klassen perceived that Christianity distracted whites and forced them to believe in "myths" and ultimately produced confused and weak white males. According to Klassen, if Christianity continues to be the most popular religion for whites, then whites will become an extinct species and ultimately lose the race war.[54]

Klassen argued that the Jews needed a strategy to overpower the Roman Empire. Saul of Tarsus, later St. Paul of Christianity, weaponized this strategy, called it Christianity, and took it to Rome in order to destroy the Roman Empire from within. Klassen rejected the Christian concept of loving one's enemies but rather openly hated them stating that it is one's purpose to destroy their enemies. Creativity focused on selective breeding to advance the white race instead of racial interbreeding, which he called mongrelization. He also stated that while Christianity indicates that sex in certain contexts is a sin, those in Creativity believe that the attraction between a man and woman is the most natural thing and should promote the propagation of species. He also asserted that Christianity stifles productivity, destroys creativity, and concentrates on "laying up treasures in heaven" or focusing on aspects of life after death or a morbid death culture. Klassen contended that Christianity is suicidal to the white race, because it was contradictory to the laws of nature and common sense. Finally, he maintained that Christianity has a lack of evidence and that it is much easier to believe the laws of nature than the stories that are indicated in the Old and New Testaments.[55] He also argued that another shortcoming of Christianity was the fact that they did not appreciate the power of ideas, propaganda, and religion which ultimately made them fall from ideas that came within.[56]

Klassen explored other white religions and found them problematic. He stated that Christian Identity was inspired by Jews, that it was hopelessly misguided, and that its followers should be characterized as enemies. He perceived Norse Neopaganism as a step backward, but agreed with more of its ideology than Christian Identity. He corresponded with the founder of the Odinists Fellowship, Else Christensen, but found the religion lacked a racial component that would mobilize the white race. The fact that it was the religion of the Druids was not an advantage. Klassen then began to design a new religion for the white race.

> The idea that the white race needed a completely new religion to promote its own best interest grew within my mind. Not just a political party such as the Nationalist White Party, but a complete, fundamentally new religion that established new moral values. Moral values we had been accepting and taking for granted were not ours. . . . They were, as I had said, Jewish shibboleths. We needed more values that reflected the heritage of our own great white race, not that of the parasitic Jews.[57]

Klassen decided to establish a racial religion, and its goal would be the survival, expansion, and advancement of the white race. He turned to the laws of nature, searching for the foundation on which to base his new religion. Laws of nature were selected because they were more predictable and reliable than the myths or superstitions in other religions. He argued that humanity was not above nature, but was integrated with it. White survival depended on a close-knitted relationship with nature. The highest aim for any species is to survive and prosper. He believed that conflict was necessary for survival because ultimately it strengthened the species.[58]

Klassen needed to overcome some of the "theological" challenges of Christianity. Christianity is death oriented, frames the Jews as the chosen people, and focuses on the pointlessness of life. Conversely, Creativity advances the white interests in order to promote, preserve, propagate, advance, and expand the white race to enjoy nature, work productively, eat well, and serve the interests of their own people. Creativity presents itself as a total religion in such a way that answers the important questions of the white race.

Klassen exhorts whites to practice the sixteen commandments of Creativity[59] and racial loyalty in order to have large families to be absolutely committed to their faith:

1. It is the avowed duty and the holy responsibility of each generation to ensure and secure for all-time existence of the white race on the face of this planet.
2. Be fruitful and multiply. Do your part in helping to populate the world with your own kind. It is our sacred goal to populate the earth with white people exclusively.
3. Remember that the inferior colored races are deadly enemies, and the most dangerous of all—the Jewish race. It is our immediate objective to relentlessly expand the white race and keep shrinking that of our enemies.
4. The guiding principle of all your actions shall be: What is best for the white race?
5. You shall keep your race pure. Pollution of the white race is a heinous crime against nature and against your own race.
6. Your first loyalty belongs to the white race.
7. Show your preferential treatment in business dealings to members of your own race. Phase out all dealings with Jews as soon as possible. Do not employ black throated colors. Have social contact only with members of your own racial family.
8. Destroy and banish all Jewish thought and influence from society. Work hard to bring about a white world as soon as possible.
9. Work and creativity are our genius. We regard work as a noble pursuit and our willingness to work as a blessing to the race.
10. Decide early that during your lifetime you will make at least one major lasting contribution to the white race.
11. Uphold the honor of your race at all times.
12. It is our duty and privilege to further nature's plan by striving toward the advancement and improvement of our future generations.
13. You shall honor and protect and venerate the sanctity of the family unit and hold it sacred.

14. Throughout your life, faithfully uphold our pivotal creed of blood, soil, and honor. Practice it diligently, for it is the heart of our faith.
15. Be a proud member of the white race, think and act positively. Be courageous, confident, and aggressive. Utilize constructively creative ability.
16. We, the racial comrades of the white race, are determined to regain complete unconditional control of our own destiny.

Klassen's Creativity religion and his phrase, "My race is my religion," deify the white race, remove nationalistic boundaries, and make skin color an example of a spiritual master status. Members of the white race who are Christians are really traitors involved in a form of racial blasphemy and are ultimately supportive of a Jewish strategy against whites. If nature has selected the white race to be the epitome of intellectual achievement and excellence, then going against what nature has produced creates a divine traitor. Even though their skin color may be the same, they are considered to be part of the enemy because of their actions. One of the indicators of how Klassen's innovations of white deification and race traitors has evolved and became part of the neo-Nazi landscape is evident in white power music.

White power music has become an effective way to disseminate ideas, and the experiences at white power events have been significant for recruitment among white supremacists and neo-Nazis.[60] It is an effective method to reach younger audiences and solidify racist ideas with raw emotion.[61] Music can also have either hidden or overt power. Scientists studying music have demonstrated the effect music has on a listener on two different levels—the conscience and subconscious.[62] Conscious and subliminal messages do more than just generate emotions. The combination of musical lyrics and words communicates messages and conditions both intellectual and emotional responses. Lyrics are coded in such a way that the listener may or may not fully understand the message. Effects can be positive, negative, or neutral, but the research has demonstrated that music accompanying ideas is powerful in both the short-term and long-term sentiment.[63] Numerous examples are available across history about how governments have used music to indoctrinate and influence public[64]; one of the more salient examples comes from the Nazi party's particularly elaborate music program of the Hitler Youth.

White power music enables diverse neo-Nazi communities to have a common ground and minimizes geographical differences. The themes associated with the genre fall into several categories: racist themes, Nazi themes, skinhead themes, anti-Semitic themes, violent themes, racial protection themes, Viking or Norse themes, and racist martyrdom or iconic themes.[65] The white power musician, George Burdi, provides an example of how Ben Klassen's ideas intersect with this musical genre.

George Burdi, a Canadian musician born in 1970, formed a band called RAHOWA (racial holy war). RAHOWA is described as a white power band that emerged in the 1990s and produced the popular neo-Nazi songs "Cult of the Holy War" and "RAHOWA." Burdi's primary source of inspiration was Creativity, specifically the ideas in *Nature's Eternal Religion* and *The White Man's Bible*. Burdi believed that racial loyalty was imperative for the survival of the white race and that Christianity was a serious hindrance to any type of racial holy war or racial revolution.[66] Burdi believed that the best way of disseminating racial ideology was to create a music scene that harnessed young white male emotions and aggression. He believed that music was effective because it would link ideas and emotions and could catalyze a population. In 1993 Burdi and Mark Wilson launched Resistance Records, a white power recording company in Detroit, Michigan. Accompanying the music, *Resistance Magazine* was also produced and disseminated.[67] In 1995 it was estimated that it had a circulation of over 13,000 periodicals.[68]

Ben Klassen's ideas can be found in Burdi's lyrics listed below.

RAHOWA LYRICS[69]

Our race is our religion, it is our reason and our creed, rid the world of the Nazarene—pathetic Christ not of our kind!

Now our future is secure, our sacred blood kept pure . . . the racial holy war has been won.

Burdi believed that the white race was the apex of nature's evolutionary process and one's race is one's religion.[70] Equating race with religion meant that the white race was no longer just a physiological trait but was the demarcation of divine superiority and a call to war. The lyrics of the song, RAHOWA, create the space to divide the white race along two lines, those that are racially loyal and those that are divine traitors to their race. The same message is also communicated by other white power musicians, which illustrates the need to connect the white race to a religious concept and implies that acting in treason against whites makes one guilty of being a divine traitor.

NOTES

1. Zimmerman, John C. Zimmerman. "Sayyid Qutb's Influence on the 11 September Attacks," *Terrorism and Political Violence* 16, no. 2 (January 1, 2004): 222–52, do: 10.1080/09546550480993.

2. Sivan, Emmanuel. *Radical Islam: Medieval Theology and Modern Politics.* New Haven: Yale University Press, 1985.

3. "CF2R—Analysis of the Influence of Sayed Qutb's Islamist Ideology on the Development of Jihadism," accessed August 29, 2015, http://www.cf2r.org/fr/ foreign-analyzes/analysis-of-the-influence-of-sayed-qutbs-islamist-ideology-on-the-development-of-djiha.prh; "ISIS, Abu Bakr Naji, and Applied Qutb | The American Conservative," accessed August 29, 2015, http://www.theamericanconservative.com/ dreher/isis-abu-bakr-naji-sayyid-qutb-jihad-islam/.

4. Shepard, William E. "Sayyid Qutb's Doctrine of Jāhiliyya," *International Journal of Middle East Studies* 35, no. 4 (November 1, 2003): 521–45.

5. Dohratz, Betty A. "The Role of Religion in the Collective Identity of the White Racialist Movement," *Journal for the Scientific Study of Religion* 40, no. 2 (June 1, 2001): 287–301.

6. Klassen, Ben P.M. *The White Man's Bible.* CreateSpace Independent Publishing Platform, 2011.

7. Klassen, Ben. *Nature's Eternal Religion.* Milwaukee, WI: Church of the Creator, 1992.

8. "Creativity Movement," *Southern Poverty Law Center*, accessed August 29, 2015, https://www.splcenter.org/fighting-hate/extremist-files/group/creativity-movement-0.

9. Qutb, Sayyid. *Milestones.* Islamic Book Service, 2006. Print. Pp. 20.

10. Wright, Lawrence. *The Looming Tower: Al-Qaeda and the Road to 9/11.* New York: Vintage Books, 2006.

11. Toth James. *Sayyid Qutb: The Life and Legacy of a Radical Islamic Intellectual.* Oxford: Oxford University Press, 2013.

12. Musallam, Adnan. *From Secularism to Jihad: Sayyid Qutb and the Foundations of Radical Islamism*, First Edition. Praeger, 2005. p. 70.

13. Kepel, Gilles. *Muslim Extremism in Egypt: The Prophet and Pharaoh.* Berkley: University of California Press, 1985.

14. Calvert, John. *Sayyid Qutb and the Origins of Radical Islamism.* New York: Columbia University Press, 2010.

15. Adnan, Musallam. *From Secularism to Jihad: Sayyid Qutb and the Foundations of Radical Islamism.* Westport, CT: Praeger, 2005.

16. Mitchell, Richard P. *The Society of the Muslim Brothers.* London: Oxford University Press, 1969.

17. Kepel, Gilles. *Muslim Extremism in Egypt: The Prophet and Pharaoh.* Berkeley: University of California Press, 1985.

18. Calvert, John. *Sayyid Qutb and the Origins of Radical Islamism.* New York: Columbia University Press, 2010.

19. Tal, Nahman. *Radical Islam in Egypt and Jordan.* Sussex Academic Press, 2005.

20. Kramer, Martin. "Fundamentalist Islam at Large: The Drive for Power." *Middle East Quarterly*, June 1, 1996, http://www.meforum.org/304/ fundamentalist-islam-at-large-the-drive-for-power.

21. Zimmerman, John C. "Sayyid Qutb's Influence on the 11 September Attacks." *Terrorism and Political Violence* 16, no. 2 (2004): 222–52. doi:10.1070/09546550490480993.

22. Qutb, Sayyid, M.A. Salahi and A.A. Shamis, *In the Shade of the Qur'ān.* London: MWH, 1979.

23. Shepard, "Sayyid Qutb's Doctrine of 'Jāhiliyya.'"

24. Qutb, Sayyid. *The Political Thought of Sayyid Qutb: The Theory of Jahiliyyah.* London: Routledge, 2006.

25. "Sayyid Qutb's Milestones," p. 9

26. Ibid.

27. Ibid.

28. Shepard, "Sayyid Qutb's Doctrine of 'Jāhiliyya.'"

29. Sheikh Terra feat Soul Salah Crew Dirty Kuffar—YouTube. (n.d.). Retrieved June 8, 2016, from https://www.youtube.com/watch?v=SWP_95eSLBI

30. "Profile: IS-Held Jordanian Pilot Moaz Al-Kasasbeh," *BBC News*, accessed August 29, 2015, http://www.bbc.com/news/world-middle-east-31021927.

31. AYAT at-Taubah 9:14 مِهْيَلَع مُكْرُصنَيَو مِهِزْخُيَو مُكِيدْيَأِب ْمُهْلِّا ا مُهُبِّذَعُي مُهوُلِتاَق نَ ينِمُؤْمٍمْوَق َروُدُص ِفْشَيَو

32. "Jordanian Pilot Kasasbeh Burned Alive by Islamic State; Jordan Executes IS Requested Prisoner Rishawi in Response," *LeakSource*, accessed August 29, 2015, http://leaksource.info/2015/02/04/jordanian-pilot-kaseasbeh-burned-alive-by-islamic-state-jordan-executes-is-requested-prisoner-rishawi-in-response/.

33. "ISIS Burns Hostage Alive," MovingImage, *Fox News*, (February 3, 2015), http://video.foxnews.com/v/4030583977001/warning-extremely-graphic-video-isis-burns-hostage-alive/.

34. Qutb, *The Political Thought of Sayyid Qutb.*

35. "The ISIS Murder of Jordanian Pilot Moaz Al-Kasasbeh: 'Healing the Believer's Chests' (Complete Uncensored Video) | Sharia Unveiled," accessed August 29, 2015, https://shariaunveiled.wordpress.com/2015/02/08/the-isis-murder-of-jordanian-pilot-moaz-al-kasasbeh-healing-the-believers-chests-complete-uncensored-video/.

36. Klassen, Ben. P.M. *The White Man's Bible*. CreateSpace Independent Publishing Platform, 2011. Print.

37. Klassen, Ben. P.M. *Trials, Tribulations, Triumphs: A History of the Church of the Creator During Its 10 Year Domicile in the State of North Carolina, Coordinated with Biographical Details During the Same Period.* Niceville, FL: Church of the Creator, 1993

38. Ibid.

39. Ibid.

40. Ibid.

41. Ibid.

42. Ibid.

43. He recommended Latin as a universal language for the white race because it was phonetically perfect, incorporated white traditions, and historically could be used as a neutral language.

44. Klassen, *Trials, Tribulations and Triumphs.*

45. Dobratz, "The Role of Religion in the Collective Identity of the White Racialist Movement"; "Creativity Movement."

46. Brian Kozel is the first recognized martyr of the Church the Creativity.

47. In South Africa, the incident involved two South African members, Juergen Matthews and Johannes Juergens Grobbela, who were killed in a gun battle with South African police after attempting to smuggle weapons to a survivalist compound in Namibia. After being arrested, they detonated a smoke bomb in an attempt to escape. Police caught up with them, and a gunfight ensued in which two officers were shot. One of them died, and the two Creativity members were killed when the officers returned fire.

48. Klassen, *Trials, Tribulations and Triumphs*.

49. In 1993, eight individuals with ties to the COTC were arrested in Southern California for plotting to bomb a black church in L.A. and assassinate Rodney King, whose videotaped beating by white police officers in 1991 had sparked national outrage. Later in 1993, Jeremiah Knesal, a member of the COTC, was found with weapons, ammunition and hate literature in his car; he later confessed to his involvement in a July 1993 firebombing of an NAACP office in Tacoma, Washington. Later, a close associate of the group's leader would go on a murderous racist rampage before police killed him.

50. "Matt Hale," *Southern Poverty Law Center*, accessed August 29, 2015, https://www.splcenter.org/fighting-hate/extremist-files/individual/matt-hale.

51. Hale graduated from Southern Illinois University School of Law in May 1998 and passed the bar in July of that same year but was denied a license to practice law. Benjamin Smith, a World Church of the Creator member, resigned from The Church and went on a three-day shooting spree in Illinois and Indiana. Smith shot nine Orthodox Jews on July 2, 1999, walking to and from their synagogues in Chicago's West Rogers Park neighborhood. He killed two people, including former Northwestern University basketball coach Ricky Byrdsong, in Evanston, Illinois, and a twenty-six-year-old Korean graduate student, Won-Joon Yoon, who was shot as he was on his way to church in Bloomington, Indiana. Smith wounded nine others before committing suicide on July 4. Smith may have acted in retaliation after Hale's application to practice law was rejected.

52. Klassen. *Nature's Eternal Religion*.

53. Ibid.

54. Klassen, *Trials, Tribulations and Triumphs*.

55. Ibid.

56. Jonathan R. White, "Political Eschatology A Theology of Antigovernment Extremism," *American Behavioral Scientist* 44, no. 6 (February 1, 2001): 937–56, doi:10.1177/00027640121956601.

57. Klassen, *Trials, Tribulations and Triumphs*. p. 47.

58. Klassen. *Nature's Eternal Religion*.

59. "Creativity Alliance—Sixteen Commandments," accessed August 29, 2015, http://creativityalliance.com/16commandments.htm.

60. White power music is a music genre that promotes white nationalism, neo-Nazism, and racist views against Jews, nonwhites, and race traitors. It can include rap, folk, heavy metal, pop, and country. The phrase "white power" was coined in

the 1960s by George Lincoln Rockwell, the founder and leader of the American Nazi Party. There are also specific white power music genres that include national socialist white metal, hate core, rock against communism, nationalist folk music, and Nazi punk. One of the central purposes of white power music is to link the power of music to lyrics and ideas that advocate racial pride, demonizing nonwhites, and the promotion of violent ideas in a way that other forms of propaganda could not accomplish. White power music was initially perceived to be an important tool to gain revenue, new recruits, and correlate ideas with emotion. The white power music industry is considered to be a leading source of young recruits, money, and resources from charismatic racists. Since the 1990s, the industry has emerged into a multimillion dollar, worldwide enterprise, and in the early 2000s, Resistance Records, a neo-Nazi music company, was selling over 70,000 CDs a year. In the year 1999, it was estimated that the neo-Nazi music industry was worth $3.4 million a year. The music itself is a global phenomenon which has a larger market in Europe and in Russia than in the United States.

61. "Music and the Holocaust: Music amongst the Hitler Youth," accessed August 29, 2015, http://holocaustmusic.ort.org/politics-and-propaganda/third-reich/music-hitler-youth/.

62. Honigsheim, Paul K., Peter Etzkorn, and Paul Hongisheim. *Sociologists and Music: An Introduction to the Study of Music and Society*. New Brunswick: Transaction Publishers, 1989.

63. Sakolsky, Ronald B. and Fred Wei-han. Ho. *Sounding Off!: Music as Subversion/resistance/revolution*. Brooklyn, NY: Autonomedia, 1995.

64. Ibid.

65. Simi, Pete, and Robert Futrell. *American Swastika: Inside the White Power Movement's Hidden Spaces of Hate*. Lanham, MD: Rowman & Littlefield Publishers, 2010.

66. "Former Hate Music Promoter George Burdi Discusses His Experiences with Racism and the White Power Music Industry," *Southern Poverty Law Center*, accessed August 29, 2015, https://www.splcenter.org/fighting-hate/intelligence-report/2001/former-hate-music-promoter-george-burdi-discusses-his-experiences-racism-and-white-power.

67. Tally, Stephan. "The Method of a Neo-Nazi Mogul," *The New York Times*, February 25, 1996, sec. Magazine, http://www.nytimes.com/1996/02/25/magazine/the-method-of-a-neo-nazi-mogul.html.

68. Burdi was arrested on May 29, 1993, after getting into a confrontation with a series of counterprotesters. He was also arrested in 1995 for assaulting a woman after a speech he gave. In April 1997, the offices of Resistance Records were razed by authorities in order to investigate nonpayment of taxes.

69. "RAHOWA LYRICS," accessed August 29, 2015, http://www.metallyrica.com/r/rahowa_us.html.

70. "Former Hate Music Promoter George Burdi Discusses His Experiences with Racism and the White Power Music Industry." *Southern Poverty Law Center*, accessed July 11, 2016. https://www.spolcenter.org/fighting-hate/intelligence-report/2001/former-hate-music-promoter-george-burdi-discusses-his-experiences-racism-and-white-power.

Chapter 2

The Need to Weaponize Ideas
Anwar Al-Awlaki and William Pierce

A dark idea can remain dormant if it is never transformed into an easily disseminated message. For example, an ideologue may have an original idea but may not effectively advance it in such a way that it is accepted by audiences. Weaponizing ideas is defined as a process in which ideas are translated into effective propaganda messages. The work from both Anwar al-Awlaki, a leading Al Qaeda propagandist in Yemen, and William Pierce, founder of the National Alliance, one of the largest neo-Nazi groups, illustrates how to weaponize ideas to the masses. This chapter examines specific events that were influenced by the weaponized ideas from Anwar al-Awlaki and William Pierce.

On April 15, 2013, two pressure cooker bombs exploded near the finish line of the Boston Marathon. The explosions resulted in the deaths of three people and wounded more than 260 others, some critically. Two brothers were responsible for the attack, Dzhokhar and Tamerlan Tsarnaev. The ensuing investigation revealed that both brothers were frequent consumers of violent jihadi propaganda and websites. The younger brother, Dzhokhar, specifically mentioned to investigators that they were influenced by *Inspire Magazine*, which is the online publication produced by Al Qaeda's Yemeni affiliate.[1] The title of the magazine indicates its purpose. Its objective is to communicate ideas, strategies, and tactics to Muslims living in Western countries. *Inspire Magazine* is the product of Anwar al-Awlaki, a Yemeni American who later returned to Yemen to become an Al Qaeda propagandist.[2]

Al-Awlaki indirectly influenced the Tsarnaev brothers in target selection, ideological motivation, and construction of an improvised explosive device. Every *Inspire* issue endorses lone-wolf jihadi attacks, and the summer 2010 issue was no exception.[3] The issue also suggested that a sports venue would maximize the casualties of an explosive device. Dzhokhar specifically

Figure 2.1   Depiction of Tamerlan Tsarnaev, Boston Bomber, in Al Qaeda's Inspire Magazine Issue #13.

mentioned that they listened to al-Awlaki's online sermons and were cata-lyzed by them. The summer 2010 *Inspire* issue included an article entitled, "Make a Bomb in the Kitchen of your Mom."[4] The article described in detail how to construct a pressure cooker bomb and marketed it as one of the most effective improvised weapons. The Tsarnaev brothers learned how to fabricate pressure cooker bombs from the magazine. In *Inspire* issue number 13, the magazine glorified Tamerlan Dzhokhar as a glorious martyr and one who should be emulated.

Almost exactly eighteen years before the Boston Bombing, a truck-bomb exploded outside the Alfred P. Murrah Federal Building in Oklahoma City, Oklahoma, on April 19, 1995. The results of the explosion left 168 people dead and hundreds more injured. The blast was set off by anti-government militant Timothy McVeigh, who in 2001 was executed for his crimes in a super Max facility in Indiana. His co-conspirator, Terry Nichols, received life in prison.[5]

Until September 11, 2001, the Oklahoma City bombing was the worst terrorist attack to take place on U.S. soil. Timothy McVeigh was pulled over by Trooper Charles Hanger for driving without a license plate and eventually was arrested for possessing an unregistered firearm. McVeigh was almost released from jail until investigators identified him as a prime suspect in the Oklahoma City bombing. A sealed envelope was found in Timothy McVeigh's yellow Mercury after his arrest. FBI agent William Eppright found several documents that included clippings from *The Turner Diaries*.[6] *The Turner Diaries* is a fictional account of a violent Aryan revolution written by Dr. William Pierce, who self-published the novel in 1978 under the pseudonym Andrew McDonald. Since its publication, it has been considered to be one of the most influential neo-Nazi documents.[7]

The clippings from *The Turner Diaries* were the first pieces of evidence introduced in McVeigh's trial, and witnesses later testified that he was inspired by the text, read it repeatedly, and sold copies at local gun shows.[8] Timothy McVeigh's case brought national attention to *The Turner Diaries* in the late 1990s, but the Anti-Defamation League (ADL) had documented cases since the 1980s where incidences of violence by individuals and groups credited Pierce's novel as influential.[9] As a vehicle for hate propaganda, Pierce's novel can be listed as one of the most effective methods in weaponizing ideas.

ANWAR AL-AWLAKI

We will implement the rule of God on earth by the tip of the sword.[10]

Anwar al-Awlaki became one of the most noted violent jihadists in the last decade.[11] His impact can be attributed to his ability to communicate effectively and to use the World Wide Web to disseminate his propaganda. The term "effectiveness" is used as a measure to correlate the number of attacks that were either directly or indirectly connected to his ideas, mentoring, or propaganda. He also represents a series of English-speaking violent jihadists who trace their ideological roots back to 1980s and 1990s in the United Kingdom and America. Scholars argue that he is one of the most effective English-speaking violent jihadis to date because of his understanding of Western political and social culture and his ability to weaponize ideas into contextual social media forms.[12] He used blogs, email, Facebook pages, numerous YouTube video sermons, and Al Qaeda's *Inspire Magazine* as dissemination tools.[13]

Al-Awlaki's radicalization process is considered unique because he was once considered to be a leading moderate Muslim and a popular Islamic preacher in the United States. He criticized Al Qaeda in *National Geographic, The New York Times,* and other media sources immediately after 9/11.[14] After the 9/11 attacks, he attended a luncheon hosted by the U.S. secretary of the army, Tom E. White, who was engaged in efforts to ease tensions with Muslim Americans. In 2002, he was granted permission to conduct the first Muslim prayer service at the U.S. Capitol. During this service, Anwar specifically prayed for Muslim congressional staffers and for officials of the Council on American Islamic Relations (CAIR).[15]

He weaponized both a strategy and methods to radicalize Muslims living in Western nations with a message in contextualized English propaganda. Specifically, he advocated lone-wolf attacks against a myriad of targets and provided the literature that outlined the required training, methods, and equipment to carry out the attack. He is known to have direct contact with several infamous violent extremists, most notably Umar Farouk Abdulmutallab, Nidal Malik Hassan, and Zachary Adam Chesser. In 2009, Abdulmutallab attempted to detonate Northwest Airlines flight 253 over Detroit. Hassan carried out a shooting attack in November 2009 and was charged with thirteen counts of premeditated murder and thirty-two counts of attempted murder. Chesser was involved in death threats against the producers of the popular animated television show "South Park."[16] Awlaki is known to have some degree of connection to at least seventeen other incidents.

The Man

Awlaki was born in 1971 to Yemeni parents in Las Cruces, New Mexico. His father, a Fulbright Fellow and former president of Sana University, was well educated and worked as a member of Yemeni president Ali Abdullah Saleh's ruling party. He returned to Yemen seven years later, where he lived for eleven years while his father helped establish Ibb University. Al-Awlaki returned to the United States in 1991 in order to attend Colorado State University and later graduated with a BS in civil engineering in 1994. Soon afterward, he was the president of the Muslim Student Association and later earned a master of arts in education leadership from San Diego State

University. He also worked on a doctorate degree in human resource develop-ment at George Washington University from January to December 2001, but never completed the program. Although he interacted with several Islamic scholars in Saudi Arabia, Yemen, and United Kingdom, he lacked any formal Islamic training or study.[17]

In the United States, he served as imam in several mosques across the country. His preaching career began in 1994 at Colorado State University in Fort Collins, Colorado, where he delivered Friday sermons at the Fort Collins Islamic Center. One year later, he moved to Denver and took up a part-time position as the imam at the Denver Islamic Society. From 1996–2000, he lived in San Diego, California, where he was the imam at the Al-Ribat al-Islami Mosque, and in 2001 he served as imam at the Dar al Hijrah Mosque near Falls Church, Virginia, while also serving as the Muslim chaplain at George Washington University. He was arrested in 1996 and 1997 in San Diego for soliciting prostitutes, but this information was never made public and is speculated to be a motive for moving back to the East Coast.[18]

In the early 1990s there were indicators that he was progressing toward the path of violent jihad. In 1993, he took a trip to Afghanistan to person-ally see the impact of the Soviet-Afghan War. From 1998–1999 he was the vice president for an organization that was later known to finance terrorist activities, The Charitable Society for Social Welfare. During this time he met with Ziyad Khalil, who was thought to be affiliated with bin Laden and blind Sheikh, Omar Abdul Rahman, who was a leading plotter in the 1991 World Trade Center bombing. Al-Awlaki developed a relationship with two of the 9/11 hijackers, Nawaf al-Hazmi and Khalid al-Mindhar. The 9/11 com-mission report states that they both respected Awlaki's spiritual leadership. The full details of al-Awlaki's involvement with the 9/11 hijackers remain unknown. He was investigated by the FBI pre- and post- 9/11, but no formal charges were filed. Specifically, after the 9/11 attacks, he was interviewed by the FBI four separate times in eight days. Shortly afterward, he moved to London in March 2002. There's speculation that he left the United States because of the investigations or that he felt a toxic climate toward Muslims.[19]

Before his affiliation with Al Qaeda, his ideological work was closely aligned with the Muslim Brotherhood. In the United Kingdom, he became an established and popular member of the English-speaking violent jihadis based there. He had a reputation of being an engaging speaker because he was able to connect contextually to his audience. His listeners describe his style as charismatic and direct. While in the United Kingdom, he was involved with the Association to Revive the Way of the Messenger or JIMAS, a Salafi organization influenced by the Muslim Brotherhood, and the Islamic Forum Europe (IFE). During his speaking engagements, he would fill auditoriums as audiences listened to him address subjects like jihad, the war on Mus-lims, or Muslim community roles. His name was even brought up by Louise

Ellman, the MP for Liverpool Riverside, during a Parliament session in 2003.[20] His messages warned audiences of increased Western threats, while he chastised passive Muslims regarding their obligation to mobilize against these threats. His sermons pointed toward a political, religious, and cultural awakening, but at this time he was not advocating violent jihad against the United States and United Kingdom.[21]

In 2004, he left the United Kingdom and moved to Yemen. He attended Islamic classes at Zindani's Imam University while continuing to lecture. In August 31, 2006, he was arrested by the Yemeni Police and charged with kidnapping a Shiite teenager for ransom and for being involved in an Al Qaeda plot to kidnap a U.S. official. It was during this imprisonment in Yemen that he began to read Sayyid Qutb's work. Awlaki would later state that he was "so immersed with the author I would feel him with me in my cell speaking to me directly."[22] One year later, he was released and gave an interview to Mozzam Begg, former Guantánamo Bay detainee and the founder of Cageprisoners. In this interview al-Awlaki stated that he'd been arrested for his arbitrator role in a tribal dispute and then was held because FBI agents wanted to speak with him about his association with three 9/11 hijackers. He also stated that he was held in solitary confinement until his last month.[23]

Al-Awlaki's influence on violent jihadists was known by the highest members of the U.S. intelligence community. In June 2008, al-Awlaki officially launched his blog, www.Anwar-Awlaki.com, where the message of global jihad and his connection with Al Qaeda was clear. He was mentioned by James Klapper, the director of National Intelligence, in October 2008 and in late 2009.[24] Awlaki's association with Nidal Hassan, the Fort Hood attacker and the Christmas Day bomber,[25] led to the Obama administration authorizing his extrajudicial assassination in early 2010.[26] Due to Anwar's role as catalyst to violence, the United States continued to put pressure on the Yemeni government to capture Awlaki and have him extradited to the United States. Diplomatic pressure was ineffective. The Yemeni government claimed that Al Qaeda moved him so secretively and regularly that they could not arrest him, while Awlaki's father argued that it was not Al Qaeda that was hiding his son, but his tribe.[27]

On April 6, 2010, *The New York Times* reported that President Obama had authorized a targeted killing of Awlaki.[28] In July of that year, Awlaki's father worked with the Center for Constitutional Rights and the American Civil Liberties Union on a lawsuit with the goal of removing his son from the targeted killing list. On August 30, 2010, both groups filed a targeted killing lawsuit against Barack Obama, CIA director Leon Panetta, and Secretary of Defense Robert Gates.[29]

On September 30, 2011, after previous failed attempts, two predator drones fired hellfire missiles that killed al-Awlaki, his sixteen-year-old son, and three other suspected Al Qaeda members. Over the course of his life, he had married three times and had five children. President Barack Obama commented on his death. The fact that the president of the United States issued a message about a man who had never personally engaged in violence indicates Awlaki's effectiveness in weaponizing ideas. President Obama stated:

> The death of Awlaki is a major blow to Al Qaeda's most active operational affiliate. He took the lead in planning and directing efforts to murder American citizens. . . . And he repeatedly called on individuals in the United States and around the globe to kill innocent men, women, and children to advance a murderous agenda. The strike is further proof that Al Qaeda and its affiliates will find no safe haven anywhere in the world.[30]

Weaponizing Jihad: Branding Open Source Jihad

Al-Awlaki was effective in weaponizing ideas for three reasons. First, he possessed a dynamic personality, and audiences liked listening to him. Although Awlaki's physical characteristics left something to be desired, the way he delivered his messages was described by his listeners as powerful. In his online preaching cache, he synthesized complex conceptual material and transformed it in a way that was both understandable and relevant to his audiences. The ideas that he shared were readily available from a variety of published and digital sources, but it was the charismatic manner in which he illuminated complex thoughts that made al-Awlaki resonate with audiences.[31]

Second, he targeted an underutilized audience niche—Muslims living in Western countries. His background of having lived in Yemen and in the United States afforded him a cultural and contextual understanding that enabled him to package ideas effectively. He mastered the ability to contextualize a message for audiences whose primary language was not Arabic, who may have grown up or been born in a Western environment, but who felt that they were caught between two different worlds because of their parents and their faith. Because he used examples that tapped into the way some Western Muslims felt about living in the West, he demonstrated that he understood their environment. He was then able to connect to feelings of shame and then direct the listeners to violent jihadi doctrines.

Third, he effectively disseminated his message through the use of blogs, email, Facebook pages, numerous YouTube video sermons, and *Inspire Magazine*. Since his death, al-Awlaki's sermons have still been broadcasted across the internet in video and audio. The first issue of *Inspire Magazine* appeared in July 2010, and thirteen issues have been published since that time with the most recent being December 2014. This magazine is not the first of its kind to address English-speaking audiences or introduce new material. What is new is the emphasis placed on branding, targeting a Western marketing gap, connecting individual jihadism to the actual techniques/methods to be used in an attack, and the fact that it has actually inspired violent extremist acts.

The idea of the magazine was thought to be the creation of Anwar al-Awlaki. The very first edition included an editorial by Awlaki, entitled, "May Our Souls be Sacrificed for You," which reads like the equivalent of leaderless resistance or lone wolfism. The doctrine in the magazine aligns within a violent jihadist perspective, and the authors assert that they are the true Islamic caliphate. The general tone of each edition highlights various conspiracy theories, describes what and how Muslims should live in the West, and issues a constant call to individual jihad. There is a consistent message of ultimate victory despite military defeats. Despite the current hardships, each edition promotes ways to identify Western weaknesses and exploit them.

The potency of the magazine can be found in its title, *Inspire*. Its sole purpose is to serve as a type of "auto propaganda" where doctrines are legitimized, morale is solidified, and a passive audience becomes engaged at the individual level. The magazine also discusses the phrase "open source jihad."[32] Open source jihad is defined in the spring 2014 edition as: "A resource manual for those who loathe the tyrants; includes bomb making techniques, security measures, guerrilla tactics, weapons training and all other jihad related activities."[33]

Open source jihad is a strategy in which all the necessary ideological training, technical training, and encouragement are available wherever an internet connection is accessible. Instead of traveling to a foreign training camp or having to train domestically with others, open source jihad makes it possible for any individual to train anywhere under any circumstances without becoming a security concern for Western law enforcement. Articles published in the magazine are used to generate anger against nonbelievers and apostates. Because of the current difficulties to confront the West with conventional weapons and tactics, the authors suggest that it is an individual obligation to carry out individual jihad while the true Islamic nation is militarily weak. Individual jihad is discussed in every issue as are the necessary techniques required to inflict violence. Some of the individuals who were inspired by Anwar al-Awlaki's weaponized ideas of open source jihad are listed in Table A.1 in the Appendix.

WILLIAM PIERCE

Dr. William Pierce, a former physics professor, is often described as one of the most infamous and influential neo-Nazi ideologues, authors, and organizers. In 1974, he founded the National Alliance, an anti-Semitic organization grounded in neo-Nazism. He led the organization until his death in 2002. At the time of his death, the National Alliance was the largest neo-Nazi-influenced organization in the United States with a reported million-dollar annual income, seventeen full-time staff members, and 1500 members. The National Alliance Headquarters was located on a compound in Mill Point, West Virginia, where Pierce hosted a weekly radio/internet show, "American Dissident Voices." On the compound he published the "National Alliance Bulletin," managed the National Vanguard Books Incorporated publishing firm, and disseminated music from his record company, Resistance Records. Pierce believed that the National Alliance was the racial Vanguard who would usher in a white nationalist revolution in the United States.[34]

Pierce argued that unless a revolution occurred, the existing cultural, political, and religious systems would ultimately lead to the demise of the white race. A revolution is necessary in order to establish white-only geographic locations, usher in a new education system, establish a government whose first priority is a racial agenda, and set up a new economic system. Pierce argued that liberalism is a submissive worldview alien to whites, while conservatism is a reformist mentality that operates from a position of weakness. He contended that whites need an alternative worldview whose objective is to create living space completely separate from other races.[35]

Pierce is described as one of the staunchest advocates of anti-Semitism and Holocaust denial. The existing culture in the United States is being bombarded by a media that he described as liberally bent on creating a passive and weak population. He argued that Jews intend to destroy the white race and have used Holocaust fabrication to gain sympathy in order to advance their cause. He believed Jews to control the media and promote a weak education system by subversively working to eradicate white culture, history, and character. He asserted that feminism, egalitarianism, and multiculturalism are Jewish creations that will eventually turn whites against whites, similar to what happened during World Wars I and II. Pierce argued that all blacks have degenerative influence over whites, but the Jewish threat should be prioritized above other threats.[36]

Pierce had been engaged in the process of weaponizing ideas since the late 1960s. Resistance Records has appealed to neo-Nazis across the globe and National Vanguard Books has disseminated neo-Nazi literature through the mail and the internet. His weekly radio/internet broadcasts and monthly publications provided listeners with a frame in which they should be interpreting current events and race. However, Pierce is most widely known for disseminating ideas through fiction, specifically in the novel *The Turner Diaries*, which is a futuristic account of racial revolution and violence.[37]

The Man

William Luther Pierce was born in Atlanta, Georgia, in 1933. He claimed that his family was part of the old Southern aristocracy, where his great-grandfather served as the governor of Alabama and as attorney general of the

Confederacy during the Civil War. Pierce's father was an insurance agency salesman and often traveled outside of the home until his death in a car accident in 1942. Pierce attended Virginia public schools until his father's death, and he and his mother then moved to Montgomery, Alabama. He spent the last two years of high school at the Allen Military Academy in Bryan, Texas, where he excelled academically. In 1951, he entered Rice University in Houston, Texas, on a full academic scholarship. In college he had an interest in space, particularly rocket engineering, and he graduated with a bachelor's degree in physics in 1955. After graduation, he was employed at the Los Alamo's Scientific Laboratory in New Mexico as a member of a team that worked on controlled nuclear fusion.[38]

He attended graduate school at the California Institute of Technology, and he worked in a jet propulsion laboratory. He continued his graduate studies at the University of Colorado in Boulder where he earned his PhD in 1962. Pierce was hired by Oregon State University (OSU) as an assistant professor and taught there from 1962 to 1965. He stated that an academic career appealed to him because he was able to set his own schedule, work at his own pace, and focus on subjects that interested him. He began to transition to neo-Nazi ideas as an OSU professor and soon resigned. He left academia to work for Pratt and Whitney in Connecticut as a senior research scientist before moving to Arlington, Virginia, to partner with George Lincoln Rockwell's American Nazi Party.[39]

Pierce's time at OSU was influenced by the counterculture revolution, civil rights, and his own reading list. It was during this time that he was confronted with the changing social world around him. Civil rights activism and protests against the Vietnam War were always in the news and were common on campus. The ideology associated with these protests and the support of the North Vietnamese against United States confounded him. Pierce was being drawn into the social and political upheaval and discovered that he needed to formulate his own beliefs on the current issues.[40]

Pierce stated that he drew inspiration from several key authors. He drew inspiration from Frederick Nietzsche's *Thus spoke Zarathustra*, specifically on the points of the power of the will and that one can be the master of his own life.[41] From August Kubizek's *The Young Hitler I Knew*, Pierce was inspired by Hitler's belief that he was the patriotic hero who fought against the corrupt oligarchy and achieved his destiny to lead Germany.[42] Dietrich Eckhart, in *Bolshevism from Moses to Lenin*,[43] provided an ideological grounding in Pierce's anti-Semitism, and from Savitri Devi's *Lightning in the Sun*[44] he incorporated racial mysticism with his beliefs. He read Adolf Hitler's *Mein Kampf* and drew parallels between the German society in the 1920s and the American society in the 1960s and felt that Jews were the antithesis of the white race. He also agreed with Hitler's concept that race carried genetic and cultural DNA; therefore, race mixing was evolutionarily destructive. He read William Galey Simpson's *Which Way, Western Man* and believed that Christianity was destructive to the white race because of its focus on egalitarianism, its emphasis on rituals, and its universal message that all are alike. Pierce believed that the pagan traditions of northern Europe were better suited for the white race than the traditions of Christianity.[45]

Before founding the National Alliance in 1974, he was involved in four other organizations: the John Birch Society (1962), the American Nazi Party (1963–1967), Youth for Wallace (1968), and the National Youth Alliance (1968–1974). Pierce criticized Birchers because they ignored race issues and the Jews. In 1963, he saw George Rockwell, the leader of the American Nazi Party, on television. The two would later meet in Washington D.C., and Pierce would soon become Rockwell's editor for *National Socialist World*. Rockwell functioned as a mentor for Pierce until his assassination in 1967. Due to irreconcilable differences with the American Nazi leadership, Pierce left the organization and joined Youth for Wallace, an organization that supported Governor George Wallace's failed bid for the presidency. After the election, he partnered with Lou Byers and Willis Carto to transform the Youth for Wallace organization into the National Youth Alliance. By 1974, Pierce gained control over the organization and renamed it the National Alliance.[46]

The National Alliance intended then and intends now to be the racial Vanguard party that leads whites to a revolutionary racial victory. Rather than gaining power through the existing political process, Pierce believed that a complete revolution was required. Pierce stated that the prime purpose of the National Alliance was to assist white Americans to regain guiding principles, promote the idea that evolution has produced its highest form in the white race, safeguard whites, and continue white greatness.

His strategy was to propagandize whites and catalyze them into a violent revolution which included ethnic cleansing. Pierce used national conventions, leadership conferences, comic books, Sunday night lecture series, National Vanguard Books, the weekly American Dissident Voices radio/internet program, books, and periodicals to transmit his ideas. The central message in all propaganda formats was usurp political power and establish white territories and nations. Like Klassen, he also believed that a race based on religion was necessary to unify whites.[47]

Cosmotheism was the name of the complex and failed religious philosophy developed by William Pierce in the 1970s. Cosmotheism can be understood from a pantheistic context where all matter and organisms are connected into an integrated whole. Cosmotheism rejects supernatural beliefs and instead relies on scientific investigation grounded in an observable phenomenon. The life rune, part of the runic alphabet of northern Europe, which represents transformation and regeneration, was selected to represent Pierce's religion. Although the life rune would identify the National Alliance as an organization, Cosmotheism, because of its esoteric and complex beliefs, would not have any lasting impact on neo-Nazism.[48]

Pierce was married five times. While at Caltech, Pierce met Patricia Jones, and after dating for some time they were married in 1957. Patricia was a mathematician who received her master's degree in math from Oregon State University. They had twin sons born in 1962, and they were divorced in 1982 after twenty-five years of marriage. His second marriage was to Elizabeth Prostel in 1982, which lasted three years. Elizabeth worked with the National Alliance office in Arlington, Virginia. In 1986, he married his third wife, Olga Skerlecz, who was a Hungarian immigrant. Four years later the marriage ended and she moved to California. His next two marriages were to Eastern European women who responded to Pierce's advertisement for a spouse in a Hungarian women's magazine.[49]

At the beginning of 2002, William Pierce was diagnosed with cancer and died several months later on July 23 in his home in Mill Point, West Virginia. Pierce gave his last public speech at the 2002 National Alliance Annual Leadership Conference held at the National Alliance compound. In his address on April 20, Hitler's birthday, he attempted to motivate those in attendance to continue to advance the National Alliance cause. Due to some of Pierce's own divisive comments against other neo-Nazi groups, subsequent fall-out between members, and inept leadership, the National Alliance in 2016 is barely a shadow of what it was during the 1990s.[50]

Weaponizing Ideas: Using Novels to Instruct and Radicalize

Pierce's most influential innovation was the use of fiction to inculcate ideology, radicalize to violence, and function as a revolutionary handbook. *The Turner Diaries*, published in 1978, has been described as "the Bible of the racist right" and stands as one of the most influential documents for recruitment and inciting racial violence. It was the first effective use of neo-Nazi fiction in a first-person narrative written to motivate and inform. Because it is written from main character Earl Turner's point of view, it enables the reader to identify with the central character of the novel while also providing a frame to interpret Turner's world. The novel is meant to make ideology entertaining and describes a future setting where Jews and nonwhites have triumphed over the white race. The novel has inspired several individuals and groups since its publication in addition to encouraging a number of imitations.[51] Table 2 lists correlations known or suspected by law enforcement.

The Turner Diaries reads as a series of two-year diary entries by the leading neo-Nazi hero, Earl Turner. The novel's setting is based in a futuristic United States that has been purged of Jews and nonwhites via an Aryan revolution. The Aryan revolution has resulted in putting whites in political power after eradicating Jewish and nonwhite threats. Turner is

Figure 2.2 Screen shot taken from YouTube's audio version of the Turner Diaries read by Dr. William Pierce.

an active member of an underground group, the Organization, engaged in asymmetric warfare against The System. The System is portrayed as an antigun, antiwhite, Jewish-controlled U.S. government that is constantly limiting the rights of its citizens. Turner manufactures explosive devices used by the Organization to inflict a maximum number of casualties against

blacks, Jews, and white racial traitors all over the United States. The violence depicted in the text is meant to be both graphic and informative. The
graphic content entertains and appeals to an audience that gravitates toward
violence. The novel is also meant to be informative by listing targets,
weapons, and tactics in such a way that the book can be used as a technical manual. Toward the end of the novel, Turner joins an elite survivalist
group called The Order. As the racial war escalates, Turner is preparing for
a suicide mission that would target the Pentagon. His plan is to fly a modified crop-duster plane equipped to carry a nuclear warhead directly into the
Pentagon. This mission would turn Turner into a martyr and would destroy
The System's last remaining stronghold.[52]

The original idea of utilizing fiction can be traced to 1974. Revilo Oliver,
one of the founding members of the Birch Society, had a lunch meeting
with Pierce in Washington D.C. to discuss a novel review for Pierce's periodical, *Attack!* Oliver asked Pierce if he had ever considered writing fiction.
Oliver stated that fiction would reach a broad range of people that would not
typically respond to nonfiction material. Oliver sent him a copy of the John
Birch Society-sponsored novel, *The John Franklin Letters* (1959), in order to
provide an example. While the author is unknown, Revilo Oliver or Harley
Ogden, a professor of American history at the University of Illinois, remain
suspects. The novel is an account written by the main fictional character,
John Semmes Franklin, to his ninety-three-year-old uncle. The novel reads
as a series of letters that record the activities of the Rangers, an underground
patriotic military force. Franklin, as a Ranger, combats a government determined to limit American freedoms. The novel emphasizes a paternalistic
federal government, a disastrous welfare system, gun control issues, and a
corrupt British government. William Pierce used *The Franklin Letters* as an
example, and the following statement illustrates his mental state when writing the novel.[53]

> What I did with *The Turner Diaries* was to imagine myself a member of the
> Revolutionary Organization, Earl Turner. I put myself inside the skin and
> looked at the fictional situation he had created through his eyes. Or maybe it
> is through my eyes; it is kind of me as Earl and Earl as me. Anyway, I tried to
> imagine how to react to various situations he was in, what I would do, and how
> other people the organization would react to behave, and proceeded from there.
> What came out of that is going to get more sympathetic reading from people
> with a similar mentality to mine, I understand that.[54]

The novel was first printed through the National Alliance Vanguard Press
until 1998 when Barricade Books also began to publish editions. At first, *The
Turner Diaries* was serialized in the National Alliance's newsletter, *Attack!*

(later renamed *National Vanguard*), from 1975 through 1978. The twenty-six chapters of *The Turner Diaries* were written over three and a half years and the complete work was initially sold in underground markets, advertisements in survival and gun magazines, and gun shows.

The novel has been linked to Timothy McVeigh and the Oklahoma City bombing. One of the scenes in the novel describes Earl Turner's guerrilla unit detonating a homemade fertilizer bomb at FBI headquarters inflicting hundreds of casualties. Timothy McVeigh regularly sold copies of *The Turner Diaries* at gun shows, and excerpts from the novel were also found in the front seat of McVeigh's yellow Mercury getaway vehicle.[55] The following excerpt illustrates how Pierce used the novel to convey "real world" tactical details in a fictional novel which foreshadows the Oklahoma City bombing:

> The plan, roughly, is this: Unit 8 will secure a large quantity of explosives—between five and ten tons. Our unit will hijack a truck making a legitimate delivery to the FBI headquarters, rendezvous at a location where Unit 8 will be waiting with the explosives, and switch loads. We will then drive into the FBI building's freight-receiving area, set the fuse, and leave the truck.

> My job will be the design and construction of the mechanism of the bomb itself.

> I packed about four pounds of the blasting gelatin into an empty applesauce can, primed it, placed the batteries and timing mechanism in the top of the can, and wired them to a small toggle switch on the end of a 20-foot extension cord. When we load the truck with explosives, the can will go in back, on top of the two cases of blasting gelatin. We'll have to poke small holes in the walls of the trailer and the cab to run the extension cord and the switch into the cab.
>
> Either George or Henry—probably Henry—will drive the truck into the freight-receiving area inside the FBI building. Before he gets out of the cab he will flip the switch, starting the timer. Ten minutes later the explosives will go off. If we're lucky, that will be the end of the FBI building—and the government's new three-billion-dollar computer complex for their internal-passport system.
>
> October 13, 1991. At 9:15 yesterday morning our bomb went off in the FBI's national headquarters building. Our worries about the relatively small size of the bomb were unfounded; the damage is immense. We have certainly disrupted a major portion of the FBI's headquarters operations for at least the next several weeks, and it looks like we have also achieved our goal of wrecking their new computer complex.[56]

Timothy McVeigh's bomb exploded in Oklahoma City at 9:02 a.m. on April 19, 1995. This date was the 200th anniversary of the Battle of Lexington, the first military engagement in the American Revolutionary War, of which is often attributed the "shot heard around the world." McVeigh believed that the explosion would be the "shot" that would inspire a white racial and anti-governmental revolution in 1995.

NOTES

1. Khan, Azmat. "The Magazine That 'Inspired' the Boston Bombers—Al Qaeda in Yemen," *FRONTLINE*, accessed August 30, 2015, http://www.pbs.org/wgbh/pages/frontline/iraq-war-on-terror/topsecretamerica/the-magazine-that-inspired-the-boston-bombers/.

2. Gessen, Masha. *The Brothers: The Road to an American Tragedy* New York: NY. Riverhead Books, 2015.

3. "Inspire Magazine | JIHADOLOGY," accessed August 30, 2015, http://jihadology.net/category/inspire-magazine/.

4. "Inspire Magazine—Make a Bomb in the Kitchen of Your Mom," accessed August 30, 2015, https://whitehouse.gov1.info/cyber-warfare/inspire-magazine.html.

5. Michel, Lou and Dan Herbeck. *American Terrorist: Timothy McVeigh and the Oklahoma City Bombing*. New York: Regan Books, 2001.

6. "CNN—'Turner Diaries' Introduced in McVeigh Trial—April 28, 1997," accessed August 30, 2015, http://www.cnn.com/US/9704/28/okc/.

7. Macdonald, Andrew. *The Turner diaries: A novel*. Fort Lee, NJ: Barricade Books, 1996.

8. Michel, Lou, and Dan Herbeck. *American terrorist: Timothy McVeigh and the Oklahoma city bombing*. New York: Regan Books, Harpers Collins, 2001.

9. Anti-Defamation League. "Turner Diaries—Extremism in America," accessed August 30, 2015, http://archive.adl.org/learn/ext_us/turner_diaries.html.

10. MacEion, Denis. "Anwar Al-Awlaki: 'I Pray That Allah Destroys America,'" *Middle East Quarterly*, Spring, Vol. 17, no. 2 (March 1, 2010): 13–19. http://www.meforum.org/2649/anwar-al-awlaki-pray-allah-destroys-america.

11. Shane, Scott. "The Lessons of Anwar Al-Awlaki," *The New York Times*, August 27, 2015, http://www.nytimes.com/2015/08/30/magazine/the-lessons-of-anwar-al-awlaki.html.

12. Chesney, Robert. "Who May Be Killed? Anwar Al-Awlaki as a Case Study in the International Legal Regulation of Lethal Force," in *Yearbook of International Humanitarian Law—2010*, ed. M. N. Schmitt, Louise Arimatsu, and T. McCormack, Yearbook of International Humanitarian Law 13 (T. M. C. Asser Press, 2011), 3–60, http://link.springer.com/chapter/10.1007/978-90-6704-811-8_1.

13. "Exclusive: Who Is Anwar Al-Awlaki? (Hasan's Va. Imam)," accessed July 11, 2016. http://www.freerepublic.com/focus/f-news/2383383/posts.

14. "Anwar Al-Awlaki Describes Post-9/11 Mood in U.S.: Watch the Interview," *PBS NewsHour*, accessed August 30, 2015, http://www.pbs.org/newshour/rundown/a-post-911-interview-with-anwar-al-awlaki/.

15. MacEoin, "Anwar Al-Awlaki."

16. "Obituary: Anwar Al-Awlaki," *BBC News*, accessed August 30, 2015, http://www.bbc.com/news/world-middle-east-11658920.

17. Figueira, Daurius. *Salafi Jihadi Discourse of Sunni Islam in the 21st Century: The Discourse of Abu Muhammad Al-Maqdisi and Anwar Al-Awlaki*. Bloomington, IN: iUniverse, 2011.

18. "Exclusive: Who is Anwar Al-Awlaki? (Hasan's Va. Imam)."

19. As American As Apple Pie: How Anwar al-Awlaki Became the Face of Western Jihad / ICSR. (2011,September 11). Retrieved July 11, 2016, from http://icsr.info/2011/09/as-american-as-apple-pie-how-anwar-al-awlaki-became-the-face-of-western-jihad/

20. "House of Commons Hansard Debates for 18 Dec 2003 (pt 18)," accessed August 30, 2015, http://www.parliament.the-stationery-office.co.uk/pa/cm200304/cmhansrd/vo031218/debtext/31218-18.htm.

21. "Exclusive: Who is Anwar Al-Awlaki? (Hasan's Va. Imam)."

22. "Cageprisoners.com—Serving the Caged Prisoners in Guantanamo Bay," accessed August 30, 2015, http://old.cageprisoners.com/articles.php?id=22926.

23. Ibid.

24. "The Awlaki Effect," *The Investigative Project on Terrorism*, accessed August 30, 2015, http://www.investigativeproject.org/2323/the-awlaki-effect.

25. Of particular interest is where the relationship began with the Fort Hood shooter and the Christmas Day bomber. Awlaki conducted the funeral of Nidal Hassan's mother, and it is believed that he came into contact with the Christmas Day bomber during his lectures in Yemen.

26. "Targeting Anwar Al-Awlaki Was Legal, Justice Department Said—The New York Times," accessed August 30, 2015, http://www.nytimes.com/2014/06/24/us/justice-department-found-it-lawful-to-target-anwar-al-awlaki.html.

27. Sullivan, Cheryl. "Why Yemen Claims Role in U.S. Drone Strike on Cleric Anwar Al-Awlaki," *Christian Science Monitor*, May 7, 2011, http://www.csmonitor.com/USA/2011/0507/Why-Yemen-claims-role-in-US-drone-strike-on-cleric-Anwar-al-Awlaki.

28. Shane, Scott. "U.S. Approves Targeted Killing of American Cleric—The New York Times," accessed August 30, 2015, http://www.nytimes.com/2010/04/07/world/middleeast/07yemen.html.

29. "Al-Aulaqi v. Panetta—Constitutional Challenge to Killing of Three U.S. Citizens," *American Civil Liberties Union*, accessed August 30, 2015, https://www.aclu.org/cases/al-aulaqi-v-panetta-constitutional-challenge-killing-three-us-citizens.

30. "Remarks by the President at the 'Change of Office' Chairman of the Joint Chiefs of Staff Ceremony," *Whitehouse.gov*, accessed August 31, 2015, https://www.whitehouse.gov/the-press-office/2011/09/30/remarks-president-change-office-chairman-joint-chiefs-staff-ceremony.

31. Shane, "The Lessons of Anwar Al-Awlaki."

32. "Open Source Jihad On America | SOFREP." SOFREP. May 12, 2014. Accessed July 11, 2016. https://sofrep.com/35355/open-source-jihad-americans/.

33. Maher, Shiraz. November 25, 2011 at 4:30 a.m. http://www.gatestoneinstitute.org/2609/Inspire-Magazine-Open-Source-Jihad, "'Inspire' Magazine: Open Source

Jihad," *Gatestone Institute*, accessed August 30, 2015, http://www.gatestoneinstitute.org/2609/inspire-magazine-open-source-jihad.

34. "National Alliance," *Southern Poverty Law Center*, accessed August 30, 2015, https://www.splcenter.org/fighting-hate/extremist-files/group/national-alliance.

35. Griffin, Robert S. *The Fame of a Dead Man's Deeds: An Up-Close Portrait of White Nationalist William Pierce*. Bloomington, IN: AuthorHouse, 2001.

36. Ibid.

37. Ibid.

38. Ibid.

39. "William Pierce," *Southern Poverty Law Center*, accessed August 30, 2015, https://www.splcenter.org/fighting-hate/extremist-files/individual/william-pierce.

40. Griffin, *The Fame of a Dead Man's Deeds*.

41. Nietzsche, Friedrich, Thomas Common, and H. James. Birx. *Thus Spoke Zarathustra*. Buffalo, NY: (Prometheus Books, 1993).

42. Kubizek, August. *The Young Hitler I Knew*. London: Greenhill Books, 2006.

43. Hitler, Adolf and Dietrich Eckart. *Bolshevism from Moses to Lenin: A Dialogue between Adolf Hitler and Me*, Hillsboro, WV: National Vanguard Books, 1999.

44. Savitri Devi. *The Lightning and the Sun*. Buffalo, NY: Samisdat, 1958.

45. Griffin, *The Fame of a Dead Man's Deeds*.

46. Pierce, William. "Rockwell: A National Socialist Life" | Counter-Currents Publishing, accessed July 11, 2016. http://www.counter-currents.com/2012/03/rockwella-national-socialist-life/.

47. Ibid.

48. Whitsel, Brad. "The Turner Diaries and Cosmotheism: William Pierce's Theology," *Nova Religio: The Journal of Alternative and Emergent Religions* 1, no. 2 (April 1, 1998): 183–97, doi:10.1525/nr.1998.1.2.183.

49. Griffin, *The Fame of a Dead Man's Deeds*.

50. Johnston, David Cay. "William Pierce, 69, Neo-Nazi Leader, Dies," *The New York Times*, July 24, 2002, sec. U.S., http://www.nytimes.com/2002/07/24/us/william-pierce-69-neo-nazi-leader-dies.html.

51. Some of the imitations are *Angle Iron (2003)*, attacking a U.S. power grid; 2001's *Dark Millennium*, the extermination of the African American genocide by a white president; 2001's *Hold Back This Day* and 2004's *Deep Blue*, neo-Nazi science-fiction; *One in a Million (1999)*, a white separatist war with IRS; *The Outsider (2001)*, a white lone-wolf terrorist killing African Americans; and *Serpent's Walk (1991)*, Nazis regain power.

52. Macdonald, *The Turner Diaries*.

53. Griffin, *The Fame of a Dead Man's Deeds*.

54. Ibid., p. 154.

55. Michel and Herbeck, *American Terrorist*.

56. Macdonald, *The Turner Diaries*.

Chapter 3

Strategizing New Violence
Abdullah Azzam and Louis Beam

New doctrines, strategies, and tactics reflect the changing nature of warfare. Doctrine is defined as a general statement of *how* a conflict is fought, strategy is defined as the *method* to accomplish a mission, and tactics are the specific *actions* to implement a strategy. Strategizing new doctrines, strategies, and tactics is applicable to asymmetric warfare by dissident violent jihadists and neo-Nazis. This chapter addresses a violent jihadi strategy and a neo-Nazi strategy that have proven to be some of the most significant dark ideas to emerge in the past thirty years. These ideas have in turn influenced the entire U.S. security apparatus, specifically, the Department of Defense and the U.S. Justice Department. Abdullah Azzam's reconceptualization of jihad and Louis Beam's modifications to the concept of leaderless resistance are examined.

Presently, the ideas from both Azzam and Beam are normalized strategies for many subcultural groups and individuals. Specifically, Abdullah Azzam is known as the "Father of Jihad" and is largely responsible for shifting the jihadi strategy to a violent strain.[1] During the Soviet-Afghan War, he argued that jihad is a necessary obligation to the Islamic faith. From his perspective, jihad should be equal to or of greater value than the other five pillars of Islam. He would state that only a truly dedicated Muslim would volunteer to fight after he learned that other Muslims were being attacked by an atheist communist regime in Afghanistan. Those who did not fight to protect other Muslims under assault were in fact not true Muslims. Conversely, Louis Beam, a self-declared white nationalist, wrote a document that popularized the concept of leaderless resistance, now known as lone-wolf terrorism. Lone-wolf terrorism is defined as a terrorist act carried out by an individual who "operates alone" and does not belong to an organized group or network, who carries out an

43

ideologically fueled self-planned and self-directed attack to inculcate fear, inflict violence, and convey a message. Beam modified leaderless resistance to counter effective law enforcement practices toward racist and anti-governmental subcultural organizations.[2]

Beam argued that a conventional hierarchal system, like the KKK, was not only problematic but would ultimately fail. When an organization operates from a weaker position, individuals and cells are not only more efficient strategically but should be the central strategy to overthrow a much more powerful governmental system. Lone-wolf terrorism as a strategy has been implemented by a myriad of violent extremist groups that range from eco-terrorism to religious terrorism.[3] Two examples are used to illustrate how Abdullah Azzam and Louis Beam's ideas have shaped new forms of violence over the past several decades.

Osama bin Laden, the leader and founder of Al Qaeda, the organization ultimately responsible for the 9/11 attacks on American soil, was a disciple of Abdullah Azzam and adopted his jihadi strategy. In recent years, almost every aspect of bin Laden's life and organization has been scrutinized by scholars, journalists, and governmental officials. Three of the most authoritative sources, Lawrence Wright, Peter Bergen, and Michael Scheuer all indicate that bin Laden's time in Afghanistan with Azzam was a critical point in his radicalization process.[4] While bin Laden was a student at the King Abdul Aziz University in Saudi Arabia, Abdullah Azzam, a member of the Muslim Brotherhood, and other Muslim Brotherhood-affiliated scholars like Mohammed Qutb, Sayyid Qutb's brother, created opportunities for bin Laden to immerse himself in radical ideologies.[5]

Michael Scheuer states that Abdullah Azzam is described as one of the six most influential men in bin Laden's life.[6] Abdullah Azzam falls in line behind the prophet Mohammed, Ibn Taymiyya, Saladin, Mohammed bin Laden, and Mullah Omar. Bin Laden respected Abdullah Azzam because he was an educated religious scholar, and he personally engaged in combat. More specifically, Azzam was a man of action; his faith epitomized the notion of being a warrior cleric. Bin Laden was influenced by Azzam's call for mujahedeen to fight the Soviets in Afghanistan. The brief description of their relationship forms the cornerstone of how Azzam's jihad informed bin Laden's decision to attack Western targets.[7]

In Afghanistan, Abdullah Azzam served as bin Laden's mentor in a master/apprentice relationship. Azzam was older, more experienced, and had the religious background that made him an ideal mentor to bin Laden. Azzam's insistence on the importance of jihad in spite of Muslim oppression and the only means by which to unite the Muslim world was also adopted by bin Laden. A tangible product of this relationship was the creation of the Service Bureau, Mahktab al-Khadamat, in 1984.[8]

Initially, bin Laden financed the Services Bureau's operating costs and provided logistical support while Azzam served as the Emir. Abdullah Azzam was on a global campaign to proselytize and disseminate his version of jihad and how it should be manifested in Afghanistan. Abdullah Azzam's version indicated the shame of Muslim men in other parts of the world after hearing of the atrocities inflicted on their Afghan brothers and sisters if they did not join the fight to assist them. The Services Bureau posed as an NGO organization whose mission was to acquire and channel funds to those already fighting in Afghanistan and to simultaneously prepare non-Afghan recruits to enter the Afghan fight.[9]

Although Osama bin Laden did not earn any official military recognition for his involvement in Afghanistan as part of a formalized Army, he would wear the jihad badge of honor for the rest of his life. While in Afghanistan, Osama bin Laden did have a chance to directly engage forces. The specialized AK-47 that often appears in Al Qaeda's propaganda videos serves as a signal that he not only embraced Abdullah Azzam's strategy of jihad but also saw it as an obligation and practiced what he preached. Osama bin Laden was now a firm believer that where Muslims are oppressed, true Muslims should fight on their behalf. Al Qaeda fighters soon went to fight Bosnia, Africa, Yemen, and New York City in support of this idea. Osama bin Laden adopted Azzam's doctrine and developed tactics to take the fight to the United States.[10]

Almost ten years after the 9/11 attack, on July 22, 2011, Anders Behring Breivik detonated a car bomb in Oslo, Norway, made from a mixture of fertilizer and fuel oil packed in a van. The van was placed in front of the prime minister's Jens Stoltenberg office, and the bomb's detonation resulted in the death of eight people and injuries to 209 others. A second attack took place two hours later on Utoya Island, where Breivik, disguised as a police officer, took a ferry to the island. He had decided to target the summer Workers Youth League of the ruling Norwegian Labour Party. The attack resulted in sixty-nine deaths and the wounding of over 110 people, making it the deadliest attack in Norway since World War II.[11]

The attack had been meticulously planned for over three years. The weapons used were obtained legally. Breivik moved to a rural area in order to escape detection and spent time practicing for the attack. It was during this time that he wrote a 1500-page manifesto entitled *2083: A European Declaration of Independence*. Approximately ninety minutes before he detonated the bomb in Oslo, he sent the document to 1003 email addresses. The manifesto outlines his grievances against multiculturalism, cultural Marxism, Muslims, leftists, feminists, and cultural genocide. His manifesto identifies his concerns about race, but his ideas have placed him in a different category than what is traditionally believed to be a neo-Nazi, a Christian fundamentalist, or white supremacist.[12]

Breivik is classified as a lone-wolf terrorist engaged in leaderless resistance. In 1983, Louis Beam argued that small unconnected cells and individuals are far more effective than large hierarchical organizations. Even though leaderless resistance was intended for a domestic audience, the idea, now known as lone-wolf terrorism, is used to describe acts of violence from the far right to ISIS. The concept has moved beyond its origin and has become a much-touted strategy among violent extremists and their organizations. Even if Breivik was unaware of Louis Beam's role in promoting an individual act of violence, he followed his strategy and modified the tactics to a Norwegian context. An argument could be made that Breivik studied and modeled his attack after Timothy McVeigh in the Oklahoma City bombing, but the dark idea originated with Beam.[13]

Bin Laden and Breivik exemplify concrete examples of how ideas are the foundation for new forms of violence. Their actions are now part of the evolutionary chain that serves as examples for others.

ABDULLAH AZZAM

Abdullah Azzam, the Striving Sheikh, did more than any other ideologue to create the theological foundation for the violent jihadist movement.[14] In the 1980s, he personally recruited Arab fighters from all over the globe to implement his version of a reborn caliphate in the modern age. Azzam was involved in international recruitment and established funds to fight the Soviets in Afghanistan. In 1984, he formalized the process and formed the Service Bureau, Mahktab al-Khadamat, that Osama bin Laden would later restructure as Al Qaeda. Azzam revived classical jihad and marketed it to young Muslims in such a way that enabled them to channel their energies in a practical way of fighting for God in reversing the decline of Muslim power.

The Man

> And something more beautiful than this is when the blood is one and the pen is one, so that the hand of the scholar which expends the ink and moves the pen is the same as the hand which expends its blood and moves the ummah.[15]

Abdullah Azzam was born in 1941 in the village of Silat al-Harithiyya near Jenin. At the time, his village was under the Palestinian British Mandate. In his youth, he experienced the influx of Jewish immigrants, the creation of Israel as a nation in 1948, and in 1967, the Six Day War. As a result, he settled in a refugee camp at Zarqa before moving to Amman, Jordan. From all accounts, Abdullah Azzam was a gifted student as a youth and in college. He attended al-Khaduriyya Agricultural College in the West Bank and after graduation taught in several villages in Jordan in the West Bank. He pursued a growing interest in religion at Damascus University, specifically in the faculty of law to study sharia. He finished his thesis on Islamic rulings on divorce and graduated with his degree in 1966. He would finish his PhD in the principles of jurisprudence in 1971 from Egypt's great madrasah, Al Azhar University, in 1973. His advanced degrees enabled him to use the Quran as well as other religious scholarship to formulate and frame his theology as a credible interpretation of jihad.[16]

Azzam was impacted by the Muslim Brotherhood and Egyptian ideologues. The Israeli 1967 victory had a tremendous impact upon Azzam, his family, and fellow Palestinians, and he joined the Amman Brotherhood branch. Azzam was drawn to the Muslim Brotherhood because it was against Arab nationalism and combined a message of Islamic revival with an organizational structure. Azzam specifically believed that the national focus in the left-leaning ideology of the Palestinian Liberation Organization (PLO) benefited from Western powers because the focus was still dividing the Muslim world along territorial lines rather than creating a unified spiritual ummah or community. In contrast to Yasser Arafat's gradual approach, the PLO's chairman, Azzam identified quick solutions that incorporated the use of armed guerrilla operations to liberate Jerusalem from Israeli control. During his time in Egypt, he was exposed to Sayyid Qutb's work and interacted with members of Qutb's family. It is also speculated that Sayyid's brother-in-law, Kamal al Sananiri, was responsible for convincing Azzam to travel to Afghanistan for the sake of jihad.[17]

After completing his doctorate from Al Azhar, Azzam returned to Jordan in order to teach at Belmont University. He left Jordan for Saudi Arabia in 1980 to continue to teach and study at the King Abd Aziz University in Jeddah. At that particular time in history there was a significant Muslim Brotherhood presence in Saudi Arabia, most notably Mohammed Qutb, Sayyid's younger brother, who taught at Mecca's Umm al-Qura University. Saudi Arabia was an ideal place for ideological, political, and religious debate which gave Abdullah Azzam a rich environment to form the ideological groundwork for his version of Islamic jihad. Azzam began to infuse his Muslim Brotherhood background with the teachings of Hassan Al Banna, Sayyid Qutb, and Wahhabi conservatism. This blended ideology would become the ideological foundation that catalyzed thousands of violent jihadists.[18]

In April 1978, a Marxist political party seized political control in Kabul, Afghanistan—the Saur Revolution. After a bloody internal conflict by the ruling Khalq faction and the Parcham faction, the Soviet Union deployed military forces to protect Parcham's leadership.[19] This action initiated the

Soviet-Afghan War during which thousands of young Muslims from Arab countries and southern Asia traveled to Afghanistan in order to fight Soviet forces. This particular environment served as a breeding ground for organizations and training that would include Osama bin Laden and the Al Qaeda. After the conclusion of the Soviet-Afghan War in 1989 and the final defeat of the communists in 1992, the Taliban emerged as the "Arab Afghans" and traveled to other fronts in defense of Muslims in Chechnya, Kashmir, and Bosnia.[20]

In 1979, during the pilgrimage to Mecca, Abdullah Azzam met Kamal al-Sananiri, a member of the Egyptian Muslim Brotherhood and one of the first Arabs to assist Afghan mujahedeen. Also that year, the Soviets had invaded Afghanistan in order to strengthen a small Afghan communist contingent attempting to establish a communist regime in the country. Al-Sananiri discussed Soviet Red Army atrocities against Muslims in Afghanistan. He provided Azzam with miraculous stories of Allah's intervention on behalf of the mujahedeen and how the faithful were answering the call to protect their Muslim brothers under attack. What initially was supposed to be a brief intervention, the Soviets were drawn into an extended conflict from various mujahedeen commanders. Azzam perceived the Soviet invasion of Afghanistan as an atheist attack on Afghan Muslims and the larger Muslim community.

Abdullah Azzam left his post at the University and traveled to Pakistan. Pakistan at the time formed the external base of operations for mujahedeen and their supporters against Soviets. The existing conflict in Afghanistan was quite different from Azzam's experience in Palestine and Israel. The military might of the Israelis, the power and influence of the PLO, and the lack of effective geographic terrain made Palestine problematic for asymmetric warfare. Additionally, a large cache of weapons already existed in Afghanistan, and Afghans knew how to fight. However, without foreign support from other Muslim countries and organizations, resources were exhausted. A global jihadi-recruiting movement ensued that saw tens of thousands of Muslims from around the globe travel to Afghanistan to fight.

While in Pakistan, Azzam accepted a teaching position at the International Islamic University in Islamabad. Azzam arrived in Islamabad in 1981 and traveled to Peshawar and Afghanistan in order to be close to combat. In Pakistan and Afghanistan he met with numerous mujahedeen commanders in order to understand the conflict and to receive updated information from the battlefield. Azzam provided material support through propaganda and speeches which outlined the necessity for supporting the fighting in Afghanistan. Azzam in particular held a high degree of respect for the Tajik commander, Ahmed Shah Massoud, to whom Azzam gave the lofty title of being the most brilliant commander in Afghanistan.[21] After three years in Islamabad, he relinquished his position at the University and pursued violent jihad full-time.

In 1984, he established Mahktab al-Khadamat, the Service Office or Service Bureau. The Service Bureau was formed in order to provide foreign fighters logistical and travel support in getting them from their home countries to the battlefield. The need for this type of organization became evident when larger numbers of foreign fighters were coming from outside of Afghanistan to fight the Soviet Red Army. The vast majority of these fighters were from Saudi Arabia, Egypt, and Algeria, and many more also came from Indonesia. The International CRISIS group estimates that between 300 and 600 fighters made their way to the Afghan battlefield through Azzam's organization. Although it is hard to estimate the number of fighters that went through Azzam's logistical support network, Lawrence Wright estimates that as many as 50,000 Arabs entered Afghanistan during the war against the Soviets.[22] The defeat of the Soviet Union in 1989 was framed as a miracle from God and justification that jihad was the righteous path ordained by God.[23]

Azzam saw the current conflict as an opportunity for thousands of pure Muslims to harness the necessary training and techniques used in combat. It would become an environment that would provide the basis for liberation of other Muslim countries beyond Afghanistan that were dominated by non-Muslims. Azzam perceived that Afghanistan's liberation was the path in which Palestine, Kashmir, the Philippines, and Andalusia would follow. He acknowledged the need for a group of committed fighters to form a base for global Muslim liberation. The name that he gave to this force was "al Qaida al-Sulbah" which literally means "the solid base." After Azzam's death, his disciple, Osama bin Laden, would make the name Al Qaeda known throughout the world.[24]

Azzam's attempt to strengthen the Muslim fighting force in Afghanistan came from both ideological support and material support, primarily through recruiting. Abdullah Azzam was engaged in a global violent jihadi speaking circuit in which he went to various organizations in a number of North American cities in order to publicize jihad among ordinary Muslims. He visited the Muslim Arab Youth Association and the Islamic Association for Palestine at the Oklahoma Convention in 1989.[25] He gave speeches in New York City and other North American cities during which he captivated audiences by his powerful oratory abilities, his use of imagery of the fighting in Afghanistan, and his in-depth knowledge of the Quran. He inspired many Muslims to join the fighting against the Soviets. It was often stated that his charisma and his style of delivery cast a hypnotic spell on the listeners to the degree that no one wanted to confront him.[26]

During his travels and speeches he seemed to understand the current need in Muslim communities across the globe. It was through his speeches that he was able to reconnect modern Muslims to the sense of adventure, power, and dedication in his modified version of jihad. Many Muslim men were trapped under the pressures of materialism, secular ambition, and the governmental structures of "apostate" Islamic regimes which led to a sense of powerlessness and depression. It was through his powerful orations and the call to jihad that he was able to give these men an opportunity to tap into deep core issues, lifting them out of their current unsatisfying situations. Azzam tapped into the notion of Islam's rightful place as leading the other nations in matters of morality, government, and faith.[27]

Azzam provided a tangible way for Muslim men to assist in jihadi revival. He gave them an opportunity to be part of this purist Vanguard that would revitalize Muslim communities across the globe to retain their rightful position of power and authority over non-Muslims. He outlined the path in which an individual Muslim could contribute in a way that was heroic and that was part of something far greater than his individual existence. His emphasis was not so much on societal diagnosis—this would come from Sayyid Qutb and others, but he was able to provide the solution through violent jihad in Afghanistan and other countries as the method and mechanism to revive Islam. It was also during his captivating speeches that he was able to harness the essence of the global community unified in violent jihad against a Muslim oppressor. This type of unity, uncommon at that time, also provided a universal symbol of what Islam should be devoid of national boundaries and misguided regional conflicts, particularly when Muslims take arms against other Muslims.[28]

In 1989, Azzam and his two sons were in route to a mosque in Peshawar. They never reached the mosque. Both Azzam and his sons were killed in the car after an explosive device detonated. Although no solid evidence links the assassination with any particular group, Ayman Zawahiri is sometimes suggested as a suspect due to his interest in wooing Osama bin Laden away from Azzam. Zawahiri took over Azzam's role as bin Laden's mentor and assumed a leadership role in bin Laden's organization.[29]

The Innovation: Redefining Jihad

Throughout the history of Islam, from the seventh century until today, jihad literally translated means to "strive or exert."[30] Briefly, there are two different forms of jihad. The greater jihad is that in which an individual strives for increased morality, closeness to God, and devotion. This is considered a struggle against the self, against those things which counter spiritual progress.

The lesser jihad is considered actual warfare against those who are encroaching against Islam. This is also known as warfare on the behalf of God, which is intent in defending geographic territory. When jihad is defined as a military struggle, it takes two forms. The first is defined as warfare against non-Muslim lands in order to advance Islam's domain and the second is warfare against non-Muslim aggression in order to defend Muslim lands. Defensive jihad in the modern age is greatly influenced by the Afghan war against the Soviet Union.

Jihad on any level is not one of the five pillars of Islam. However, violent jihadists elevate the lesser jihad to a sixth pillar of Islam. At this level violent jihadists intend to make the "lesser" jihad the greater jihad. They use quotations from the Quran and cite current events to build their arguments about their use of the jihad.[31] "Fighting is above all a spiritual journey. It is the ultimate proof of the reform of the self."[32] The problem is that their version supersedes all other tenants of their faith. Oliver Roy states, "A line is drawn between those who consider *jihad* to be defensive and those who advocate a fight to the death against the West. Offensive *jihad* nowadays is the dividing line between mainstream Islamists and radicals."[33]

History is often cited to reflect on a larger issue, that the West or Christianity is trying to destroy or hinder Islam. This is a pitting of West against East, Christianity against Islam. Violent jihadis cite the real first engagement between the West and Islam in the Crusades. The Crusades are constantly cited as evidence of this continuing theme and violent jihadists assert that it was not by chance that President Bush used this term to outline the attacks against Al Qaeda.[34] The events that occurred some 800 years ago with the Crusades are perceived to be just as relevant today as they were then. The fact that an event occurred in 1251 has no relevance. These events of history are known and are not at all distanced by how long ago they occurred. The purpose of the Crusades was to establish European dominance in Palestine. The battles and atrocities that occurred during this time are still told, despite the time elapsed. The metaphor of what the Crusades represent beyond the historical recollection is just as powerful as what unfolded in 2009.

Violent jihadists also believe that the United States is the puppet master that controls the corrupt regimes in the Muslim world. This is often cited in the governing body of Saudi Arabia and its close ties with the United States.[35] The West is perceived as being bent on extracting the wealth from the Middle East into their own coffers at the expense of the majority of the Muslim population. Violent jihadists believe that the current regimes are held in place so that they can maintain a dominant control over the region and the resources of the Middle East. Israel is at the center of the grievances. It is not only that Israel currently occupies what was once Muslim lands, but it is also a staging ground for the West, particularly for the United States.[36] This is a focus on attempting to strike at the head rather than the body that is represented in local regimes or even in Israel. Specifically for Israel, violent jiihadists argue that a more effective strategy is to attack the United States in order to weaken it's support of Israel or focus on a propaganda campaign to turn the international community against Israel. Either strategy is considered to be more effective than conventional warfare which historically resulted in defeat.

Violent jihadists assert that the reason for their current weaker state is the fact that the majority of Muslims are not following the true faith, and Allah therefore is allowing them to be dominated in order to incite a call to purification. Reform of the soul should occur before a political system can be purified. Political systems will not purify humanity; rather it is a system comprised of purified individuals that will make the political system work.[37] It is from this call to the purification of individuals that Abdullah Azzam emerges within the context of the Israeli-Palestinian conflict and the Soviet-Afghan War.

Abdullah Azzam formulated his thoughts on jihad through three specific events: his own experience of the defeat of paramilitary forces by the Israeli forces during 1967; his active participation in armed resistance against Israelis; and his Afghan experiences with the mujahedeen. Azzam argued that the final revelation of jihad requires Muslims to wage jihad against all non-Muslims without conditions and that this perspective supersedes any previous Quranic verses where jihad is defensive. He stated that jihad necessitates this view because all non-Muslims are inherently hostile and are engaged in the collective action to encourage Muslims to abandon their faith. Abdullah Azzam added that the vast majority of Muslim jihadists are zealous for violent jihad but lack religious education and theological grounding.[38]

Conversely, Azzam recognized that a "final" version of jihad needed to be grounded in Quranic verses and judicial sources. Azzam described jihad as depicted in the Quran and the hadiths as fighting the infidels, which is a position that is maintained by all four major schools of Islamic jurisprudence. Azzam argued that the meaning of jihad needed to be broadened and then focused on its etymological meaning, the struggle, inferring against infidels. He believed it was an obligation that is absolutely central to Islam and second only to declaring the oneness of God. He contended that jihad is greater than prayer, fasting during Ramadan, the hajj (the pilgrimage to Mecca), or any other obligation. He argued that jihad is a way of life that brought glory to the early Muslims and eventually brought down the Roman and Persian Empires. Jihad is considered by him to be absolutely necessary in order to achieve global recognition and Islam's survival and security. Jihad was the concept given to true Muslims in order to combat Jahiliyyah. Azzam also framed jahiliyyah as a process that produces pure Muslims and the standard by which one's faith is measured. In his messages he argued that jihad was necessary for Afghanistan and also necessary for the propagation of Islam.[39]

He classified jihad into two different types: defensive jihad, jihad al daf, and offensive jihad, jihad al-Talab. Azzam placed the bulk of his theoretical work on defensive jihad and used Afghanistan as a case study. Azzam outlined four required steps of any Muslim who desires to participate in jihad. First is hijrah, or the migration away from lands that are not governed by sharia law to those that are. The second step, I'dad, involves military preparation in addition to rigorous intellectual spiritual education. The third step, ribat, entails an operational lifestyle in the way of jihad by carrying out military operations against the enemies or defending other Muslims from enemy attacks. The final step is jihad; offensive operations are carried out at all the levels against the enemy.[40]

Azzam also commented on several issues related to violent jihad. He argued that individual participation in jihad did not necessitate parental permission or consent from other authorities. He believed that the legitimate targets of jihad were infidel fighters, Qutta' Al-Turuq (miscreants) and Bughat (rebels) and stated that women, children, and unarmed citizens should not be targeted unless they directly contributed money or other forms of support to Azzam's version of anti-Islamic activity. He mandated that it was permissible to kill Jews in America, and he argued against killing Muslims indiscriminately; however, he stated that Muslims who are fighting on the side of communism or working for intelligence agencies or non-Muslims are considered apostates. He denounced suicide but supported the use of explosive-laden vehicles or vests as an offensive tactic and called those engaged in such tactics martyrs. Azzam also discussed the role of individual jihad for women. He was adamant that the call of individual jihad is equal upon both men and women. He provided present and past examples of women, such as Sufiyya bint Abd al-Muttalib, who fought in the battle of Uhud with the prophet Mohammad, and emphasized the importance of raising children to become warrior-clerics.[41]

In this light, the Afghan war enabled the mixing of religious doctrine interpreted through a modernist lens. It was unique because it transcended national boundaries. Azzam was thus able to create a transnational version of jihad, grounded in chronic jurisprudence and flavored with the conservatism found in Wahhabism.

Azzam's jihadist ideology was built upon previous works from individuals like Jamal al-Din, Sayyid Qutb, Hassan al-Banna, al-Afghani, al-Madudi, and al-Salam Faraj. Azzam's approach toward ideological doctrine differs from bin Laden and Zawahiri because of his focus on the classical canon of jurisprudence and the honor and integrity of the system. It was an absolute requirement that jihad was framed primarily as a combat force against nonbelievers and apostate Muslims and as a primary method for true Muslim revival. He discussed his vision of jihad in separate publications. The first is called *Defense of the Muslim Lands* and the second is *Join the Caravan*. He penned both of these pieces of propaganda in the mid-1980s, and they are written in a style that has broad appeal. In these works, Azzam argued that the Afghan jihad was the true jihad and not some radical offspring as it was being discussed by other clerics at the time. *Defense of the Muslim Lands* makes the argument that is the absolute obligation of a true believing Muslim to physically fight to defend Muslim territory and oppressed Muslims.[42]

He separated this obligation into two different forms, the first being a collective jihad and the second an individual jihad. Collective jihad manifests itself in the collection of Muslim armies to fight on behalf of Muslim causes, similar to the example set by the prophet. Individual jihad is the responsibility of every Muslim, even if the larger Muslim community remains passive. The foundation for this argument is the belief that the Muslim community is united by faith, not by geographic boundaries drawn by Western powers. Therefore, the loss of Muslim territory in the Philippines, Palestine, Kashmir, Chad, and Eritrea are examples of how Muslims have neglected individual jihad and accepted a passive and malaise mentality instead. Because of Allah's displeasure toward Muslims, these lands were lost, and now Afghanistan has an opportunity to engage in an obligation to God and provide a redemptive action for Muslims who did not stand by their brethren in land lost to non-Muslims. Azzam believed that Afghanistan would be the starting point for a series of revivals that would move from country to country and reclaim all land lost, reviving a puritanical version of Islam.[43]

Azzam's ideal warrior was a Muslim both well versed in strategies and tactics of warfare and who had the entire Quran or large portions of the Quran memorized. He believed that this warrior was strong both in intellect and physical combat, a warrior scholar. Abdullah Azzam would inspire a contingent of influential violent jihadists. This contingent of fighters learned that jihad is Islam's only means of victory and long-term survival against any internal or offensive attacks. For the thousands who have adopted this version of jihad, it is *the* unifier of the Muslim world.

LOUIS BEAM

Louis Beam is a decorated Vietnam War Veteran and former KKK member who currently lives in New Braunfels, Texas. He was most active in the three decades following the Vietnam War and at the time was seen as one of the more prominent strategists. He is described as a paradigmatic figure in the neo-Nazi white supremacist movement at the height of involvement for contextualizing a form of asymmetric warfare for neo-Nazis and using computers to disseminate hate ideology. It was not until he posted a revised version on a dial-up bulletin board that the leaderless resistance concept began to gain traction in neo-Nazi groups. The idea has been implemented since 1992 by the Earth Liberation Front and in 2016 is the modus operandi for ISIS and Al Qaeda in the Western nations.[44]

The Man

I'm here to tell you that if we can't have this country, as far as I'm concerned, no one gets it. The guns are cocked, the bullets are in the chamber. . . . We're going to fight and live or we're going to die soon. If you don't help me kill the bastards, you're going to be required to beg for your child's life, and the answer will be no.[45]

—Speech at the 1983 Aryan World Congress

Louis Beam was born in 1946 in Lufkin, Texas. As a child he attended segregated schools in Lake Jackson, Texas, and by junior high school, he had supposedly read every book in the school library on Southern history. In 1966, he volunteered to join the U.S. Army during the Vietnam War. He served eighteen months as a 50-caliber machine gunner on Huey helicopter gunships with the 25th Aviation Battalion, A Company, and on February 20, 1968, he was awarded the Distinguished Flying Cross for his actions in the Republic of Vietnam.[46]

He returned to the United States in 1968, and his Vietnam experience gave him a new-found hatred both for communism and his own country's government. Acting on his disdain of the existing federal government and the civil rights movement, he joined the Texas chapter of United Klans of America (UKA), an Alabama-based group that was behind a significant amount of civil rights violence in the 1950s and 1960s. In the early 1970s, he was accused of bombing a left-wing radio station and firing gunshots into a local Communist Party's headquarters, although he was never tried. In 1976, he joined David Duke's Knights of the Ku Klux Klan and quickly rose to hold a state leadership position. He was known to lead guerrilla warfare workshops and paramilitary camps. He was instrumental in leading the Klan's efforts to recruit active duty Army personnel from Fort Hood, Texas. In 1977, he earned a bachelor of arts degree from the University of Houston at Clear Lake City. In 1981, he was a member of a KKK maritime unit, "USS Vietcong" harassing Vietnamese fisherman and burning at least two Vietnamese-owned boats.

That same year he became an Aryan Nations "Ambassador at Large" and moved to the Aryan Nations compound in Idaho to work with Richard Butler, the leader of the Aryan Nations at that time. A couple of months after his move to the Aryan Nations compound, The Order was formed. The Order was a secret domestic terrorist group also known as the Bruder Schweighen or The Silent Brotherhood. Robert Matthews led the group, and although his exact ties to Louis Beam are not known, Matthews passed out copies of Beam's "Leaderless Resistance" essay to his members. Matthews published an Order document that used the code name "Lone Star" to indicate that after the upcoming racial revolution, Beam would be in charge of the Western District of America.[47]

In 1984, Beam and two other white supremacists established Aryan Nations Liberty.net. Liberty.net was the first white supremacist neo-Nazi online bulletin board and made Beam one of the first Americans to use computers as a method to organize followers and ideas. In 1987, he fled to Mexico to evade law enforcement after being indicted by a grand jury in Arkansas for allegedly conspiring to overthrow the government. Beam was then added to the FBI's Ten Most Wanted list and was subsequently apprehended in Chapala, Mexico, and extradited to the United States after a gun battle with Mexican authorities that left one officer critically wounded. In April 1988, he was acquitted of all federal charges at Fort Smith, Arkansas, and then launched a quarterly racist magazine titled *The Seditionist*.[48]

In 1992, he revised an earlier leaderless resistance essay and published it in *The Seditionist*. The central message of the essay was that all white revolutionaries should abandon large groups and engage in small cells of one man in order to counter the effective law enforcement actions being conducted on behalf of the United States. Beam's last public speech was given in 1996, and although he has written an occasional essay, he apparently is only active through email correspondence and on his website. His written work is posted on his website and is available in five different languages.[49]

Leaderless Resistance

In 1983, Louis Beam self-published "Leaderless Resistance" in the *Inter Klan Newsletter* and *Survival Alert* and again in his journal, *The Seditionist*, in 1992. The central argument of the essay is that the U.S. federal government is threatening American civil liberties and that a change in strategy is needed in order to overcome this threat. Despite the diminished communist threat, Beam argued that U.S. freedoms are still at risk and that anyone who disagrees with the current policies of the United States will likely be labeled a domestic terrorist or cultist. Therefore, conventional strategies, organizational structures, and tactics used by current resistance organizations will ultimately fail. He stated that a new form of asymmetric warfare is needed in order to circumvent the superior military strength, the U.S. federal government, its law enforcement, and its intelligence abilities.[50]

Beam attributes the leaderless resistance idea to Colonel Ulius Louis Amoss, the founder and chairman of the International Service of Information Incorporated in Baltimore, Maryland. Amoss documented his thoughts on leaderless resistance in April 17, 1962, to counter the communist threat. However, Beam states that he has taken these ideas and contextualized them in order to be effectively used against the United States federal government. Beam also argues that leaderless resistance is part of the original thirteen colonies' strategy and tactics during the American Revolution. In order for the white separatist movement to be successful in overcoming a superior opponent, individual resistance cells and small unconnected cells are required in order to maintain operational security. There are some challenges associated with leaderless resistance, most notably the inability to carry out coordinated and sustained engagements. However, individuals and small cells are necessary in order to evade federal informants and intelligence-gathering mechanisms that have been effectively constructed to eradicate large, open-to-the-public organizations. Individual cells are even more difficult to detect, reconnoiter, and disrupt. These small, autonomous cells and individuals will only prove effective if they maintain the same resolve and commitment that was seen during the Revolutionary War.[51]

It was due to a combination of current events and Beam's ideas that leaderless resistance gained traction within the white supremacist movement. Beam was invited to speak in October 1992 at a Christian Identity meeting hosted by Keith Peters at Estes Park, Colorado. This conference was held three months after Randy Weaver and his family were engaged in a firefight with federal agents. This incident, known as Ruby Ridge, resulted in the deaths of Weaver's wife, young son, family dog, and a federal agent. Ruby Ridge was framed as evidence that the federal government was targeting true patriots. From February 28 to April 19, 1993, the Waco siege occurred at the Branch Davidian compound, ultimately resulting in a total of seventy-eight Davidian deaths. These two events were the primary catalysts that gave context to the notion of leaderless resistance. Leaderless resistance was popularized and resonated with other neo-Nazi leaders such as Tom Metzger, Richard Kelly Hoskins, David Lane, and William Pierce. Leaderless resistance was a central theme in William Pierce's *Hunter*, Richard Kelly Hoskins' *Vigilantes of Christendom,* and David Lane's *Wotan is Coming.*[52]

Tom Metzger, former KKK Grand Dragon, founder of White Aryan Resistance (WAR), and well-known neo-Nazi, effectively promoted the leaderless resistance idea and created the phrase "lone wolf." He used his magazines *The Insurgent* and *White Aryan Resistance Magazine*, WAR's website, his "Race and Reason" television show, and video games to publicize the idea.

In May 2000, the *White Aryan Resistance Magazine* published "Advice for the Lone Wolf" from a supposed anonymous contributor. The following are excerpts from that publication:

THE LONE WOLF CREED:
Anonymous
I am the Lone Wolf; I am covert. I conduct surveillance, reconnaissance and intelligence on my opponents. I do not join groups and/or organizations due to informants, agent provocateurs and troublemakers. I avoid being on a list.
I have studied and researched people like the Unabomber, BTK Wichita, Kansas serial killer, Eric Rudolph, Robert Mathews and others and learned from their errors.
I am preparing for the coming War. I am ready when the line is crossed.
If need be I will pretend to be an anti-racist or very liberal as a cover. If I am in a position of authority I will not disclose to anyone my true objectives. My actions must be totally covert in nature.
I am the underground Insurgent fighter and independent. I am in your neighborhoods, schools, police departments, bars, coffee shops, malls, etc.
I am, The Lone Wolf! I am always listening.[53]

Over two decades have passed since the leaderless resistance model became prominent in the neo-Nazi movement. Fortunately, there have only been a limited number of successful lone-wolf attacks and the envisioned army of lone wolves carrying out hundreds or thousands of attacks never materialized. However, it is important to note that Beams' idea was also adopted by left-wing extremists such as the Earth Liberation Front and the Animal Liberation Front and have now been adopted by violent jihadists. Although it is difficult to determine the exact time and ideologue that introduced the idea of violent jihadism, the most likely suspect could be Abu Musab al Suri.[54]
The notion of individual jihad existed before Beam, but it was always used in the confines of a group, an organization, or community. In some of his writings, al Suri promotes the concept of individual jihad after witnessing the dismantling of the Al Qaeda group following 9/11 and recognizing that their strength was extremely limited, particularly in their ability to carry out a successful attack in the West.[55] Organizationally, additional groups declined new members to join their organization because of the dangers associated with surveillance, intelligence community, and elements of the military and law enforcement. Al Suri eventually was captured in November 2005 in Pakistan.[56] His idea of individual jihad was embraced by Al Qaeda in the Arabian Peninsula, specifically the Al Qaeda franchise group in Yemen. *Inspire Magazine*, the Al Qaeda magazine, published long excerpts from al Suri's written material on individual jihad. In 2010, Adam Gadahn, U.S.-born

Al Qaeda spokesman, called for Muslims in the West to adopt the leaderless resistance model. ISIS has also adopted this model that is reflected in the following statement. Below is an excerpt from a communication released by the Islamic State in September of 2014:[57]

> *You must strike the soldiers, patrons, and troops of the tawāghīt [those who do not rule by that which Allah has revealed]. Strike their police, security, and intelligence members, as well as their treacherous agents. Destroy their beds. Embitter their lives for them and busy them with themselves. If you can kill a disbelieving American or European—especially the spiteful and filthy French—or an Australian, or a Canadian, or any other disbeliever from the disbelievers waging war, including the citizens of the countries that entered into a coalition against the Islamic State, then rely upon Allah, and kill him in any manner or way however it may be. Do not ask for anyone's advice and do not seek anyone's verdict. Kill the disbeliever whether he is civilian or military, for they have the same ruling. Both of them are disbelievers. Both of them are considered to be waging war (the civilian by belonging to a state waging war against the Muslims). Both of their blood and wealth is legal for you to destroy, for blood does not become illegal or legal to spill by the clothes being worn.*
>
> *The best thing you can do is to strive to do your best and kill any disbeliever, whether he be French, American, or from any of their allies.*
>
> *If you are not able to find an IED or a bullet, then single out the disbelieving American, Frenchman, or any of their allies. Smash his head with a rock, or slaughter him with a knife, or run him over with your car, or throw him down from a high place, or choke him, or poison him. Do not lack. Do not be contemptible. Let your slogan be, "May I not be saved if the cross worshipper and taghūt (ruler ruling by manmade laws) patron survives."*
>
> *If you are unable to do so, then burn his home, car, or business. Or destroy his crops.*
>
> *If you are unable to do so, then spit in his face. If yourself refuses to do so, while your brothers are being bombarded and killed, and while their blood and wealth everywhere is deemed lawful by their enemies, then review your religion.*

NOTES

1. Hassan, Muhammad Haniff. *The Father of Jihad:'Abd Allāh "Azzām"s Jihad Ideas and Implications to National Security*: 2. ICP, 2014.

2. Michael, George. *Lone Wolf Terror and the Rise of Leaderless Resistance.* Nashville: Vanderbilt University Press, 2012.

3. "SEDITIONIST." Leaderless Resistance. Accessed July 11, 2016. http://www.louisbeam.com/leaderless.htm.

4. Bergen, Peter L. *Manhunt: The Ten-year Search for Bin Laden from 9/11 to Abbottabad.* New York: Crown Publishers, 2012.

5. Wright, Lawrence. *The Looming Tower: Al-Qaeda and the Road to 9/11.* New York: Vintage Books, 2006.

6. Scheuer, Michael. *Osama Bin Laden.* Oxford: (Oxford University Press, 2011).

7. Hassan, *The Father of Jihad.*

8. Wright, Lawrence. *The Looming Tower.*

9. Hassan, Muhammad Haniff. *The Father of Jihad: 'Abd Allah 'Azzam's Jihad Ideas and Implications to National Security*: 2. ICP, 2014.

10. Burke, Jason. *Al-Qaeda: The True Story of Radical Islam.* London: Penguin, 2004.

11. "Timeline: How Norway's Terror Attacks Unfolded," *BBC News*, accessed August 30, 2015, http://www.bbc.com/news/world-europe-14260297.

12. "'Breivik Manifesto' Details Chilling Attack Preparation," *BBC News*, accessed August 30, 2015, http://www.bbc.com/news/world-europe-14267007.

13. Pantucci, Raffaello. "What Have We Learned about Lone Wolves from Anders Behring Breivik?," *Perspectives on Terrorism* 5, no. 5–6 (July 12, 2011), http://www.terrorismanalysts.com/pt/index.php/pot/article/view/what-we-have-learned.

14. Calver, *John* C. M. "The Striving Shaykh: Abdullah Azzam and the Revival of Jihad." *Journal of Religion and Society.* Supplement Series 2 (2007).

15. Azzām, Abdullah. *Defence of the Muslim Lands.* London: (Azzam Publications, 2002).

16. Calvert, "The Striving Shaykh."

17. Hassan, *The Father of Jihad.*

18. Calvert, "The Striving Shaykh."

19. Braithwaite, Rodric. *Afgantsy: The Russians in Afghanistan, 1979–89.* New York: Oxford University Press, 2011.

20. Burke, *Al-Qaeda.*

21. Yusuf Azzam, Abdullah. *Join the Caravan*, 2nd Revised edition, Azzam Publications, 2001.

22. *The Looming Tower* by Lawrence Wright.

23. Another unique development in the war in Afghanistan involves the material support provided by the United States and Saudi Arabia. The spread of communism in Afghanistan was seen as the ever-expanding role of communism across the globe and the United States not wanting to invest lives in this particular conflict, with support from local fighters against the communist resistance gene and a proxy war. Their support came primarily through money and equipment, most notably the Stinger ground to air missile. This particular missile had a huge impact on the war and provided a tipping point against the Soviet Union because it took away their air superiority.

24. Haroro J. Ingram. *The Charismatic Leadership Phenomenon in Radical and Militant Islamism.* Routledge, 2016.

25. Emerson, Steven. *American Jihad: The Terrorists Living Among Us.* New York: Free Press, 2002.

26. "Asharq Al-Awsat Interviews Umm Mohammed: The Wife of Bin Laden's Spiritual Mentor," *ASHARQ AL-AWSAT*, accessed August 30, 2015, http://english.

aawsat.com/2006/04/article55266896/asharq-al-awsat-interviews-umm-mohammed-the-wife-of-bin-ladens-spiritual-mentor.

27. Suellentrop, Chris. "Abdullah Azzam," *Slate*, April 16, 2002, http://www.slate.com/articles/news_and_politics/assessment/2002/04/abdullah_azzam.html.

28. Bergen, Peter L. *Holy War, Inc.: Inside the Secret World of Osama bin Laden.* New York: Free Press, 2001.

29. Hassan, *The Father of Jihad.*

30. Firestone, Reuven. *Jihād: The Origin of Holy War in Islam.* New York: Oxford University Press, 1999.

31. Mastors, Elena and Alyssa Deffenbaugh. *The Lesser Jihad: Recruits and the Al-Qaida Network.* Lanham, MD: Rowman & Littlefield, 2007.

32. Roy, Olivier. *Globalized Islam: The Search for a New Ummah.* New York: Columbia University Press, 2004. Pp. 289.

33. Roy, Oliver. *Globalized Islam: The Search for a New Ummah.* p. 112.

34. Carroll, James. "The Bush Crusade. Sacred violence, again unleashed in 2001, could prove as destructive as in 1096." *The Nation.* September 20, 2004. https://www.thenation.com/article/bush-crusade/

35. "The Islamic State's (ISIS, ISIL) Magazine | Clarion Project." ClarionProject.org. Accessed July 11, 2016. http://www.clarionproject.org/news/islamic-state-isis-isil-propaganda-magazine-dabiq.

36. Solomon, Ariel Ben. "Al-Qaida Faction Calls Its New English Magazine 'Palestine'" (August, 20, 2014) The Jerusalem Post. Accessed July 11, 2016. http://www.jpost.com/Middle-East/Al-Qaida-faction-calls-its-new-English-magazine-Palestine-371579.

37. Roy, "Globalized Islam." p. 248.

38. McGregor, Andrew. "'Jihad and the Rifle Alone': 'Abdullah Azzam' and the Islamist Revolution," *Journal of Conflict Studies* 23, no. 2 (February 21, 2006), https://journals.lib.unb.ca/index.php/JCS/article/view/219; Azzam, Join the Caravan.

39. Azzam, *Join the Caravan.*

40. Kepel, Gilles, Jean-Pierre Milelli, and Pascale Ghazaleh. *Al Qaeda in Its Own Words.* Cambridge, MA: Belknap Press of Harvard University, 2008.

41. Calvert, "The Striving Shaykh."

42. Azzam, "Defence of the Muslim Lands" and "*Join the Caravan.*"

43. Kepel, Milelli, and Ghazaleh, *Al Qaeda in Its Own Words.*

44. Michael, George. *Lone Wolf Terror and the Rise of Leaderless Resistance.* Nashville: Vanderbilt University Press, 2012.

45. "Louis Beam," *Southern Poverty Law Center*, accessed August 30, 2015, https://www.splcenter.org/fighting-hate/extremist-files/individual/louis-beam.

46. Ibid.; "Essays by Louis Beam on History, Government, Politics, Vietnam, Police State," accessed August 30, 2015, http://www.louisbeam.com/.

47. "Louis Beam," accessed August 30, 2015, http://archive.adl.org/learn/ext_us/beam.html; "Leadership vs. Leaderless Resistance: The Militant White Separatist Movement's Operating Model | Foundation for Defense of Democracies," accessed August 30, 2015, http://www.defenddemocracy.org/media-hit/leadership-vs-leaderless-resistance-the-militant-white-separatist-movement/.

48. "Louis Beam."

49. "Essays by Louis Beam on History, Government, Politics, Vietnam, Police State."

50. George Michael, *Lone Wolf Terror and the Rise of Leaderless Resistance.*

51. "Leaderless Resistance."

52. Ibid.

53. Selections from "The Lone Wolf Creed." Anonymous. (2000, May). Advice for the Lone Wolf. *White Aryan Resistance Magazine*, p. 5. Often attributed to Tom Metzger.

54. Samuels, David. "The New Mastermind of Jihad," *Wall Street Journal*, April 7, 2012, sec. Life and Style, http://www.wsj.com/articles/SB100014240527023032996045773237508559163544.

55. Michael, George. *Lone Wolf Terror and the Rise of Leaderless Resistance.*

56. Roggio, Bill. "The Arrest of Abu Musab Al-Suri?," *The Long War Journal.* November, 3, 2005. Accessed August 30, 2015, http://www.longwarjournal.org/archives/2005/11/the_arrest_of_a.php.

57. Holton, Christopher. "'Lone Wolf' or Jihadi?," *Center for Security Policy*, (July 31, 2015) accessed August 30, 2015, https://www.centerforsecuritypolicy.org/2015/07/31/lone-wolf-or-jihadi/.

Chapter 4

Shifting the Targeting Paradigm

Osama bin Laden and George Lincoln Rockwell

Target selection is both a strategic and tactical decision. In both conventional and asymmetric warfare, a target symbolizes the source of conflict, and if destroyed, it represents a vehicle to change the existing political, social, or religious order. Significant attention has been given to target symbolism in terrorism studies.[1] From the violent extremist's perspective, the target conveys information about the source of grievances and the nature of the conflict. A targeting paradigm within violent extremism is defined as a framework of strategic and tactical decisions used to advance a particular ideology. A shift in a targeting paradigm reflects a shift in strategy and potentially the tactics used to support the shift. Historical examples include the first Irish Republican Army attack on the British outside of Ireland in 1939 or when Black September members took Israeli Olympic athletes hostage in Munich, Germany, in 1972. Although these two examples indicate innovation in target selection on a tactical level, they do not illustrate a complete targeting paradigm shift on the strategic level. This chapter will highlight two of the most important targeting paradigm shifts at a strategic level within neo-Nazism and violent jihadism. Strategic levels indicating shifts in targets are important to identify because they signify an ideological and logistical change.

Violent jihadis and neo-Nazis perceive that their way of life is threatened by outsiders and by other Muslims or whites. A violent jihadi can target outsider threats that originate from the West, atheists, Eastern faiths, or internal threats like apostate Muslims and secular Muslim governments. Neo-Nazis can target blacks, homosexuals, Jews, and Hispanics or internal threats such as whites whom they stigmatize as race traitors. Internal and external threats do not pose the same threat level, and for both ideologies, it has been increasingly critical to identify the most strategic and dangerous threat.

Osama bin Laden and George Lincoln Rockwell have contributed to a targeting paradigm shift within violent jihadism and neo-Nazism. They have done so by identifying who and what they perceive to be the most central threat to whites and to Islam. Bin Laden identifies the West, the United States and Europe, as being the primary target instead of local Muslim governments. George Lincoln Rockwell identifies the American and Global Zionist Jewish threat as being the most strategic target over blacks and other nonwhite groups. Bin Laden shifted the target away from Middle Eastern "puppet apostate" governments (or the near enemy) to the West (the far enemy), while Rockwell directed neo-Nazis and the white supremacy movement away from racial minorities to Jews. It is important to note that both men did not originate these particular ideas; however, their actions, organizations, and ideological advancements in speech and in written form have shifted the targeting paradigm in both movements. The following two examples illustrate the results.

David Lane believed that Jews were the number one threat to the white race, and the assassination-style murder of Alan Berg was meant to be a message to all Jews. Alan Berg was a Jewish American attorney and a popular radio talk show host in Denver, Colorado. His radio style was known to be controversial, and his viewpoints were generally classified as those of a liberal socialist. His radio program was broadcasted in thirty states and had a loyal following in some venues. Berg was known and often criticized for abusing callers and radio guests. Some of these guests and callers belonged to white supremacist groups, and Berg's response would often target and humiliate those groups. Months before his murder, David Lane had called into Alan Berg's show, and in typical Berg fashion, Lane was berated. On June 18, 1984, at 9:30 p.m., Alan Berg pulled up in his driveway after a dinner date. As Berg exited the vehicle, he was shot twelve times by a semi-automatic weapon. The group that claimed responsibility for his death was called The Order or Bruder Schweighen (the Silent Brotherhood). In 1987, four members were indicted on federal charges for Berg's death; David Lane was one of the four. He was convicted and sentenced to serve 190 years for racketeering, conspiracy, and violating the civil rights of Alan Berg. David Lane was the getaway driver for the incident.[2]

Berg's death was ideologically symbolic. The incident represented a point in time where decades of propaganda shifted the targeting paradigm to Jews as the primary racial threat. Lane was a self-described American white nationalist leader, a racist Odinist, which Lane renamed Wotanism, and a self-described political prisoner. Over the course of his life, he was a member of the Aryan Nations, White Aryan Resistance, David Duke's Knights of the Ku Klux Klan, and The Order. While incarcerated, his publications had a significant influence within neo-Nazism until his death from cancer in 2007.

He published frequently in *White Aryan Resistance, Racial Loyalty, The Klansman,* and *Jew Watch.* He coined a universal neo-Nazi slogan called the fourteen words: "We must secure the existence of our people and a future for white children." He drafted the eighty-eight precepts which are supposed to be strategic guidelines for establishing a white society. Lane also advocated the creation of a white ethnic state and promoted a racist religion and white procreation.[3]

Eight years later an incident in Aden, Yemen, was meant to signal another targeting paradigm shift. The shift would be formally declared in *The Declaration of Jihad on the Americans Occupying the Country of the Two Sacred Places,* issued in August 1996.[4] Al Qaeda's first recorded attack targeted U.S. Marines bound for Somalia as part of Operation Restore Hope on December 29, 1992. Two bombs were intended to kill a larger number of Marines staying in Yemen; one destroyed the fourth floor at the Gold Mohur Hotel while a second bomb prematurely detonated at the Aden Movenpick Hotel. Although there were three injuries from the second explosion, no Americans were killed by either bomb. The two Al Qaeda operatives involved in the bombing were Tariq Nasr al-Fadhli, an Afghan veteran, and Jamal al-Nahdi, who lost a hand in the premature explosion.[5] Although this event is eclipsed by the 1998 embassy bombings, the Yemen hotel bombings were significant because they identified a specific point in time when Al Qaeda's targeting paradigm shifted at the strategic and tactical level. In 1998, Osama bin Laden stated,

> The United States wanted to set up a military base for U.S. soldiers in Yemen, so that it could send fresh troops to Somalia. . . . The Arab mujahidin related to the Afghan jihad carried out two bomb explosions in Yemen to warn the United States, causing damage to some Americans staying in those hotels. The United States received our warning and gave up the idea of setting up its military bases in Yemen. This was the first al-Qaeda victory scored against the Crusaders.[6]

Bin Laden was able to successfully shift a targeting paradigm from the near enemy to a far one. It is important to see bin Laden through their eyes, because he was inspirational to many violent jihadists then and now. To them, bin Laden was a skilled speaker who was fluent in both classical Arabic and poetry. He ran a multiethnic, multinational, multilingual organization while demonstrating cost-benefit calculations both in tactical and diplomatic affairs. He was generous and lived frugally despite being born into a privileged family. He gave up a one-billion dollar lifestyle and shared his wealth with others to fight for his faith in some of the harshest places on earth. Bin Laden dressed modestly and associated with the poor as well as with the rich and powerful. He claimed to be fighting against foreign occupation, neocolonialism, and infidel domination. Some of Bin Laden's contemporaries and current violent jihadists describe him as pious and brave, demonstrating integrity and speaking with eloquence. According to them, he apparently had Allah's blessing because he survived numerous assassination attempts, engaged Soviet Special Forces, and endured an extensive manhunt by the United States.[7]

OSAMA BIN LADEN

Osama bin Laden's name and face are some of the most recognizable across the globe. He carried out one the most successful propaganda campaigns in history which put himself, his group, their ideology, and their grievances on the world stage. The average American citizen can be shown a picture of bin Laden, and he or she can give his name, possibly name the group in which he belongs to, and maybe even articulate some of their ideas or grievances. The 9/11 attacks, orchestrated by bin Laden's Al Qaeda also ushered in a complete change in American military equipment, tactics, and doctrine, American's understanding of Islam and the Middle East, and ultimately fulfilled the purpose of the name of his group Al Qaeda or "The Base." Bin Laden was often criticized for not being a religious scholar and for not having a plan for a Muslim government or for a unified Muslim community. He was also criticized for not being an original thinker; however, both of these arguments are derived from a misunderstanding about the man and the goals of Al Qaeda.

Bin Laden was not an ideologue or religious scholar innovating new ideas like Sayyid Qutb or Abdullah Azzam. He is, however, responsible for the creation of "a base" that put ideas into practice, specifically shifting a targeting paradigm. Osama bin Laden never claimed to be an Islamic scholar and wrote that others would draft what the new Muslim community would look like after his organization had paved the way. Michael Scheuer states that bin Laden should not be perceived as an idea generator but rather as an effective leader who reframed and implemented ideas similar to Thomas Jefferson. Comparable to bin Laden's work, there is nothing original in the Declaration of Independence; Jefferson took revolutionary ideas drawn from other philosophers and reframed them in contextual way. From bin Laden's perspective, he believed that in order to bring Muslims back to total submission to Allah and back to his favor, violent jihad against non-Muslims and apostate Muslim was necessary. Violent jihad would be the path to unity, a form of worship, and an Islamic pillar. Jihad was a way in which he was able to set an example of what it meant to follow one's faith, and to bin Laden the most important attribute of being a true Muslim was not words, but actions.[8]

Osama bin Laden perceived that an American military fighting on Afghan soil would recruit violent jihadi fighters and unite the Muslim world.

On Muslim soil, the American military would be easier to attack because of local proximity. Bin Laden knew the importance of information warfare, and through his Al Qaeda media branch, he manufactured a message focused on lightly armed fighters, strong in their Islamic faith, fighting the strongest military force. Finally, if the Americans were fighting on Muslim soil, economic attrition and political upheaval could impact America in the same way it impacted the Soviet Union during the Soviet-Afghan War.[9]

Bin Laden's death in May 2011, by U.S. Navy Seals in Abbottabad, Pakistan, can be seen from two different perspectives. The first is that his death signaled the demise of Al Qaeda as a hierarchal organization, and by killing the leader; the group would disintegrate and lose their capacity to carry out violence. This is the same erroneous perspective that correlates the death of an individual to the death of his ideas. Abdul Nasser, president of Egypt, made the same error when he executed Sayyid Qutb in 1966. A second perspective, or the long-range view of bin Laden and his ideas, is that his targeting paradigm and other ideas are now normalized, and his death gives violent jihadis greater resonance and celebrity within violent jihadi circles.[10] Al Qaeda has in fact functioned as a base for not only violent attacks but also information warfare and advancing jihad toward a Western enemy.

The Man

We declared jihad against the U.S. government because the U.S. government is unjust, criminal and tyrannical. It has committed acts that are extremely unjust, hideous and criminal, whether directly or through its support of the Israeli occupation.

—Osama bin Laden. April 1997 CNN Interview [11]

Jihad will continue even if I am not around.[12]

—Osama bin Laden, Late September 2001, in an interview with a Pakistani newspaper

Osama bin Laden was born on March 10, 1957 in Riyadh, Saudi Arabia. The name Osama can be translated to mean "lion," and according to Michael Scheuer, he was named after one of the venerable companions of the prophet. Six months after he was born, his family moved to Medina and would later live in Mecca and Jeddah.[13] Osama was part of a family comprising fifty-two siblings, twenty-eight brothers and twenty-four sisters. His family was Yemeni in origin, and the patriarchy rose to prominence through hard work, religious faith, and taking risks. Osama's father, Mohammed bin Awad bin Laden, was born in the village of al-Rubat in the Hadramut region of Yemen in 1908. Mohammed bin Laden immigrated to Saudi Arabia where he worked in construction primarily as a porter bricklayer. He later became a foreman and eventually formed the Bin Laden Group which led him to extreme prominence and wealth. Osama bin Laden's father married often, and it has been said that he had two passions, work and women. Osama's mother was Allia Ghanem, a young Syrian wife who bore Mohammed his seventh son. She was Yemeni although their family moved to Syria, and she belonged to the Ghanem family, a large secular middle-class Syrian family.[14]

Osama was the only one of his brothers not to have attended school outside of the Saudi kingdom. He developed a love for the Quran and Muslim history and later saw the actions of his organization and the jihadis as part of a continuum rather than a complete revolution. He attended one of the top two schools in the country, the al-Thagher Model School, supported by Crown Prince Faisal, near downtown Jeddah. His classmates were comprised of some of the kingdom's most notable citizens, including those of the royal family. He studied science, mathematics, biology, and English and was a member of an afterschool religious study group led by a Syrian gym teacher speculated to be an exiled Muslim Brotherhood member. In 1978, Osama was a student at King Abdul Aziz University in Jeddah where he studied economics, business administration, and management.[15]

Osama's development into young adulthood was impacted by several factors. Bin Laden's' father blended his religious thought into action, was decisive, hated Israel, and had a strong work ethic. Personally, bin Laden enjoyed the outdoors and agriculture and preferred a rural lifestyle over an urban one. He would hunt, swim, hike long distances, often in harsh terrain, and spent as much time as possible at al-Bahra, the family farm fifteen miles outside of Jeddah. Both he and his father believed that a rural lifestyle made society stronger and better able to resist threats because it preserved a person's spirit instead of it decaying in urban societies. Bin Laden was not materialistic, and his preference for the rural life would enable him to endure the rugged Afghan conditions. These preferences reflected the philosophical underpinnings of Ibn Khaldun, whose work theorized that rural, tribal, and pastoral societies experience greater solidarity as well as an increased will to fight.[16]

After the Soviet-Afghan War broke out in 1979, bin Laden assisted Abdullah Azzam in establishing the Service Bureau, an organization that facilitated foreign Muslim fighters into the fight against the Soviets. At the beginning, the Service Bureau was engaged in assisting refugees, producing educational materials, and staffing clinics. Soon the organization would recruit and train foreign fighters because so many other organizations were involved in charity and humanitarian work, and the Services Bureau was competing for resources. The Service Bureau changed its focus to military activities against the Soviets.

Bin Laden was twenty-two years old when he first went to Afghanistan. Although the exact date of Osama bin Laden's arrival in Afghanistan is contested, it is estimated that he arrived sometime in December 1979. He also at that time devoted a significant amount of personal funds to supporting the Services' office and providing stipends for Arab fighters. Bin Laden would meet with members of the Saudi Embassy in Islamabad, specifically the Saudi interior minister Prince Nayef. This would later evolve into a road-building project from Pakistan to Afghanistan so that more weapons and supplies could get to the Afghan front.

Bin Laden and Ayman Zawahiri, the current leader of Al Qaeda in 2016, assumed leadership of the Services Bureau renaming it Al Qaeda after the death of Abdullah Azzam in 1989.[17] After the Soviet Army left Afghanistan in 1989, bin Laden attributed their victory to Allah's miracles and intervention, proving that any nation or army could be defeated by the faithful. He defined "faithful" as Muslims who submit to the Quran, sharia, and the jihadi obligation.[18]

After the Soviet-Afghan War, the organization focused on removing all forms of communism, tribal unification, and governmental rule in Afghanistan. Bin Laden also reassessed some of the lessons learned from the War. He determined that military training camps were an absolutely necessity for an effective insurgency. On a tactical level, motivated recruits will fail without a combat mindset and tactical competencies. On a strategic level, he learned the power of economic attrition in a protracted conflict and how it impacted Soviet national morale and economy to keep a fighting force in Afghanistan. Bin Laden asserted that the USSR fell due in part to the great economic loss in the Afghan war against the mujahedeen. Finally, he was also able to realize the power of media. Bin Laden, after studying Islamic history, recognized the importance of winning hearts and minds. He was already involved in producing *Al-Jihad*, Abdullah Azzam's magazine, in the 1980s and then later developed the Al Qaeda media wing for information warfare.

Al Qaeda intended to provide support for jihad on a global scale through its media activities, military operations, and assistance to Muslims committed to jihad. Al Qaeda was modeled off of what he saw in Afghanistan states. Bin Laden aspired to build an insurgent operation.[19] The purpose of this insurgent organization was to train individuals or small groups for combat operations. The organization would orchestrate the logistical, accounting, and administrative issues associated with training fighters. Another function was religious, issuing fatwas and offering religious training to training camp participants. Finally, a media wing maximized Al Qaeda's use of information warfare to Western or non-Muslim audiences locally and on a global scale. The purpose of each message was not only to gain recruits, but also to increase the possibility of winning hearts and minds and to outline grievances and etiology for opponents. Organizationally, all of this was overseen by a Shura Council chaired by Osama bin Laden.[20]

Afterward, bin Laden returned to Saudi Arabia somewhat a celebrity. He was asked to give speeches and interviews as he returned to work for the Bin Laden Group constructing roads, tunnels, and buildings. As a construction manager he not only led construction crews and completed projects, but he also negotiated details with Saudi officials and coordinated issues between European and American engineers. He was able to speak English fairly well, and one of his sons stated that he was fluent in Pashtun.[21]

However, his return to Saudi Arabia was not without problems. It was during this time that he gave his support to Yemenis who had Afghan battle experience and who were assisting in a campaign to overthrow South Yemen's Marxist regime. He associated with Saudi Arabia's Islamic Awakening (Sahwa) group, by which the Sahwa leaders drafted two documents, *The Declaration of Demands* and *A Memorandum Advice to Saudi Grand Mufti Sheikh Abdulaziz bin Baz* in September 1992. These documents discussed ending official corruption and aligning the government under full sharia law. These documents were received negatively, and members of the organization were incarcerated. During this time, Saddam's army invaded Kuwait in August 1990, and in response, bin Laden proposed to use his construction company and his experienced network of fighters to defend Saudi Arabia against an Iraqi invasion. The Saudi Royal family and government declined bin Laden's proposal and sought military assistance from Western militaries.

The rejection to defend his homeland by the Saudi government was a turning point. This meant that his government was permitting infidels to set foot on the Holy Arabian Peninsula while at the same time discrediting what Allah had done through the Afghanistan mujahedeen. Bin Laden's distaste of the Saudi government was apparent, and Saudi security officials raided his farm and disarmed over 100 Afghan veterans who resided there. In response, bin Laden urged religious scholars to issue a fatwa against Western militaries residing on the Arabian Peninsula. His confrontation with the Saudi government, specifically with the Saudi Royal family was public and intensified to the degree that he left Saudi Arabia for Pakistan and never returned. The Saudi government, specifically King Fahd, retracted his Saudi citizenship in 1994.[22]

Bin Laden returned to Pakistan and lived in Peshawar for a short time to mediate conflicts in the fractured Afghan political landscape before moving to Sudan. While in the Sudan, he expanded Al Qaeda, worked commercial construction contracts, engaged in import/export opportunities, and managed agricultural enterprises. Bin Laden's company, Al Higrah, was responsible for building the 500-mile highway called "the challenge road" that linked Port Sudan with Khartoum. Bin Laden owned a sizable area of southeastern Sudan, which was granted to him as payment for some of his construction work.[23]

Bin Laden's time in Sudan functioned as a time to prepare Al Qaeda to confront the West. The Sudanese years enabled bin Laden to mature in his leadership, outline strategic priorities including priorities that focused on potential targets, and fuse political, military, and media operations. It was also at this time that Al Qaeda sponsored the 1992 attack against U.S. forces in Yemen and provided support for anti-U.S. forces in Somalia between 1992 and 1994. The U.S. government and the Saudi government put economic pressure on the Sudanese to deport bin Laden. Sudanese officials eventually complied, and bin Laden returned to Afghanistan on May 18, 1996. He was welcomed by some of the Afghan mujahedeen with whom bin Laden had fought alongside against the Soviets. Several accounts demonstrate not only a warm welcome for bin Laden's return but also a contract to protect him as a guest from outside authorities.[24]

The Taliban at the time were bound to protect bin Laden on two points. Bin Laden was perceived as a great jihadist fighter and therefore brought a lot of favorable attention to the Taliban. Second, the code of Pashtunwali articulates that it is a high honor and duty to protect guests. In this particular part of the world, honor means everything, and Mullah Omar and the Taliban would sacrifice everything, including their lives, in order to protect their honor. In return, bin Laden praised the Taliban in his propaganda and also used some of his economic resources and construction experience to support the Taliban. After the bombing of the USS Cole in 2000, Mullah Omar began to come under intense pressure from the United States. In response, bin Laden continued to offer verbal praise for and even publicly pledged personal allegiance to Omar and encouraged others to do the same.[25]

After the September 11 attacks, the United States demanded that the Taliban hand over bin Laden for extradition. Mullah Omar dismissed the Americans, and the United States responded with military action on October 7, 2001. Bin Laden, his family, and organizational members fled to the Tora Bora Mountains before crossing into Pakistan and eventually building a compound in Abbottabad. Until his death, he continued to engage in sporadic information warfare focusing on religious justification for war, discrediting apostate Muslim governments and religious scholars, and criticizing U.S. military and policy.[26]

Osama bin Laden was killed on May 2, 2011, in Operation Neptune Spear, a CIA joint operation by U.S. Seal Team Six and the U.S. Army Special Operations Command, 160th Special Operations Aviation Regiment.[27] By the time of his death, bin Laden had been married five times.

The Far Enemy

On August 23, 1996, bin Laden issued a declaration of war against the United States, also known as the Ladense Epistle. This declaration was published in *Al-Quds al-Arabi*, a London-based periodical, and also published on the U.K.-based Saudi dissident website Al-Islah on September 2 of the same year.[28] This declaration formalized an ideological shift that was already present in Al Qaeda. Instead of focusing on the corrupt regimes in the Middle East like Saudi Arabia or Egypt, the near enemy, he focused on the United States, the far enemy. The purpose of the document was to implicate the United States as the most threatening enemy to Muslims around the world. The document then argued that it was the duty of all true Muslims to wage jihad against the United States.

The declaration of war outlined a sequenced long-range strategy. Bin Laden's four objectives were: drive United States out of Muslim territory, eliminate Israel, destroy and replace oppressive secular Muslim regimes, and resolve the Shia issue. In the declaration, bin Laden clearly outlined six major grievances with the United States. He outlined his case for jihad citing the presence of U.S. military and civilians on the Arabian Peninsula, Washington's support of jahiliyyah Muslim governments, support for Israel, support for other nations that target Muslims, the exploitation of Muslim resources, and the placing of U.S. military personnel on Muslim lands. He argued that governments in Jordan, Algeria, Egypt, and Saudi Arabia were able to maintain power because of the economic, military, and political support from the United States. He maintained that Israel would be defeated if the United States was economically threatened and lost their military superiority and will to fight. Eighteen months after this declaration was issued, a fatwa was signed by several fully credentialed Islamic scholars. The fatwa gave violent jihadists the religious authority to kill Americans and their allies anywhere in order to liberate the Al-Aqsa mosque and the holy mosque.[29]

An excerpt from the document:

> Men of the radiant future of our *umma* of Muhammad, raise the banner of *jihad* up high against the Judeo-American alliance that has occupied the holy places of Islam. God told his Prophet: "He will not let the deeds of those who

are killed for His cause come to nothing; He will guide them and put them in
a good state; He will admit them into the Garden He has already made known
to them." And the Prophet said: "There are one hundred levels in Heaven that
God has prepared for the holy warriors who have died for Him, between two
levels as between the earth and the sky." And the *al-Jami al-Sahih* notes that the
Prophet said: "The best martyrs are those who stay in the battle line and do not
turn their faces away until they are killed. They will achieve the highest level
of Heaven, and their Lord will look kindly upon them. When your Lord looks
kindly upon a slave in the world, He will not hold him to account." I say to our
Muslim brothers across the world: Your brothers in Saudi Arabia and Palestine
are calling for your help and asking you to share with them in the jihad against
the enemies of God, your enemies the Israelis and Americans. They are asking
you to defy them in whatever way you possibly can, so as to expel them in
defeat and humiliation from the holy places of Islam.[30]

The initial impact of the declaration of jihad was limited. Part of this was
due to the fact that bin Laden had just returned to Afghanistan and was there
during the time the Taliban regime was reorganizing after years of civil war.
On August 7, 1998, two bombs exploded in the U.S. embassies of Kenya
and Tanzania. This was the first large strike against the United States, and it
demonstrated Al Qaeda's ability to carry out complex synchronized attacks.
After these two attacks, bin Laden continued to conduct a media campaign
focused on increased global support for Al Qaeda, identifying those whom he
believed were enemies or supported the United States, while the Taliban was
also experiencing rhetorical pressure from diplomatic channels.

However, the 1998 American embassy attacks in East Africa put bin
Laden's targeting paradigm shift in the forefront of almost all jihadi debates.
In retaliation, cruise missiles were sent to Al Qaeda's base in Afghanistan
and were directed toward Khartoum, Sudan, where Washington suspected
that biological weapons were being manufactured at a pharmaceutical company. Two years later in October 2000, the USS Cole was attacked in Aden,
followed one year later by the 9/11 attack. The United States responded by
invading Afghanistan in 2001, implementing a War on Terrorism, creating
the Department of Homeland Security, and invading Iraq in 2003.[31]

The Afghan and Iraqi American invasions fit bin Laden's strategic paradigm shift. Western forces were now the near enemy. In this capacity, the
United States could be targeted first, then Israel, and then apostate Muslims.
Additionally, Western forces in Iraq and Afghanistan became legitimate reasons to call for defensive jihad, reminiscent of the calls for foreign fighters
during the Soviet-Afghan War. Bin Laden used both invasions as evidence of
a Western crusade to occupy Muslim lands and eradicate sharia law.

It is difficult to measure the exact impact of this idea on violent jihadism.
One way is to examine the number of groups and attacks that have emerged

since 1998. The START database, housed at the University of Maryland, boasts one of the largest terrorism databases. As of August 10, 2015, eleven different Al Qaeda organizations were listed with a total of 1722 incidents attributed to the organization.[32] Out of the 1722 incidents, 61% of these attacks were divided among government, military, and police targets. Due to the coding of the database, it is not possible to tell which are Western targets or localized government targets. However, a cursory qualitative search of the attack reveals that the targets in some way are connected either directly to the United States or served as a proxy for them. It is also important to note that although theoretically the first targets were supposed to be Western nations, the data reveals that many victims have also been Muslims. Still, these Muslims were in some way connected to the West, which differs from ISIS targeting Shia and other Muslim groups simply because they are considered to be apostates.

GEORGE LINCOLN ROCKWELL—CHANGED THE FACE OF RACISM IN AMERICA

For the first time, with the arrival on the American scene of the American Nazi Party, there is now a spiritual force to look these Jew terrorists in the eye when they start that "You're-a-Nazi"-bit and reply, "You're damned right we're Nazis, and we will soon enough take care of you traitors, thieves, liars, terrorists and communist enemies!"[33]

George Lincoln Rockwell, 1918–1967, has been called the American Fuhrer and is considered to be one of the most influential neo-Nazi ideologues by changing the face of racism in America. He learned important lessons as a navy pilot in World War II, graphic designer, publisher, and speaker. These experiences informed how he advanced neo-Nazism in the United States.[34] In 1958, he founded the American Nazi Party (ANP), later known as the National Socialist Party, and continued to lead the organization until his death on August 25, 1967. During these nine years, Rockwell's work and ideas launched neo-Nazism in the United States.[35]

He influenced a generation of neo-Nazi leaders, not necessarily through his organization, but by his ideas and his endeavors. He promoted the use of Nazi images and slogans,[36] advanced Holocaust denial, created the phrase "white power," and expanded the "white" definition to include Catholics, Poles, Greeks, Armenians, Turks, Spaniards, and Russians. He shared the Nazi's view of eugenics and perceived interracial marriages and children as suicide for the white race. Finally, he believed in an upcoming race war that would eventually purge or relocate all nonwhites and Jews.

Rockwell was inspired by Adolf Hitler's *Mein Kampf*, and argued that Jews were the white race's primary enemy, not blacks or other minorities. He asserted that American Jews controlled the U.S. media, the government, banks, and commerce. He argued that communism, feminism, immorality, homosexuality, racial integration, and Hollywood were either created by Jews or promoted by them. George Lincoln Rockwell was one of the first American neo-Nazi leaders to identify the strategic necessity of Holocaust denial in order to advance their racist doctrine. [37]

Rockwell recognized that unless history could be revised, the Holocaust would continue to be the single greatest impediment to Rockwell's vision of a post-Nazi movement. Anti-Semitic views were forever correlated to the Nazi Party and Hitler's slaughter of six million Jews. Rockwell's strategy was to distort historical memory so that the stigma that associated the Holocaust with Nazism would be reduced. Rockwell's first documented activity of Holocaust denial occurred in 1964 in a speech that he gave at the University of Hawaii. Three years later, in 1967, Rockwell drafted some basic Holocaust denial tenets and disseminated these concepts across his speaking circuit and in the media. In fact, since 1964, Holocaust denial was standard fare in almost all of Rockwell's presentations.[38]

Rockwell understood that if any idea is to resonate with a population, it is more likely to be effective if it is framed as entertainment. He asserted that the propaganda must focus on media that address limited attention spans and frames of reference. Unless a political or racist message was entertaining, it would be unable to hold the public's attention and the message would not be transmitted. For example, Rockwell continued to berate African Americans because he believed that a majority of American whites shared some degree of his racist views. He would then use debate, protest, or stagecraft to state that Jews were using blacks as pawns to advance a Jewish agenda. He told blacks that it was for their own good, and they should return to Africa, lose their citizenship, or be forced to a relocation center.[39]

Rockwell's strategy was to come to political power by unifying the white race. His plan was to instigate the Jews and blacks into violence against him, effectively turning him into a victim. This victimization would gain publicity, unify whites against a common enemy, and gather more support. Using Hitler's model, this support would then translate into political power. After achieving political power, he would then mobilize an effective base and pass a series of racist policies focused on the institution of the systematic execution of Marxist Zionist traitors and disloyal Jews from positions of influence in the media, government, education, and legal system. He argued that an international treason tribunal be formed in order to investigate, try, and publicly hang all non-Jews who have collaborated with Jews, which he labeled as treasonous behavior.[40]

The Man

> The secret world of the Jews not only exists—if it continues to exist and flourish, WE will cease to exist.[41]

George Lincoln "Link" Rockwell was born on March 9, 1918, in Bloomington, Illinois. His parents were George Lovejoy "Doc" Rockwell and Claire Schade Rockwell. Both parents were rising vaudeville comics of the 1920s and headlined at Radio City Cusic Hall in New York City, making his father one of the most popular and well-paid vaudevillians in the nation. George Lincoln Rockwell's father dominated both room and stage. Some of his friends were the most well-known entertainers at the time, including Jack Benny and George Burns. The couple divorced in 1924, and George Lincoln, then six years old, moved with his mother to Atlantic City, New Jersey, to live with her sister, Arlene. Throughout his childhood, Rockwell idealized his father, though he rarely spent time with him. He was often physically and mentally abused by his mother's sister.[42]

Even before his foray into Nazi ideology, he was an activist. For example, during his high school years, 1931–1936, he organized a student boycott over bad cafeteria food and held a one-person strike against a civics teacher. He was given an ultimatum by the administrators to either end the strike or resume classwork. Rockwell continued the strike and was not allowed to graduate. Because of school problems and abuse from his aunt, Arlene, he was sent to live with his paternal grandmother, Mary MacPherson Rockwell, in Providence, Rhode Island. Under his grandmother's supervision, he did well in high school and became the editor and cartoonist for the school newspaper. He graduated in 1936 and then attended Hope High School in Providence in order to increase his chances in being accepted into Harvard. He received his second high school diploma in less than a year. However, he was rejected by Harvard and did not apply to another school. Rather than spending a year outside of school, he was enrolled in Hadron Academy, a boarding school for boys in central Maine. He was accepted into Brown University in 1941 based on his college aptitude test scores, and he was given a place in the incoming class of 1942. At Brown, Rockwell revived a campus humor magazine, *Sir Brown!*, Where he worked as the magazine editor, and he contributed his own cartoons to the college newspaper, *The Brown Daily Herald*. Rockwell majored in philosophy, though he described the environment as stifling creativity and intellectual freedom, being infected with communism and riddled with intellectual dishonesty.[43]

He dropped out of Brown, and in March 1941 Rockwell joined the U.S. Navy hoping to fly. He was accepted as an aviation cadet in order to receive flight training at the naval air station at Squantum, Massachusetts. He was commissioned as a naval aviator on December 9, 1941, two days after the

Japanese attack on Pearl Harbor. In 1944, he was promoted to lieutenant and then to lieutenant commander in October 1945. He was considered a competent pilot and an efficient officer. During World War II, he flew primarily in support of reconnaissance, transport, and training functions aboard the anti-submarine vessels. After the war, he left active duty and maintained his commission as an officer in the Naval Reserve. In 1950, he was recalled to active duty by the United States Navy at the onset of the Korean War. Rockwell was assigned as an instructor to the Naval Air Support School in California, specifically at the San Diego Naval Air Station, and he was promoted to full commander. In 1952, he was transferred to the Keflavik Naval Air Station in Iceland where he served two one-year tours of duty. He was released from active duty on December 15, 1954, after returning to the United States. He would remain in the Naval Reserve until 1960 when the Department of the Navy revoked his commission because of his racial and religious actions.[44]

He supported his family through several venues before he become fully invested in neo-Nazism. Between World War II and the Korean War, Rockwell moved back to Boothbay Harbor, Maine. In 1946, he entered the Pratt Institute of Commercial Art in Brooklyn, New York, which was one of the most respected institutions for commercial illustration. Rockwell wanted a career as a commercial artist and saw the Pratt Institute as the pathway to a lucrative career. While at Pratt, he won a National American Cancer Society illustration competition. He was awarded a thousand dollars and national recognition for winning this competition. He never completed the program but later moved back to Maine to start a company, Main Advertising Incorporated, with two other partners. In 1949, he produced *The Olde Maine Guide* and *What's Next?*, which was virtually identical in content and format to a periodical soon to be known as the *TV Guide*. He left his startup and published *US Lady*, a magazine designed to target military spouses across the globe and then began working as an independent contractor for William F. Buckley's *National Review*. In 1957, he worked as a salesman for Cleworth Company and then moved to Newport News, Virginia, to work on *The Virginian Magazine*. His work for *US Lady* led him to move his family from Maine to Washington, and it was during this time from 1955 to 1957 that Rockwell became engaged in conservative political groups.[45]

In 1956, Rockwell became an organizer for Robert Snowden's Americans for Constitutional Action and worked for Russell Maguire's *American Mercury* as assistant publisher. He also established the American Federation of Conservative Organizations through which he tried to organize and mobilize the extreme conservative groups under a central ideological umbrella. The organization failed. He believed that almost all contemporary right wing groups and leaders shared his anti-Semitic beliefs but were fearful of Jewish retribution and therefore focused on secondary issues. He then met a financial supporter, Harold N. Arrowsmith, who assisted him in publishing *National Committee to Free America from Jewish Domination.* Now residing in Arlington, Virginia, he began distributing a series of documents on the Jewish question. He then led the first anti-Jewish picket in the United States since World War II in front of the White House on July 29, 1958, with members of the Nationalist Youth League. Two other simultaneous anti-Jewish protests were held in Atlanta, Georgia, and Louisville, Kentucky. After the Hebrew Benevolent Congregation, an Atlanta synagogue, was bombed on October 12, 1958, initial reports correlated Rockwell to the attack. Rockwell's home became a target for Molotov cocktails, police raids, telephone death threats, and abusive mail.[46]

In 1958, Rockwell proclaimed himself a Nazi and formed the American Nazi Party in March 1959. Rockwell incorporated the Nazi uniform, the swastika, and the "sieg heil" salute to demonstrate his solidarity with the Third Reich and the power of the white race. His clean-cut look, sharp dress, and corn cob pipe was intended to create a progressive/positive image. By integrating these seemingly divergent sociopolitical strands, Rockwell's group would form the ANP. Rockwell used visual imagery in public rallies, civil rights counterprotests, and speaking engagements to gain attention for the ANP. Rockwell was center stage in the media due to his controversial public appearances and debates, therefore giving the white power movement ample national coverage.[47]

Rockwell did everything he could to gain publicity. He organized protests, countermarches, and controversial speaking engagements that received national media attention. Rockwell entered into the public domain as a Nazi in the summer of 1960 in Washington D.C. and in New York City. In April 1960, he began giving speeches on the crowded Washington D.C. mall. A riot eventually broke out between the American Nazi Party storm troopers and counterprotesters, ending in Rockwell's arrest. The event and arrest were publicized nationally. Rockwell and his storm troopers picketed the opening of the movie *Exodus* in several East Coast cities, created hate riders to mock freedom riders, produced the Hatenanny record label, and enrolled racist singers and musicians to perform at fundraisers. In July 1960, he organized another neo-Nazi protest that sparked a riot at the State Supreme Court in New York City. In 1962, he hosted a rally in New York City's Union Square on Hitler's birthday, April 20, and addressed the Nation of Islam's National Convention in Chicago. In August 1963, he planned a Martin Luther King, Jr. countermarch in Washington D.C. He entered politics and qualified for the 1964 presidential primary ballot, running for the governor of Virginia in 1965. In 1966, he led an American Nazi Party parade in the town of Skokie,

Illinois, which at the time had a large number of Holocaust survivors as residents.[48]

The American Nazi Party had a significant media presence which inflated the size of the organization. California's Department of Justice investigated the American Nazi Party in 1965. The purpose of the investigation was to determine if the American Nazi Party was staged to commit violence in California.[49] The Department of Justice noted that Rockwell's Arlington, Virginia, headquarters was staffed with more than two dozen storm troopers, and the full potential of mobilization was 150 storm troopers nationwide. The American Jewish committee and the Anti-Defamation League also conducted surveillance on the American Nazi Party. Their reports provided the most accurate assessment of Rockwell's followings from 1958 until his death. Jewish Community Council of Greater Washington also stated that his followers consisted of some thirty to fifty people. Rockwell would state that if needed, the ANP could muster at least 500 individuals, but this would include many nonmembers.[50]

The financial status of the American Nazi Party was always precariously on the verge of bankruptcy. Sometimes the ANP headquarters was without power or water. Storm troopers had to make headquarter repairs and were asked to find outside employment and donate their paycheck to the cause. Rockwell depended on cash sent from his mother, members, and sympathizers. In 1966, due to problems with his taxes, the American Nazi Party's first headquarters on Randolph Street in Arlington was sold at auction with all of its contents in order to meet a tax lien.[51]

Rockwell tried to combine Nazi racial and political ideology with a spiritual foundation.[52] Although a self-proclaimed agnostic, he recognized the power that spirituality had across socioeconomic classes, and he also recognized the need to harness a religious belief for his own racial purposes. Rockwell reasoned that if politics and religion are fused together, a population is likely to demonstrate a higher level of commitment to a cause. Therefore, in the mid-1960s, Rockwell entertained the notion of merging Nazi political philosophy with the Christian Identity Movement. Christian Identity was a good starting point because a racial theology and anti-Semitic views were already present. Christian Identity seemed to be a productive channel to intertwine theology with racism and anti-Semitic beliefs.[53] Rockwell believed the term "Christian" had mass appeal and therefore should be retained for that purpose as it could masquerade as less offensive. He wanted to harness a new-found racial passion into a religion, the Christian Nationalist Church. Rockwell insisted that a white political philosophy and spiritual grounding were needed for the white race because a race war was inevitable.[54] Rockwell was killed before the Christian Nationalist Church materialized. William Pierce, one of

Rockwell's followers, founded the National Alliance and merged a political philosophy to a spiritual foundation.[55]

Three important events occurred in 1967. On January 1, 1967, George Lincoln Rockwell changed the name of the American Nazi Party to the National Socialist White People's Party in order to create a more palatable image. Early that year he also published a new book, *White Power*, which is an influential text in neo-Nazism. Finally, John Patler, a former disenfranchised ANP member, ended Rockwell's life on August 25, 1967. John Patler was twenty-nine years old and fired the shots that killed Rockwell in a Laundromat strip mall in Arlington, Virginia.[56] At the time of his death, Rockwell himself had been married twice. He had three children with his first wife, Judith Aultman. They divorced in 1953. He had one son with his second wife, Thora Halligrimsson, who was Icelandic. They separated in 1958. As he led the ANP he became estranged from all family members with the exception of his mother.

Rockwell's impact can be felt to this day in the neo-Nazi movement. His use of literature and music and the creation of a visual identity and organizational structure are still used by the National Alliance, Aryan Nations, and the National Socialist Movement. Rockwell's death is considered by neo-Nazis as a martyr's death by a race traitor, solidifying his prominence in the white power movement.[57]

Identifying the Enemy—Jews, the #1 threat

When they do, the reaction of the American White Man will make the Jews get on their knees and pray for Adolf Hitler to save them. The revenge taken upon them by other outraged host people will seem like heaven compared to the ferocity of the White American, once he has had all he is going to take from these arrogant Jews.[58]

If I am successful, we can find a just solution to the Jewish problem.

If I am unsuccessful, there will be Jews swinging from every lamp post in America.[59]

George Lincoln Rockwell believed that the Jews were the number one threat to the white race. Despite the social upheaval and riots that involved blacks in the 1960s, Rockwell believed that the Jews were behind all of the civil unrest and felt that they were trying to change the fabric of the existing American culture. In his autobiography, *This Time the World*, and in his book, *White Power*, he blames the Jews for moral depravity, communism, the control of the media and the American government, both world wars, the hijacking of the Holocaust to create the nation of Israel, taxpayer dollars sent to support Israel, the movie industry, liberalism, and using blacks as strongmen. He still believed that African Americans, homosexuals, white race traitors, and other minorities were deplorable, but he held that the needed action was the dismantling of the most strategic target—the Jews.[60]

Rockwell had studied Hitler and his propaganda machinery. He stated that the plight of the African Americans was being manipulated by Jewish leaders who were using them to advance their own cause. He cited as evidence that the first president of the National Association for Colored People was a Jew. Rockwell's propaganda was similar to that of Hitler's framing Germany's problems in 1930s on the Jews as a way to unite the German people. Rockwell understood that if he could promote the Jews as a race, then he would not only be able to dismantle the Jewish threat, but he would also weaken the networks of all other nonwhites. Essentially, he saw the Jewish people providing the strategic goals and leadership in an eternal campaign against whites.[61]

When the American Nazi Party was organized in 1959 in Arlington, Virginia, the leadership core of the organization agreed to seven immutable principles. Rockwell did not hide his admiration of Adolf Hitler; the seventh principle agreed upon by the core group stated that "Adolf Hitler was the gift of an inscrutable providence to the world on the brink of Jewish Bolshevik catastrophe."[62] Rockwell openly made claims that he is not anti-Semitic and was only opposed to treasonous Jews, but he also did believe that about 95% of American Jewry is guilty of treason.[63] In his headquarters he had a sign which read "The Jews are thru [*sic*] in 72."

George Lincoln Rockwell had aspired for political power. Rockwell maintained that after the American Nazi Party united whites in 1972, he would implement a program that called for[64]:

1. Execution of all Jews proven to have taken part in Marxist communist plots of treason.
2. Removal of all disloyal Jews from positions where they can control Jewish thoughts or actions, particularly from the press, government, education, entertainment, and courts.
3. Establishment of an international treason tribunal to investigate, try, and publicly hang, in front of the United States capital, all non-Jews who are convicted of having consciously acted as fronts for Jewish treason or subversion or who have violated their oaths of office or participated in any form of treason against their nations or humanity.

Rockwell was involved with an organization called the World Union of National Socialists. This organization attempted to unify the neo-Nazi parties and groups under a single vision and leadership and to form an international combat-efficient organization to oppose international Jewish communism. The long-term strategy was the unification of the white race into a world order in which complete racial apartheid existed. This particular organization was unique from other supremacy or extreme right organizations because it acknowledged Adolf Hitler as its spiritual leader and demanded that there be a final settlement to the world wide Jewish problem. Rockwell was the leader of the organization and saw it as a way to propagate, agitate, and recruit members to their cause and to fight the Jewish threat.[65]

In 1962, Rockwell secretly traveled to England and Ireland to attend a clandestine meeting of National Socialist leaders from seven nations: the United States, Great Britain, West Germany, France, Austria, Ireland, and Belgium. Rockwell met with the British neo-Nazi, Colin Jordan, the French Fascist, Savitri Devi, and German neo-Nazi, Bruno Armin Ludtke. This meeting took place in a remote countryside of Cotswold Hills in Gloucestershire.[66] Participants drafted a consensus document, the Cotswold Agreement, which laid out a plan for a National Socialist world revolution and the final settlement of the Jewish problem.[67]

The major objectives of the World Union of National Socialists were set up in the terms of the Cotswold Agreement wherein Rockwell and the leaders of other foreign national socialist parties formed the Confederation. Major objectives of the agreement were as follows[68]:

1. To form a monolithic, combat-efficient, international political apparatus to combat and utterly destroy the international Jew–communist in sinus apparatus of treason and subversion.
2. To protect and promote the area and race and its Western civilization wherever its members may be on the globe, and whatever their nationality may be.
3. To protect private property and free enterprise from communist class warfare.

The ideas from the Cotswold Agreement were already evident in Rockwell's American Nazi Party. He now ensured that the idea of the Jew as the number one threat was declared internationally and continued efforts to marginalize, persecute, detain, and eliminate the Jews.

It is difficult to measure the impact of Rockwell's strategic target shift of focus on the Jews. Two measures are illustrated. The first measure is the content on websites and blogs. Stormfront is one of the largest neo-Nazi websites available on the web. When the term "Jew" is typed into their search engine, 322 blogs contain the term. In their Global Tag Cloud, Jewish Media Control, Jewish Power, Jewish Subversion, and Jews and Civil Rights appear. When the term "Jew" is entered in the search domain as a blog title, out of 291 total blogs, thirty-one of them have the term "Jew" listed in the blog title.

The second measure of impact is from the anifesto of Dylann Roof, the 2015 Charleston Church Shooter in South Carolina. He wrote[69]:

But Europe is the homeland of White people, and in many ways the situation is even worse there. From here I found out about the Jewish problem and other issues facing our race, and I can say today that I am completely racially aware. Unlike many White nationalists, I am of the opinion that the majority of American and European jews are White. In my opinion the issues with jews is not their blood, but their identity. I think that if we could somehow destroy the jewish identity, then they wouldn't cause much of a problem. The problem is that Jews look White, and in many cases are White, yet they see themselves as minorities.

NOTES

1. Sandler, Todd and Harvey E. Lapan, "The Calculus of Dissent: An Analysis of Terrorists' Choice of Targets," *Synthese* 76, no. 2 (August 1988): 245–61, doi:10.1007/BF00869591; Philip Keefer and Norman Loayza, *Terrorism, Economic Development, and Political Openness* New York: Cambridge University Press, 2008).

2. Kleg, Milton. *Hate, Prejudice, and Racism.* Albany: State University of New York Press, 1993.

3. David Lane and Katja Lane. *Deceived, Damned & Defiant: The Revolutionary Writings of David Lane.* St. Maries, Idaho. HC 01 Box 268K, St. Maries 83861: 14 Word Press, 1999.

4. "Osama Bin Laden's Jihad." Osama Bin Laden. Accessed July 11, 2016. http://mideastweb.org/osamabinladen1.htm.

5. Burns, John F. "Yemen Links to Bin Laden Gnaw at F.B.I. in Cole Inquiry," *The New York Times*, November 26, 2000, sec. World, http://www.nytimes.com/2000/11/26/world/yemen-links-to-bin-laden-gnaw-at-fbi-in-cole-inquiry.html.

6. Scheuer, Michael. *Osama Bin Laden.* Oxford: Oxford University Press, 2011. Pp. 147.

7. Ibid.

8. Ibid.

9. Bergen, Peter L. *Holy War, Inc.: Inside the Secret World of Osama Bin Laden.* New York: Free Press, 2001.

10. Atwan, Abdel Bari. *After Bin Laden: Al Qaeda, the Next Generation.* New York, NY: The New Press, 2013.

11. Bergen, Peter L. *The Osama Bin Laden I Know: An Oral History of Al-Qaeda's Leader.* New York: Free Press, 2006 Pp. 183.

12. "Osama Bin Laden: Famous Quotes—Telegraph," accessed August 30, 2015, http://www.telegraph.co.uk/news/worldnews/asia/afghanistan/8487347/Osama-bin-Laden-famous-quotes.html.

13. Scheuer, Michael. *Osama Bin Laden.*

14. Wright, Lawrence. *The Looming Tower by Lawrence Wright.*

15. Bergen, Peter. *The Osama Bin Laden I Know.*

16. Scheuer, Michael. *Osama Bin Laden.* 1967. Arab-Israeli war is a significant marker for bin Laden's generation.

17. Bin Laden's terror unit engaged in combat for the first time on August 17, 1987. Abdullah Azzam also participated in observing the unit. The first mission was unsuccessful because of the lack of improper logistical management and tactical reconnaissance. Bin Laden personally engaged in combat around Jaji, and it is often said that he fought bravely in these conflicts; he was wounded at Jalalabad. In the end, it is estimated that a total of 500 Arab Afghans were killed in the entirety of the war, which is a small number compared to the several hundred thousand Afghan mujahedeen killed during the same time.

18 Scheuer, Michael. *Osama Bin Laden.*

19. Berner, Brad K. *Jihad: Bin Laden in His Own Words : Declarations, Interviews, and Speeches*, Peacock Books, 2007.

20. Burke, *Al-Qaeda.*

21. Scheuer, Michael. *Osama Bin Laden.*

22. Bin Laden argued that the Royal family had strayed from the original tenets of Islam even to the degree of shortchanging size-defensive forces and rerouting jihadi relief funds for their own private use. He also specifically critiqued the religious organization and stated that their rulings were based on corruption—instead of pleasing God they desired to please the Saudi family. The Saudi government responded with a series of harsh interrogations and detainment operations because of the scathing critiques by bin Laden and members of the Islamic awakening group against Saudi family and government. Bin Laden also remarked that during these crackdowns of the Muslims, the supposedly religious scholars remained silent and therefore turned their backs against the true faith.

23. Bergen, *The Osama Bin Laden I Know.*

24. Scheuer, *Osama Bin Laden.*

25. However, both bin Laden and Mullah Omar agreed on eliminating the threat posed by Ahmed Shah Massoud and his Northern alliance. Mullah Omar was interested in having Muslims eliminated because it would essentially decapitate the Northern alliance and would provide an opportunity for the Taliban power to expand. Bin Laden was interested in having Massoud assassinated because he was fully aware of a potential alliance between the United States and Massoud in the event that the United States decided to occupy Afghanistan. Massoud was assassinated by an Al Qaeda-sponsored suicide bomber film crew on September 9, 2001.

26. Riedel, Bruce O. *The Search for Al Qaeda: Its Leadership, Ideology, and Future*, Washington, D.C.: Brookings Institution Press, 2010.

27. Brown, Adrian. BBC News, "Osama Bin Laden's Death: How It Happened," *BBC News*, accessed August 30, 2015, http://www.bbc.com/news/world-south-asia-13257330.

28. "Declaration of War by Osama Bin Laden, 1996," *Council on Foreign Relations*, accessed August 30, 2015, http://www.cfr.org/terrorist-leaders/declaration-war-osama-bin-laden-1996/p13174.

29. Berner, *Jihad.*

30. "Bin Laden's Fatwa," *PBS NewsHour*, accessed August 30, 2015, http://www.pbs.org/newshour/updates/military-july-dec96-fatwa_1996/.

31. Riedel, *The Search for Al Qaeda.*

32. Al Qaeda in Lebanon, Al Qaeda in Saudi Arabia, Al Qaeda in the Indian Sub-continent, Al Qaeda Network for Southwestern Khulna Division, Al Qaeda in Iraq, Al Qaeda in the Arabian Peninsula (AQAP), Al Qaeda Organization for Jihad in Sweden, Al Qaeda in Yemen, and Al Qaeda in the Lands of the Islamic Maghreb (AQLIM).

33. Rockwell, George Lincoln. *White Power.* Dallas: Ragnarok Press, 1967.

34. Rockwell spoke at numerous venues including Ivy leagues across the country. For example, at the University of Colorado he spoke to 3000 students and to 2000 at the University of Kansas. His speaking engagements were steady, and the revenue generated from the speaking engagements in 1966 in 1967 was steady and was supporting the American Nazi Party.

35. Simmonelli, Frederick J. *American Fuehrer: George Lincoln Rockwell and the American Nazi Party.* Urbana: University of Illinois Press, 1999.

36. Rockwell also intended to. In 1966, George Lincoln Rockwell, in response to Stokely Carmichael's use of black power, promoted white power as a counter slogan. Rockwell used the slogan in 1966 in a counterprotest against the right. Chicago was a racially and ethnically segregated city and when his supporters marched in Chicago, they were met by local residents throwing items at King and his supporters and waving Confederate and Nazi flags. The dominant chant among whites lining the Chicago row was "white power."

37. Schmaltz, William H. *Hate: George Lincoln Rockwell and the American Nazi Party.* Washington, D.C.: Brassey's, 1999.

38. Willis Carto and Rockwell worked independently on the idea of Holocaust denial. However, Rockwell's popularizing the idea of Holocaust denial far exceeded Carto's efforts. Rockwell used material from Carto's magazine, *Right,* to recruit members of the American Nazi Party. Deborah Lipstadt asserts that Charles C. Tansill's book published in 1952, *Back Door,* became a classic for neo-Nazi revisionism. According to Frederick, Bruno Ludtke introduced Rockwell on elements concerning the usefulness of Holocaust knowledge 1961. It was working on this that shaped his thinking on the topic. In an attempt to minimize the Holocaust's impact, neo-Nazis highlighted the atrocities of the Allied bombing campaign against German civilians. Another argument provided by Luedtke argued that some of the killings of Jews were actually done by Zionists to discredit Atul Fidler and the neo-Nazi regime. Neo-Nazis also argued that numbers of those killed in the Holocaust were also inflated in order to increase the number of recreation payments from the German government and its increase will lessen the formation of Israel in 1948. Rockwell and Ludtke generated an arsenal of "facts" from the United States in Europe to boster their Holocaust denial campaign. For example, a German-language Argentinian monthly entitled "The Life of the Six Million" was published in a 1954 magazine, *Der Weg.* Rockwell used the data, concepts, and phraseology in this article and inserted them regularly into his speaking circuit and American Nazi Party publications.

39. George Lincoln Rockwell, *White Power.*

40. Ibid.

41. Ibid.

42. Simonelli, Frederick J. *American Fuehrer: George Lincoln Rockwell and the American Nazi Party.*

43. Schmaltz, *Hate.*

44. Rockwell, George Lincoln. *This Time the* World. New York: Parliament House, 1963.

45. Schmaltz, *Hate.*

46. Obermayer, Herman. *American Nazi Party: Northern Virginia Sun, Arlington, Virginia, 1958–1984.* Cambridge, MA: Nieman Foundation, Harvard University, 1997.

47. Schmaltz, *Hate.*

48. Simonelli, Frederick J. *American Fuehrer: George Lincoln Rockwell and the American Nazi Party.*

49. On December 28, 1962, one of the Rockwell storm troopers, Roy James, attacked Martin Luther King as he addressed the Southern Christian Leadership conference in Birmingham, Alabama. James attacked Martin Luther King on stage with his fists, and the crowd seized him following his attack on King. Rockwell awarded James the American Nazi Party's highest honor, The Order of Adolf Hitler silver medal, for his actions.

50. Obermayer, *American Nazi Party in Arlington, Virginia 1958—1984.*

51. Simonelli. *American Fuehrer: George Lincoln Rockwell and the American Nazi Party.*

52. Ibid.

53. Dobratz. Betty A. "The Role of Religion in the Collective Identity of the White Racialist Movement." *J Sci Stud Rel Journal for the Scientific Study of Religion* 40, no. 2 (2001): 287–302. doi:10.1111/0021–8294.00056.

54. George Lincoln Rockwell, *White Power.*

55. The British version was Philo somatic and benign while the Christian identity is vehemently anti-semitic. Richard Girnt Butler, who would later become the leader of Aryan Nations, was a former Lockheed aerospace engineer. Butler devoted his life to Christian identity ministry and in the early 1970s became the leader of Christian identity in the United States. Butler saw all Christian identity and Nazi politics is a way of intertwining to both were inseparable. Christian identity important Butler holds that Jews are not available Israelites but imposters and frauds, and are actually the spawn of Satan. Anglo-Saxons are the true Israelites, who are engaged in an apocalyptic struggle with satanic Jews and other interracial individuals that are called mud people. It was Butler who introduced Rockwell to Christian identity in the early 1960s. It is also important to note that even before Rockwell, Butler discussed the formation of proposed religious organization based on the world view of Adolf Hitler (Frederick page 117 Forbes followed Rockwell's directive loyally and became a Christian identity minister where Nazis who needed a religious essence were welcomed by Forbes and those that adhered to Christian identity ripped fuel in a political ambitions always by the American Nazi Party. Rockwell and Butler by the time that he was assassinated in 1967 and merged Christian identity and Nazi philosophy into a seamless synthesis of anti-Semitism and hate. R. E. Cooper, who was a current Nazi activist, perceives Swift as the founder of Christian identity, however identified Butler as the prophet and dissemination. It is important to note that it was Rockwell who reconfigured Christian identity as a safe haven for American Nazis and their

ideological protégé. Matt Koehl framed Rockwell as St. Paul in the church of Jesus Christ. Christian identity provided the spiritual grounding and also in linking actions to a cause greater than the individual or current politics. Anti-Semitism and racism became a redemptive spiritual act all of humanity.

56. *White Power* (1967) serves as a manifesto for the ANP. One of the central themes outlines that a race war will be fought based on skin color. Rockwell claimed that whites will fight against an ever-increasing nonwhite populace. Rockwell targeted desegregation and used the notion of an impending race war to forecast the devastating long-range impact on whites. Rockwell also argued that Jews across the globe used the Holocaust to leverage sympathy to accomplish their agenda. He cited examples like the United Nations vote for Israeli statehood in 1948 (Rockwell, 1979). He also contended that civil rights activists were using the same tactic, obtaining sympathy for blacks because of the oppression caused by slavery and Jim Crow laws, which Rockwell asserted that this also put the white race at risk. Rockwell stated that the civil rights movementand the Holocaust were effective weapons against the white race, because theygave immense resources, leverage, and political power to nonwhites and Jews.

57. Frederick J. Simonelli. *American Fuehrer: George Lincoln Rockwell and the American Nazi Party.*

58. George Lincoln Rockwell, *White Power.* p. 53

59. Ibid., p. 86

60. Ibid.

61. Ibid.

62. Ibid.

63. Haley, Alex. "George Lincoln Rockwell: A Candid Conversation with the Fanatical Führer of the American Nazi Party." *Playboy* 13 (1966): 71–74.

64. George Lincoln Rockwell, *White Power.*

65. "UI Press | Frederick J. Simonelli | American Fuehrer: George Lincoln Rockwell and the American Nazi Party."

66. Atkins, Stephen E. *Holocaust Denial as an International Movement* (ABC-CLIO, 2009).

67. Simonelli. *American Fuhrer: George Lincoln Rockwell and the American Nazi Party.*

68. Goodrick-Clarke, Nicholas. *Black Sun: Aryan Cults, Esoteric Nazism, and the Politics of Identity.* New York: New York University Press, 2002. p. 37.

69. Bernstein, Lenny, Sari Horwitz, and Peter Holley. "Dylann Roof's Racist Manifesto: 'I Have No Choice'" Washington Post. (June 20, 2015), accessed July 11, 2016. http://www.washingtonpost.com/national/health-science/authorities-investigate-whether-racist-manifesto-was-written-by-sc-gunman/2015/06/20/f0bd3052–1762–11e5–9ddc-e3353542100c_story.html

Chapter 5

The Need to Create Soft Extremism

Mohammed Maqdisi and David Duke

In order to build a movement into a revolution, large numbers are needed. Unless a message appeals to a wide demographic, then a revolution is unlikely. A revolution is even more unlikely if necessary violence is perceived as victimization instead of vindication. Therefore, crafting a message that makes violence seem altruistic is necessary. The violent strain is not altered, only it is presented as soft extremism.

Soft extremism is defined as the use of messages with broad appeal—like morality or communism—and is less offensive. Palatable messages should resonate with larger segments of the population that share a similar value or opinion. Frame alignment occurs when a message aligns with an audience. Ideologues engaged in soft extremism look to find common ideological ground and focus on the strength of those connections rather than the divisive issues and aggression that are also part of violent extremism. Neo-Nazis or violent jihadists' soft extremism is just as violent as the overt strains, despite its marketed appearance as a watered-down version. This chapter focuses on two ideologues who have advanced soft extremism.

David Duke and Abu Mohammad al-Maqdisi have marketed themselves and their messages as soft extremism. There are several similarities between them. Duke and Maqdisi run digital libraries, have appeared on national media shows (where they have denounced the more violent strains of their ideology), have spent time in jail, have been criticized for not actually participating themselves in violence, and argue that strategies should be implanted sequentially.

Abu Muhammad al-Maqdisi, according to West Point's Countering Terrorism Center, is one of the most read and cited contemporary violent jihadists.[1] He was a mentor to Abu Mus'ab al-Zarqawi, the violent Jordanian leader of Al Qaeda in Iraq, currently seen as the precursor to ISIS. Maqdisi is known for his harsh public criticism of the Muslim government and leaders in his writing and speeches. As a result, he has been incarcerated by the Jordanian government, yet his voluminous online library, www.tawhed.ws, is still functional and continues to be an important repository for violent jihadis around the world. His thoughts are used by violent jihadists to justify terror attacks against Muslim governments, more specifically in Saudi Arabia and Kuwait.

David Duke is arguably the most visible and well-known neo-Nazi ideologue in the United States. A former Louisiana state representative, he has promoted white supremacy and neo-Nazi ideas since the late 1960s. Although his organizational affiliations have changed over the years, he is a staunch anti-Semite and former KKK Grand Dragon. He currently resides in Austria. He is the founder of the National Association of White People and is the leader of the European American Unity and Rights Organization. He publishes articles, books, and an online talk show to promote his anti-Jewish ideology broadly but gives particular attention to Russia and the Ukraine. He is seen as the catalyst for softening and "professionalizing" the image of the Klan and neo-Nazism by stopping the use of Klan and Nazi regalia in ceremonies, replacing them instead with more acceptable, less controversial implements, like a suit and tie. He has appeared in all forms of media over the past four decades and tries to "appeal" to the masses by carefully constructing a positive image of his past and his ideas.[2]

Over the years Duke's strategy has changed but not his ideology. While a student at Louisiana State University he wore a swastika armband, carried a copy of George Lincoln Rockwell's *White Power*, and engaged in racial debates with students across campus. David Duke originally was enamored with George Lincoln Rockwell and adopted Rockwell's targeting paradigm which stated that Jews were the greatest problem and further, that if Jewish power was eliminated, then other races would follow. Unlike Rockwell, he decided to create a softer mass-produced version of these ideas. Since his college years, his public image and persona have changed drastically in such a way as to distance himself from racial stereotypes. He has engaged in a steady campaign to legitimize neo-Nazism as white nationalism through various respectable means. For example, Duke describes himself as a former Louisiana member of the House of Representatives, former U.S. presidential candidate, recipient of a doctorate degree, a teacher, and author of one of the bestselling books in the world.[3] Duke uses these titles to establish credibility in order to overcome the stereotype of the ignorant, uneducated, and unsuccessful white supremacist. Additionally, he seeks to be identified as well-traveled and internationally credible.

In the following decades, he promoted messages that emphasized morality, employment, white victimization, and the European immigrant's rights. An example of Duke's soft extremism can be seen in his Reuter's interview with Thom Hartman in 2015. David Duke was interviewed by Hartman to share his views about South Carolina governor Nikki Haley's bill which called for the removal of the Confederate battle flag from South Carolina's Statehouse grounds. This measure followed the mass shooting at Emmanuel Church by Dylann Roof.[4] In the interview, Duke discussed the Confederate flag and the rights of European Americans.

Hartman introduced him as a former Louisiana state representative and former U.S. presidential candidate, Dr. David Duke. Duke explained that the Confederate flag is a symbol of European heritage not hate. Over the course of the next ten minutes, Duke discussed the history of slavery, the origin of America's Civil War, and racism. He stated that the removal of the Confederate flag was an assault on Euro-American heritage. He tried to use broad frames to spin the mass killing in Charleston as the result of Jewish Hollywood's glorification of violence, showing African American actors killing whites, and the Jewish hate of the European Christian, Christianity, and Christian values. He stated:

> So as far as white supremacy or white racism, I'm against any sort of racism—white racism, black racism, but the most prominent racism in the world today is Jewish racism, Zionist racism and designed the state of Israel. The truth is that the real racism going on in this country right now is hatred against the European people saying that all Europeans are guilty of being racist.[5]

This interview illustrates how frame resonance functions in soft extremism. His objective is to appeal to a population who share his Confederate flag beliefs and who have come to the conclusion that they agree with David Duke despite their ignorance of his background or his true ideology. David Duke intends to create a an appropriate persona and modern message with broad appeal that neo-Nazi symbols would discredit. This interview illustrates how he has been advancing soft extremism for decades in public forums.

Maqdisi was also interviewed on television in 2015.[6] He appeared to discuss a letter he sent to ISIS's leader, Abu Bakr al-Baghdadi, in a televised interview with al-Ru'ya, a Jordanian television channel.[7] Maqdisi has been incarcerated for fifteen out of his twenty-three years in Jordan but was released by the Jordanian authorities to negotiate with ISIS for the release of Jordanian pilot, Mutah Safi Yousef al-Kasasbeh. This televised interview was not the first time that the Jordanian government had released Maqdisi to comment on a current event. Maqdisi's influence and credibility are significant, and therefore his comments on a particular subject are influential. All across Jordan, the leading news story was al-Kasasbeh's release, and this interview put Maqdisi in the center of the story. This interview, similar to Duke's Reuters interview, illustrates soft extremism.

As he was a prisoner in Jordan, it is important to ask why Maqdisi would agree to a television interview where he would discuss his negotiations with ISIS and his actions on behalf of the Jordanian people and government. Conceptually, it is illogical for an imprisoned ideologue who supports Al Qaeda to confront ISIS, representing a Jordanian position on national airtime. He granted the interview because he was able to frame ISIS as shameful and as using heinous methods. Maqdisi stigmatized ISIS as dishonest, and he stated that the level of brutality is not contextual but is rather counterproductive. From his strategic point of view, ISIS was detracting from the overarching strategy of fighting the far enemy first and the near enemy second. In this case, there is consensus between the Jordanian government and Maqdisi because both agree that ISIS is not advancing their version of society.

The Jordanian government released Maqdisi from prison in January 2015. On behalf of the Jordanian government, he wrote letters to ISIS's leader, al-Baghdadi, in order to conduct a prisoner exchange for an Al Qaeda operative in Iraq, female suicide bomber, Safida Mubarak Atrous al-Rishawi, sentenced to death for her involvement in the 2005 Ammon hotel bombings. The hotel bombing had been ordered by Zarqawi, the leader of Al Qaeda in Iraq at the time and the former disciple of Maqdisi during their Jordanian incarceration in the 1990s. Zarqawi is seen by ISIS today as the Godfather of their organization.[8]

Zarqawi was the face of Al Qaeda in Iraq until his death in 2006. In Iraq, Zarqawi targeted Shia mosques and executed Shia Muslims across the country. This caused open debate and criticism not only from Maqdisi but also from the Al Qaeda's leadership. The contention was not over the rationale behind killing Shias, who Al Qaeda considers to be apostates; it was the fact that the killings were not in line with Al Qaeda's strategy. According to Al Qaeda's leadership, the West is the primary target, followed by Israel, and then apostates.[9] Therefore, Zarqawi's actions simply were not following strategic directives, because violence at this point in time should be directed against the far enemy and should not be creating internal battles between Muslims. This distinction is essential because Maqdisi's "criticism" against ISIS in this interview was about strategy and methods, not ideology.

Maqdisi has a history of arguing that jihad should be kept free from "excesses." Excesses are defined as actions that detract from the original strategy. He is the author of *Waqafat ma`a Thamrat al-Jihad* (*Positions on the Fruits of Jihad*), which criticizes certain jihadist practices as being counterproductive.[10] It is important to note that in the interview Maqdisi never confronted the ideology of ISIS, but focused instead on their "methods" as excesses. Earlier in the interview he criticized ISIS's dishonesty during the negotiations and asserted that it was dishonorable to conduct business in this manner. But again, he was only criticizing their methods and character, not their ideology. He also made it absolutely clear that ISIS had taken a wrong path in the jihadist movement, adding that all jihadists should not be defined by ISIS's actions. It would be out of character for Maqdisi to criticize a group that he played an indirect role in forming. Maqdisi perceives al-Baghdadi, the current leader of ISIS, to be Zarqawi's successor and now claims that it is his duty to carry out a task that Zarqawi could not finish. This distinction is slight but is seen in the following statement. At the end of the interview, Maqdisi addresses the Jordanian people directly:

> Yes, I thank you for the sake of providing me this interview, and I accept your invitation directly to communicate with you. Because this is a Jordanian channel and I wanted these words of mine to reach the Jordanian people. For whom a lot of reactions have now come forth, and the images they have seen in the thing which they saw. So that they may know that the group ISIS; does not represent the Salafi jihadi's and the Salafi jihadi movement is free from these acts.[11]

In this statement and in other statements in the interview, it appears that ISIS and Maqdisi's ideology are in conflict. However, on closer examination, he emphasized "acts" and "representations" over ideas. Maqdisi's letter on behalf of al-Kasasbeh asserted more of a concern for the female suicide bomber, al-Rishawi, than the pilot. In the letter, Maqdisi made the case that she was their true Muslim sister and was closely affiliated with Zarqawi, who also wanted her freed. A document written by Abu l-'Izz al-Najdi, a Saudi member of the Shari'a Council of al-Maqdisi's website, was posted online and shared negotiation details between al-Maqdisi and ISIS. Maqdisi was involved in the negotiations for the sake of al-Rishawi, not the Jordanian pilot, because, according to Maqdisi, he was an apostate anyway.[12] His role in the ISIS negotiation demonstrated how he very cleverly promoted a soft version of extremism while maintaining support for ISIS. Whether or not he was being used by the Jordanian regime and was being forced to do the interview, he was still able to maintain his violent jihadi ideology while remaining cloaked in the appearance of caring for the release of al-Kasasbeh.

It is far more strategic to use soft extremism to build a large base and gain political and military power. This is why David Duke does not claim to be a racist and Maqdisi does not praise ISIS for killing Shia Muslims. They do not share their true beliefs in these venues because it is not advantageous to be direct and it would hinder independent unification efforts for Muslims and whites. Shias will be addressed after a violent caliphate is established, Western forces are defeated, and Israel is destroyed. After achieving some type of political power, David Duke would use the Armed Forces to regulate

American Jewry. Currently, both men do not possess any legitimate power and therefore must use the banner of soft extremism to gain broad appeal. The rigid and violent strain of ideas lays docile until the right time.

MAQDISI: THE MAN

My project is not to blow up a bar, my project is not to blow the cinema, my project is not to kill an officer who has tortured me. . . . My project is to bring back to the Islamic nation its glories and to establish the Islamic state that provides refuge to every Muslim, and this is a grand large project; it does not come by small potential acts. It requires the education of the Muslim generation, requires long-term planning, requires participation of all the learned men and sons of this Islamic nation, and since I do not have the resources for this project, then I will not implicate my brothers.

—Abu Muhammad al-Maqdisi, July 5, 2005[13]

Abu Mohammed al-Maqdisi, a Palestinian[14] known as Isam Tahir al-Barqawi, was born in Nablus in 1959. He became known as Maqdisi at the beginning of his preaching career, which refers to the Bayt Al-Maqdis in Jerusalem, close to his birthplace in the village of Barqa, near Nablus. He claims that he is from the Utaybi tribe and is a descendent of the Ruqa branch as some of his ancestors moved from Najd in Saudi Arabia to Barqa. The eldest of two, his father was a farmer before becoming a nurse. His family immigrated to Kuwait when he was three or four, and many Palestinians had a significant role in the country's newly founded oil industry.[15]

After his secondary education, he wanted to attend the Islamic University in Madinah to study sharia. His initial request was denied by his parents, and they sent him to study engineering in University of Mosul in northern Iraq. Although he was not able to study sharia formally, he began as a self-learner studying from the thirteenth-century theologian, Ibn Taymiyya up until the eighteenth century's Mohammed Ibn Abd-Wahhab. While at university, he participated in different movements, some of which were offshoots of the Muslim Brotherhood. Maqdisi was also in contact with Al-Uteibi, the Saudi leader of the group of rebels who occupied the grand mosque of Mecca for two weeks in 1979, and he visited some of the leading scholars and sheikhs at the time.[16]

Maqdisi quit his studies in Iraq and wrote letters to the sheikhs in Saudi Arabia. He asked them if he would be permitted to study at the Islamic University of Madinah instead of in Mosul where he had to study with women. He was never accepted officially as a student; however, he traveled to Saudi Arabia for the annual major pilgrimage to Mecca where he overstayed his visa and studied unofficially at the University of Madinah. After meeting with Ibn Baz, one of the most important scholars at the time, he was told that he could use the university facilities without being an official student. Maqdisi began his own independent study when a life-changing moment occurred at the library of the prophet's mosque in Madinah. There he read about the long tradition of Wahhabism. He then connected the fatwas of the Najdi imams to the current period. This experience provided him with Salafi arguments, concepts, and ideas that would become part of establishing his own ideological foundation.[17]

In the 1980s, Maqdisi moved back to Kuwait after a year in Saudi Arabia. In 1985, he wrote his famous book, *The Religion of Abraham*.[18] This text indicted from a Salafi perspective the Muslim states that failed to rule by Islamic law. After the completion of this book, he traveled to Peshawar, Pakistan, in 1989 to assist the mujahedeen against the Soviet Union for six months[19] and had the book printed there.

His time was spent teaching and spreading his ideas instead of fighting. In Afghanistan, he underwent military training but did not see combat. Besides printing *The Religion of Abraham* in Peshawar, he wrote and printed another book, *al-Jahiliya fi Kufr al-Dawla al-Sa'udiyya*, and his material became known among the Arab mujahedeen. Some of Maqdisi's ideas were not necessarily that popular, particularly among the Saudis who came to fight the Soviets and did not want to hear how their own state was unIslamic. Maqdisi did not stay very long in Afghanistan/Pakistan and did not establish close connections with Al Qaeda's leaders, but he did meet Abu Musab Zarqawi. This would become an influential encounter for both men. Zarqawi, whose original name is Ahmed Fadheel Nezzal Al-Khalayeh, was a Jordanian also in Afghanistan to engage in jihads and who later led Al Qaeda in Iraq. The men discovered that they shared common ideological views; however, the conflict in the region forced them to go in separate paths.[20]

After the Soviet Army left Afghanistan, Maqdisi returned to Kuwait until Saddam Hussein invaded in 1990. He became a manager in a bookstore where he connected with other Salafi scholars. He eventually changed jobs to a trading business. Because of Yasser Arafat's decision to support Saddam Hussein against an international coalition, all Palestinians were expelled from Kuwait. Maqdisi then left for Saudi Arabia where, through his teaching and writings, he generated a small following.[21] He left there to settle in Jordan in 1992.

Maqdisi relocated to the Palestinian refugee camp of Ruseifa near Zarqa. While in Jordan in the summer of 1993, Maqdisi was visited by Zarqawi concerning earlier conversations during the Afghan jihad. They formed the group later known as the Bay'at al-Imam. The first objective for the group was to proselytize youth in Zarqa, convert them to the idea of loyalty and renunciation, and later incite them to violence. The group began to grow, and Maqdisi's influence grew also until he was eventually noticed by the Jordanian security and intelligence services. One of the reasons that he gained the attention of the Jordanian security apparatus was his reaction to Jordanian parliamentary elections. He published a book, *Democracy is Religion*, in which he argued that turning to democracy is the same as converting from Islam into another religion. He viewed this as apostasy. Zarqawi and Maqdisi brought weapons from Kuwait in preparations for a raid on Israeli targets over the Jordanian border. However, in March 29, 1994, the attack was disrupted by Jordanian security services, and Maqdisi and Zarqawi were arrested.[22]

They were tried in the case that became known as the Bay'at al-Imam case. The case ended in November 1996 with Zarqawi and Maqdisi both receiving guilty verdicts and life sentences. Maqdisi spent time in prison from 1994 to 1999, and he recruited new followers from prisoners and guards. Both men were sent to Jordan's Mukhaberat prison where they spent the majority of time in solitary confinement before being individually transferred to various state prisons across Jordan. In April 1995, they were both sent to Suwaqa Prison. While in prison, they formed the organization Tawheed wel jihad. Maqdisi initially led the group but eventually transferred all responsibility to Zarqawi so that he could concentrate on his studies and research. Zarqawi's strong leadership and personality made him the ideal person to deal with prison management and to facilitate a group; Maqdisi remained the ideological leader focused on his work. According to Maqdisi's own estimate, the group never had more than thirty men.

Maqdisi's time in prison was one of the most important intellectual periods of his life since he was able to devote extensive time to writing. He expanded another treatise entitled *Exposing the Vagaries of Today's Marji'eh*. His work was used to denounce The Muslim Clerics Association and the Iraqi Islamic Party as Marji'eh. His writing was smuggled out of prison by family members and sometimes by guards and disseminated broadly. In this way, Maqdisi became well known among Jordanians who saw their government as illegitimate. When he was transferred to a prison in al Salt, his followers visited him in prison.[23]

After four years of incarceration, Maqdisi was released by a royal pardon on the ascension of King Abdullah II in March 1999. He was quickly arrested again in late 1999 for his involvement in a millennium plot which was supposed to take place on January 1, 2000. This attack involved four different locations, hotels in Ammon, a Jordanian Israeli border crossing, and Christian holy sites. The attack again was foiled by Jordanian authorities, and he was arrested because of his suspected role in planning the attacks. In 2000, Maqdisi was sent back to prison on charges of inspiring terrorist activities against Jordanian targets. Maqdisi states that he was arrested because some of his books were found in the homes of those planning the attacks.

Prior to 2002, Zarqawi and Maqdisi parted ways. Zarqawi pledged allegiance to Osama bin Laden in October 2004, departed to Afghanistan, and then moved on to northern Iraq. After the Americans invaded Iraq in 2003, Zarqawi and his group were involved in a spree of destruction and killing across Iraq, often against civilian targets. Maqdisi and Al Qaeda's senior leadership did not approve of his tactics and ordered him to stop. Zarqawi refused, and a feud ensued.

Maqdisi chose to stay in Jordan to study and resume his public preaching. Maqdisi had an interview with Al Jazeera that was aired on July 5, 2002, where he reiterated his earlier criticisms of the Jordanian government and defended himself by saying that these ideas were not new as they were written earlier in *The 13th Letter on Cautioning Against Excesses* and *Rendering the Verdict of Unbelief*. Maqdisi was arrested again in November 2002 for his supposed conspiracy to attack U.S. soldiers in the northern Jordanian city of Mafraq. Maqdisi launched his website in the year 2002. There he published his own work and the work of others promoting the same ideological foundations.[24]

On December 28, 2004, charges against Maqdisi were dropped and interviews were released on June 28, 2005. He was released on the explicit condition that he should not interact with the media. Maqdisi was arrested again on July 6, 2005, a week after being released, as he violated his prohibition of contacting the media, did not denounce terrorism, and did not fully denounce the actions of Zarqawi. The Jordanian authorities had hoped that the disagreement which went public between himself and Zarqawi would minimize his impact over the jihadists in Iraq. The Jordanians' rearrest of Maqdisi was an embarrassment because he did not denounce Zarqawi, who was slaughtering Shia and American soldiers in Iraq, but lauded Zarqawi as a hero.[25]

His moving in and out of prison continued. He was held in prison without charge until his release in March 2008.[26] After spending almost two years out of prison, he was arrested again in September 2010 and charged with five years' imprisonment for recruiting terrorists. He was recently released in 2015 to negotiate with ISIS.

DAVID DUKE: THE MAN

David Duke was born on July 1, 1950, in Tulsa, Oklahoma. His father, a World War II veteran, worked as a Shell Oil petroleum engineer. Duke would move to the Netherlands for a year when he was five and then to a New Orleans suburb, Gentilly Woods. Duke's mother was a homemaker and later would struggle with alcoholism as a way to cope with her husband's intense focus on work and the deaths of her sister and brother-in-law in an airline crash. In 1966, his father moved to Vietnam without the family to work for the U.S. Agency for International Development, and he also worked for the state department, programs in Southeast Asia, and the U.S. Department of Energy, where he worked until his mid-70s. Duke attended schools in Louisiana and at Riverside Military Academy, a private college preparatory school in Northern Georgia. He eventually graduated from Louisiana State University in 1974.[27]

The civil rights movement outlined his adolescent years, and he experienced rapid cultural changes in the South. As an adolescent, he developed a strong admiration for southern culture, the confederacy, and white supremacy. At thirteen, he attended a private Church of Christ school in New Orleans, the Clifton L. Ganus School. In an eighth-grade assignment, he made the case against racial integration in public education. In preparation for the assignment, he read Carlos Putnam's anti-Semitic *Race and Reason: A Yankee View*. Putnam argued that there are distinct and divergent patterns between races and that if race mixing, immigration, and differential birthrates occur at disproportionate rates, civilization will be destroyed. The text was recommended to him by Maggie Smith, a member of the Segregationist White Citizen's Council, a group that influenced his thoughts on race, anti-Semitism, and white supremacy throughout his adolescence. By the time he was in junior high school, he was convinced of the differences between races and that racial integration would have dire future consequences. He later abandoned the White Citizen's Council for the Ku Klux Klan because he believed that the Citizen Council was too passive and its members were closet anti-Semites.[28]

After doing some research, he found that the only group in his area that seemed to take a more proactive stance for the white race was the KKK. The KKK, founded in 1865 by Nathan Bedford Forrest after the American Civil War, pioneered modern guerrilla warfare tactics and became one of the most powerful American social organizations. At its height, the Klan had over million members, some of them being U.S. senators, Congressmen, and Northern and Southern state governors. During his time in the Klan, Duke was mentored by James Lindsay, an articulate Klan leader and successful New Orleans stockbroker who influenced members from Texas, Tennessee, Louisiana, Mississippi, and Alabama. Lindsay invited Duke to give brief speeches about racial threats to Klan audiences. Duke became active in a Klan Den before taking the KKK oath to officially join.[29]

At seventeen, Duke attended an integrated Kennedy High School in New Orleans. This school had a 10% black population with the majority being white students from middle to upper income families. In his autobiography, he states that it was during this time that he was able to confirm his view on blacks and Jews.[30] In his senior year of high school, he drifted away from the Klan and focused on topics such as white civil rights, integrated housing, welfare for minorities, affirmative action, and immigration. He read Madison Grant and Lothrip Stoddard, early nineteenth-century authors who discussed the rising population rate and racial extinction. He also read some of George Lincoln Rockwell's literature and found him interesting and inspiring. He was particularly impressed with Rockwell's intelligence, courage, and use of media. David Duke began to correspond with him in the months before Rockwell was killed.

Rockwell's emphasis on targeting the Jews is seen in Duke's thoughts at the time. He argues that Jews are guilty of the following[31]:

1. Teaching egalitarianism and academia and the media to destroy white racial consciousness and solidarity.
2. Spearheading the effort to open the borders of America and other Western nations to the third world.
3. Spreading guilt and supplication among whites for slavery, Third World exploitation, and the Holocaust.
4. Installing resentment and hatred and growing nonwhite racial minorities.
5. Leading the legal and governmental assault on white schools and neighborhoods.
6. Undermining the family by feminism, lower moral standards, and economic restructuring.

In August 1968 he began his college career at Louisiana State University in Baton Rouge. His residence hall became known as the Klansman dormitory because he stated that most residents shared his beliefs but did not vocalize them. He also asserted that about three quarters of the male students loved the Confederate flag. He was an active debater in LSU's free speech area. He would stand in the middle of campus on a soap box with a full Nazi uniform armed in one hand and a copy of George Lincoln Rockwell's *White Power* (1967) in the other. He would debate anyone within earshot who wanted to disagree with him on race and/or Jews. In college, he took courses that would provide a deeper understanding on race. For example, he took biology, geography, anthropology, and history and used material from each course in the debate.[32]

In 1970, Duke founded a student group, The White Youth Alliance. Duke borrowed its ideology and organizational structure from the National Socialist White People's Party, formally the American Nazi Party, and published a tabloid, *The Racialist*, which stood for the racial idealist. He stated that he wanted a more modern version of the Ku Klux Klan and made changes to soften the Klan's image. The group at one time had about 300 members and began to start chapters at other schools. He stated that the group had a national membership of 2000.[33]

Reserve Officer Training Corps (ROTC) was compulsory at Louisiana State University for all male freshmen students. Duke, with his father's support, wanted to become a commissioned officer in the armed services. He joined the Bengal Raiders, a Special Forces-oriented extracurricular part of the ROTC program. He performed well in ROTC until he was informed by Col. Joseph Dale, the Commandant of cadets at Louisiana State University, that he would not receive a commission because of his anti-Semitic beliefs and actions. He left LSU soon after the news to work overseas.[34]

In the early 1970s, his father was involved with a U.S. State Department school in Vietnam for Laotian military officers. This particular school taught the Laotian Army and Air Force officers basic and military-oriented English. David Duke's father arranged for him to have a job teaching English in Laos. His flight itinerary took him to Hawaii, Japan, Hong Kong, Saigon, Bangkok, and finally Laos. In late August he left Laos and traveled to India, Israel, and Europe. In 1971 he visited Israel and spent time in Tel Aviv, Haifa, and Jerusalem. In his autobiography, he states that he spoke with Palestinians and Israelis about a myriad of issues. After Rome, he went to Munich and then to Dachau. He also visited historic landmarks associated with National Socialism and the destruction that still remained after the War.

In the fall of 1972, David Duke and Jim Lindsay wanted to recreate the original movement and proposed to completely modernize the Klan. He was interested in creating a modern social movement as a political machine to change men's minds, granting full rights to women and shifting meeting venues. He returned to the United States, and rather than return to LSU, he started the White Youth Alliance. Duke modeled the White Youth Alliance after the South African White Youth Alliance and opened a small office at 3214 2 Main Street in New Orleans. He published a magazine, *The Nationalist*, helped organize student support groups, and carried out several demonstrations for publicity. He began a process of raising support, and Duke asserts that in 1972. The National Party had hundreds of members which included at least 100 active high school and college students in the New Orleans area. He focused on public meetings and literature distribution.[35]

In 1974, he founded the Knights of the Ku Klux Klan in order to promote a new type of Klansman. A KKK Knight should be educated, driven, handsome, professional, and articulate. Duke believed that he embodied these attributes. Attempting to maximize his public appeal, he appeared on national talk shows as a Grand Dragon. His ideology at the time focused more on Jews and Nazi ideas than grievances with African Americans. However, KKK members had problems with his personality, specifically his womanizing, his self-promotion, and his personal financial gain. Duke wrote program policies of the Knights of the Ku Klux Klan and redesigned their publications with a more modernistic style. He established twenty-two Klan Dens in Louisiana and Mississippi while also opening a day-care center at Woodlawn Baptist

Church. He was appointed a Grand Dragon in Louisiana. He also made speeches in numerous states as the national information director and focused on recruiting members in their 20s and 30s.[36]

Duke continued his speaking circuit all over the country and graduated from LSU in 1974. He started a monthly newsletter, *Klan Action Report*, and later renamed it the *Crusader*. Duke was no longer interested in overt Nazism but wanted to create a new and "softer" brand that would be more appealing to a wider audience. He wanted to soften and professionalize the Klan's image. He broadened its membership to include women and Catholics in order to expand the pool of potential members. In addition to the newsletter, he also wrote books and other pieces of propaganda.[37]

Duke's modus operandi is subversive, an approach he used in publishing both books and in pursuing political office. Duke wrote *African Atto* (1973), a street fighting manual for African Americans in urban areas and *Finders Keepers* (1976), a book for women on how to keep their male companions. He selected misleading pseudonyms for each book; Malcolm X for *African Atto* and Dorothy Vanderbilt and James Konrad for *Finders Keepers*. The strategy behind *African Atto* was to provide African Americans with better tactics and techniques to kill each other on the street. *Finders Keepers* was written to prevent white women from race mixing. Both books were published and distributed without drawing attention to the fact that behind them was a white male pushing a subversive agenda.[38]

Duke formally left the KKK in 1979, but desired to retain a softer professional image. He formed the National Association for the Advancement of White People (NAAWP) as a grass-roots effort to inflate his political base and aligned himself with Willis Carto, an influential anti-Semitic propagandist. Both Duke and Carto collaborated to disprove the Holocaust. In 1980, he collaborated with Don Black on several racist projects. Their partnership would continue over the years and despite Black marrying Duke's former wife, Chloe Hardin, they created Stormfront, one of the leading online neo-Nazi/white supremacist forums.[39]

His first run for political office was in 1975 for a 10th district seat in the Louisiana State Senate. He lost, but received 26% of the votes. He ran a Democratic presidential campaign in 1988 and received 47,047 votes or 4% of the national popular vote. However, in 1989 he changed his party affiliation to Republican and won the State House's 81st district seat with 3,995 votes or 33%. He served in this post from 1990 to 1992. Then in 1992, now as a Republican, he sought his party's nomination for president, which he failed to obtain. In 1994, he ran for the U.S. Senate seat and lost, but received 44% of the votes or 607,391. In 1996, he campaigned again for a U.S. Senate seat and again in 1999 for the U.S. House of Representatives. He failed in both attempts. After his failed political bid in 1999, Duke was finished with running for office.[40]

All future political ambitions dissolved after his conviction of filing a false tax return in December 2002. He was sentenced to fifteen months in prison, and he spent the time in Big Springs, Texas. He was released in 2004 and shifted gears. Duke organized a White Nationalism Conference where attendees agreed to unify the white movement, established peace within the movement, and fostered a new image.[41] Duke drafted a protocol that was adopted by those in attendance and has been labeled as the New Orleans Protocol. Paul Fromm, Don Black, Willis Carto, Kevin Strom, and John Tyndall signed the document. The protocol is listed on the Southern Poverty's Law Center website and has three provisions[42]:

1. Zero tolerance for violence
2. Honorable and ethical behavior with other signatory groups. This includes not denouncing others who have signed this protocol. In other words, no enemies on the right
3. Maintaining a high tone in arguments and public presentation

In 2005, Duke visited Damascus, Syria, and spoke at a televised rally about Israel and Zionist control. That same year he was awarded a Ph.D. from the Ukrainian Interregional Academy of Personnel Management.[43] His doctoral dissertation, "Zionism as a Form of Ethnic Supremacism," is a "scholarly" attempt to promote his ideology in an academic format. During his studies there, he taught courses in international relations and history.[44] In 2006, Duke was a delegate in Tehran at the International Conference to Review the Global Vision of the Holocaust, and in April 2009 Duke was invited by Czechoslovakian neo-Nazis to deliver three lectures.[45] Duke has two adult daughters from his wife, Chloe Hardin, who was an active member in Duke's LSU student group. They married in 1974 and divorced ten years later.[46]

Duke currently describes himself as a white civil rights activist, not a white supremacist or neo-Nazi. Duke has published numerous articles, has written four books, and has hosted an internet broadcast show. In 1998, he published a book that outlines his social philosophies entitled *My Awakening: A Path to Racial Understanding*. In 2002, he published *Jewish Supremacism*, which is considered a comprehensive outline of his beliefs. He currently resides in Austria and is very active on the internet, in publishing, and in streaming audio messages.[47]

NOTES

1. McCants, William and Jarret Brachman, *Militant Ideology Atlas: Research Compendium*. West Point, NY: Combating Terrorism Center, 2006.
2. "David Duke.com," *David Duke.com*, accessed August 30, 2015, http://david-duke.com.

3. Duke, David Ernest. *My Awakening: A Path to Racial Understanding*. Covington, LW: Free Speech Press, 1998.

4. "David Duke vs. Thom Hartmann: The Confederate Flag | Thom Hartmann," accessed August 30, 2015, http://www.thomhartmann.com/bigpicture/david-duke-vs-thom-hartmann-confederate-flag.

5. Ibid.

6. almuwahideenmedia, "Interview with Shaykh Abu Muhammad Al Maqdisi (English)," *Al Muwahideen Media*, accessed August 30, 2015, https://almuwahideenmedia.wordpress.com/2015/02/09/interview-with-shaykh-abu-muhammad-al-maqdisi-english/.

7. "Conclave is talking about negotiations with Daesh." . المقدسي يتحدث عن مفاوضات عداعش حول الكساسبة. accessed June 30, 2016, http://assabeel.net/local/item/90290-.

8. Jaber, Majed. "Jordan Releases Leading Al Qaeda Mentor: Security Source," *Reuters*, (September, 24, 2014). Accessed February 5, 2015, http://www.reuters.com/article/2015/02/05/us-mideast-crisis-jordan-qaeda-idUSKBN0L92GE20150205.

9. Weaver, Mary Anne. "The Short, Violent Life of Abu Musab Al-Zarqawi—The Atlantic," (June 8, 2006), accessed August 30, 2015, http://www.theatlantic.com/.

10. Meir Hatina, *Martyrdom in Modern Islam: Piety, Power, and Politics*. New York, NY: (Cambridge University Press, 2014).

11. almuwahideenmedia, "Interview with Shaykh Abu Muhammad Al Maqdisi (English)."

12. Wagemakers, Joas. "Maqdisi in the Middle: An inside Account of the Secret Negotiations to Free a Jordanian Pilot « Jihadica," (February, 11, 2015), accessed August 30, 2015, http://www.jihadica.com/maqdisi-in-the-middle-an-inside-account-of-the-secret-negotiations-to-free-a-jordanian-pilot/.

13. Kazimi, Nibras. "A Virulent Ideology in Mutation: Zarqawi Upstages Maqdisi." *Current Trends in Islamist Ideology* 2 (2005): 59.

14. Maqdisi is rather of an outlier among Palestinians because he does not seem to identify with a strong Palestinian identity.

15. Kazimi, Nibras, "A Virulent Ideology in Mutation."

16. Wagemakers, Joas. *A Quietist Jihadi: The Ideology and Influence of Abu Muhammad Al-Maqdis*. Cambridge: Cambridge University Press, 2012.

17. Ibid.

18. Maqdisi's 1985 book entitled, *Millat Ibrahim or the Religion of Abraham* (or *The second Abraham and the Preaching of the Prophets and the Deliverers*) demonstrates Uteibi's impact. He elaborates on two principles that preoccupied much of his intellectual work. This work is an exegesis of a theme in Uteibi's last letter that focuses on the concept of loyalty and renunciation, or al-wala' we bara, from the following verse in the Koran. "Sura: Al-Mumtehaan: four: you had an admirable example in Ibrahim and who was with you for they say to their nation we renounce you and what you pray to in lieu of God, we brand you unbelievers and enmity and hatred is apparent between us and you forever until you believe in God alone."

19. Maqdisi honors the founder of Wahhabism, Mohammed bin Abdel Mohammed, but then later states that the house of Saud turning to unbelievers when they turn a focus on destroying the Muslim Brotherhood.

20. Kazimi, "A Virulent Ideology in Mutation."

21. Maqdisi's books were brought into the Saudi kingdom in the late 1980s and 1990s by Saudis who had fought in Afghanistan and Pakistan. His books were at the time critical of the Saudi Arabian government. According to Wagemaker, these books were spread by hand delivering them to others and through photocopies. Another key point of criticism was the Saudi Arabian government's allowing 500,000 Americans on its soil to defend against a possible invasion from Saddam Hussein.

22. Kazimi, "A Virulent Ideology in Mutation."

23. Wagemakers, *A Quietist Jihadi*. Maqdisi continually describes Saudi Arabia as a nation that does not live up to its own Salafi Wahhabi ideology. He criticizes Saudi Arabia on three set points. First is its use and application of man-made laws instead of sharia, contrary to what governing authorities state. His second criticism accuses Saudi Arabian officials of partnering with other organizations and institutions that govern the basis of man-made laws. The final point according to Wagemaker is that the strong ties between the Saudi government and the United States illustrates a close partnership of problematic origins. Maqdisi thus frames Saudi Arabia's rulers as infidels which takes his disagreement with the state a step farther than Uteibi.

24. Wagemakers, *A Quietist Jihadi*.

25. Ibid.

26. "Zarqawi Mentor Maqdisi Free Again via @intelwire," accessed August 30, 2015, http://news.intelwire.com/2008/03/zarqawi-mentor-maqdisi-free-again.html.

27. Duke, *My Awakening*.

28. Bridges, Tyler. *The Rise of David Duke*. Jackson: University Press of Mississippi, 1994.

29. Zatarain, Michael. *David Duke: Evolution of a Klansman*. Gretna, LA: Pelican Publishing Company, 1990.

30. Duke, *My Awakening*.

31. Ibid.

32. Bridges, *The Rise of David Duke*.

33. Duke, *My Awakening*.

34. Ibid.

35. Ibid.

36. Bridges, *The Rise of David Duke*.

37. Rose, David D. *The Emergence of David Duke and the Politics of Race*. Chapel Hill: University of North Carolina Press, 1992.

38. Bridges, *The Rise of David Duke*.

39. "David Duke," *Southern Poverty Law Center*, accessed August 30, 2015, https://www.splcenter.org/fighting-hate/extremist-files/individual/david-duke.

40. Rose, *The Emergence of David Duke and the Politics of Race*.

41. "David Duke."

42. Ibid.

43. Duke, David (2005–09–09). "David Duke Achieves Doctorate in Ukraine". http://www.davidduke.com/index.php?p=394. Retrieved 2006–11–16.

44. "David Duke.com."

45. He was arrested by Czech officials and was forced out of the country a day later.

46. Bridges, *The Rise of David Duke*.

47. "David Duke.com."

Chapter 6

The Way Forward

Focus on the Source, Not Just the Symptoms

A disproportionate amount of attention is given to the violent incident than to the ideas behind the violence. This is logical since violence requires immediate attention and the loss of life is more pressing than ideological analysis. However, each act of violence is a symptom of the ideological source. Until recently, the majority of counterterrorism efforts have focused on symptom elimination rather than on eradicating the source. It is far more effective to drain the swamp that produces mosquitos that transmit malaria than to develop a strategy to kill every single mosquito. If killing one organism is the strategy, then no understanding is required of the organism, what it carries, or the environment in which it breeds. Although it is crucially important to understand all of the anatomical aspects of how a mosquito transmits malaria, this understanding does not imply an effective strategy. At some point, what the mosquito carries, the parasitic protozoan, has to be also identified and defeated. It only creates the possibility of generating an effective strategy when the carrier, the source, and the environment are understood. When applied to violent extremism, for example, it is imperative to understand all the tactical dimensions of suicide bombing, but a suicide bomber is the carrier of ideas which need equal analysis. Effective counterterrorism methods are needed to disrupt symptoms and eliminate the source.

There are specific dark ideas that resonate with populations, become normalized, and endure become the most dangerous long-term threats to security. Killing a leader or dispersing a group does have an immediate symptom reduction effect but may ultimately validate the leader and his ideas. This creates a new, different threat that can take years of incubation before another violent incident occurs. The absence of violence does not necessarily mean the threat is diminished. It could be displaced or delayed. The strategic argument here is that symptom and source reduction should occur in parallel processes. An over-the-counter drug approach can relieve the symptom, but it does not impact the cancer in any way. In fact, the cancer continues to grow, even if the symptoms are not visible.

Dark ideas will continue to emerge from violent extremists in the years to come. The context, culture, technology, and ideologues will drive each innovation. The presentation of some of the leading innovations within the two ideologies examined in this text and the following discussion outlines a path forward. Specifically, a conceptual framework is proposed to understand, identify, and counter dark ideas from the past, present, and future. Although there may be other innovations within neo-Nazism and violent jihadism, it is not within the scope of this study to identify all of them. Only two ideologies were selected to illustrate how to apply this conceptual framework to existing ideologies. At this point, it is sufficient to conclude that a multidimensional approach is required.

This chapter outlines several conceptual points to proactively address these innovations and to adequately address past innovations that still resonate with certain segments of the population. Although this book focuses on neo-Nazism and violent jihadism, the central objective of this book is to highlight the importance of identifying and understanding dark ideas across all violent extremists' ideologies.

Three important points outlined in this chapter discuss a way forward. First, it is essential to acknowledge that dark ideas are crafted by individuals and groups within a particular culture and context. If any long-range counterterrorism efforts are to be successful, it is paramount that the petri dish from which they originated should be carefully examined. In other words, in order to understand violent extremism and the ideas that originate from subcultural groups, context from the individual at the micro level to governing structures at the macro level is the required knowledge. This concept has been gaining traction within scholarship and governmental agencies over the past eight years. Second, the communication and dissemination process from which innovations are advanced needs to be analyzed from multiple dimensions. The idea itself may not resonate or be accepted by a target population; however, through the use of effective propaganda, a contagion effect may occur. A contagion effect is the mass spread of an idea that infects large segments of a target population. The process of spreading ideas, especially when it is effective, needs to be understood both from a practical standpoint and a frame resonance perspective. When innovations are identified, analyzing the potential impact of new methods and ideas related to violent extremism should be prioritized. Finally, ideas must be targeted in addition to individuals and groups. The same degree of critical analysis and debate applied to delegitimizing accepted political discourse needs to be applied to innovations produced and disseminated by violent extremist ideologues.

IDEAS AND IDEOLOGUES SHOULD BE EXAMINED
IN THEIR PROPER CULTURE AND CONTEXT

Innovations do not originate in a vacuum. The internal map of a terrorist or any group is not generated in a vacuum completely isolated from preconditions[1] that exist in the larger sociological, economic, political, historical, anthropological and psychological elements that surround the individual and the group. Gustave Morf in 1970 recognized this fact.[2] He completed a comprehensive study of the Front de libération du Québec (FLQ) terrorist network in Quebec. His sample included hundreds of interviews of FLQ members in and out of Canadian penitentiaries over a three-year period combined with a content analysis of their publications. Though this study was conducted almost fifty years ago, his method of data collection and analysis would be a welcomed addition to today's terrorism literature. He recognized that analyzing culture was central to understanding ideology, motivation, and grievances. FLQ terrorism was rooted in culture conflict being expressed in sociopolitical outlets. Morf's work correctly identified this source and mapped their ideology using ethnographic research methods. He allowed the terrorists to define their worldview to him, using their terminology, as he triangulated the validity of their data with external sources. This grounded theoretical approach led him to make etiological assertions of the role of poverty and narcissism, which are still being discussed some forty years later. Over thirty years later, Mark Juergensmeyer shared a similar sentiment when attempting to understand cultural dimensions that surround Christian Identity, Jewish activism, Islam, Sikhism, and Japanese cults.[3]

There are concentric circles of influences that assist in determining how culture according to this model is observed, experienced, interpreted, and defined. The following intervals can be defined as: individual, family, group network/organization, regional, and national. The intervals function at varying degrees of influence over the life course. What dominates also varies. The levels function together as a complex tapestry where norms imparted by the family during childhood may conflict with the culture experienced in-group network/organization during adolescence or early adulthood. Network/organization exists as part of a larger regional culture that is often distinct from other regions identified by geography, language, accent, ideology, history, dress, etc. Sub-cultural norms are imbedded in macro-level components of nationalistic culture identified by a nation/state that includes the following variables: dominant religion, type of legal system, educational/economic language, form of government, geography, and the culture associated with the nation.[4]

Another aspect to consider is the relationship between the idea and the ideologues. Certain actions on behalf of governments and law enforcement officials can propel the popularity of an ideologue but can also serve to solidify their message. For example, Egyptian president Abdul Nasser attempted to silence Sayyid Qutb through execution, but instead he made him a martyr and amplified Qutb's voice. Even though George Lincoln Rockwell was assassinated by one of his own members, he is still considered a martyr at the hands of a race traitor. However, if the assassin had been member of the federal government, law enforcement, an African American or a Jewish shooter, history may have found the impact of George Lincoln Rockwell to be even greater. Conversely, Abdullah Azzam was given almost free rein to spread his message in the Middle East and in the United States. His message at the time was not seen as a security threat, and as a result, his message and ideas were ignored. Bin Laden and Anwar Awlaki were also killed at the hands of the Americans. Within the jihadi literature both men are seen as martyrs and have joined the ranks of Sayyid Qutb, not necessarily in terms of ideological contributions to date, but it is impossible to tell how their actions will be framed in the future.

Edward Said asserted that the history, culture, and psychology of the Middle East consisted of a compilation of scholars who were writing about a social phenomenon that was being constructed from an outsider's perspective.[5] He claimed that the mental construction of the Middle East was nothing but mental fantasy projections of Western scholars to create a world that could be understood by the West. A similar statement can almost be made about the current state of approaching terrorist groups and terrorists. Attempts to analyze individual terrorists or terrorism networks/organizations without cultural dimensions communicates the irrelevance of etiological variables prevalent in social discourse, myths, philosophies, ideologies, ethics, morals, folklore, and conflict resolution.[6] Excluding these variables can lead to unintended consequences[7] or to asking questions like, "Why do they hate us?"

Terrorists live in cultures and try to establish their own value systems and subcultures, both to justify themselves and proselytize. A subcultural approach would fall within an established form of reference for analysis of violent behavior, of which political violence would be a specific subcategory. Construction of reality takes place at the individual and group level and is impacted by cultural context, historical-cultural narratives, and sociopsychological dimensions.[8] For example, selecting the dates of the September 11 attack in the United States and the March 11 attacks in Spain by Al Qaeda reveals that both had symbolic meanings understood from a cultural context. The same is true for the Oklahoma City bombing. The date of April 19, 1995, was symbolic as were Timothy McVeigh's clothing and the documents he possessed.[9] Culture is interpreted through a symbolic interactionism perspective manifested in symbols, the situation, roles socialization, role taking, and the self.[10] Understanding cultural cognitive maps of terrorists and how these impact their worldview, grievances, and use of violence will lead to an increased understanding of individual terrorists, terrorists groups, and counterterrorism "best practices." The common theme in terrorism is to categorize terrorist groups according to perceived political agendas as homogenous samples from various regions, essentially presuming that an equal correlation exists between cultures. Etiological research in terrorism follows the same trend when comprehensive theoretical models are pursued.[11]

HOW IDEAS SPREAD, RESONATE, AND BECOME NORMALIZED SUBCULTURAL VALUES NEEDS TO BE UNDERSTOOD

Before any innovation becomes an action, propaganda is necessary to promote and rationalize the idea. Propaganda, an emotive communicative form, is used in multiple formats to promote and normalize a "new" innovation. This propaganda is embedded within layers of data, and each layer requires an applicable propaganda analysis method to identify and understand how ideas are disseminated and become normalized within certain subcultures.

Propaganda analysis is often defined as the examination of a communications' social impact.[12] Propaganda analysis is also defined as a strategy tool to improve information about an opponent's intentions, strategy, and current situation, as a method to uncover overt and covert communications intended to dominate the publics' attitudes and opinions, or as a method to examine the internal/external qualities of emotionally laden communication. In this context, propaganda analysis is defined as a critical study of communication strategies intended to dominate a target audience. Communication strategies refer to the structure, context, affect, and content-specific levels associated with propaganda.[13]

Propaganda analysis is generally divided into two different approaches: top down and bottom up. Historically, propaganda analysis emphasized the top-down approach that originated from state-supported organizations. Until recently, dissident terrorist's messages, communiqués, books, or manifestos were not classified as "propaganda" on the same level as state-level propaganda.[14] Due to 9/11 and the subsequent "War on Terror," propaganda analysis devoted to violent extremist propaganda by the intelligence community and scholars increased exponentially. Since propaganda analysis was firmly embedded in communications, content or discourse analyses are common methods used to examine communiqués and the media's relationship to the tactic of terrorism. However, other propaganda analysis methods that are not commonly used also need to be incorporated for multilevel analysis. A propaganda analysis typology outlines the purposes and outcomes of five different approaches to extracting intelligence from propaganda.[15]

A propaganda analysis typology identifies the various methods of identifying intelligence in extremist propaganda for multilevel analysis. Typologies are used across academic disciplines to reconcile seemingly divergent information. Typologies provide a system to compare, contrast, and organize information that leads to a deeper, more robust understanding of a subject. A propaganda analysis typology assists in categorizing the inner workings of different approaches to identify all usable data for intelligence and counter-propaganda. The proposed propaganda analysis typology is organized into five different approaches. Each approach is guided by a specific purpose and method to exploit the full range of data being communicated in the text for intelligence purposes. An outcome of a propaganda analysis typology is to provide a propaganda analysis framework that enables researchers or analysts to identify and process overt and subversive content for intelligence purposes. Analyzing propaganda from different angles (dimensions) enables propaganda to be holistically and critically examined for complete intelligence.

Dissemination analysis examines the symbiotic relationship between propaganda and the media. The symbiotic relationship between violent extremist communication and the media is defined in two ways. Historically, terrorist groups perceive the mainstream media as the primary tactical tool to generate awareness and solicit leverage. Terrorists select targets and engage in acts of violence in order to obtain coverage from main media outlets. Dissemination analysis determines the success/failure rate of media volume, frequency, and range toward a particular terrorist incident or communication. Informative analysis identifies actionable intelligence since propaganda is a valuable source of intelligence due to the tangible information that can be extracted from the material such as names, targets, funding sources, ideology, geographic information, and weapons. Communicative analysis identifies the communicative structure of violent extremist propaganda through semantic, syntax, and grammar analysis. The communicative technical approach examines how a terrorist group's message is constructed. The communicative approach analyzes the communication techniques, the types of arguments, rhetorical fallacies, and communicative persuasion techniques.

Frame analysis is the process of understanding how information is packaged in a manner that appeals to the target population. Using multidisciplinary methods, analysts and scholars examine how groups frame their ideology into a message in order to gain political momentum and seize power. Scholars examine how a message is framed to resonate with indigenous cultural symbols, language and identities, so that it is more likely to mobilize a targeted population. Appropriate frame analysis reveals how and why political momentum is occurring and constructs the appropriate counter message.

Affect analysis identifies the emotional catalysts in violent extremists' propaganda used to incite particular emotions in a target audience. This approach examines the emotional code of propaganda. The content is used to "get at" the emotional code using a social-psychological approach. The emotional code is defined as emotional semantic or visual triggers embedded by the propagandist to stimulate positive or negative emotions in populations. It is intended to function exactly as a contagious emotional plague. It is to spread rapidly, infecting as many as possible without losing its potency. The media are defined as the fuel for terrorism, but in an emotional contagion model it is the method of contamination. It is the effectiveness of the propagandist to incite the target audience to active or passive participation. Propaganda analysis using the social-psychological approach focuses on the emotional code in order to examine what is being framed as emotional contagion and how the propagandist is using it throughout the text. Content is not the primary focus. The content of propaganda is used to expose the communicative strategy and the emotional code that lies underneath the content. This is what distinguishes the social-psychological approach of propaganda analysis from the informative or dissemination approach. Extracting content is not the sole objective nor is focusing primarily on the communicative technical structure. The primary objective is to understand how the propagandist uses information to trigger emotional responses.

FRAME ANALYSIS

Neo-Nazi propaganda is dominantly diagnostic, identifying the problems, whereas violent jihadi propaganda is prognostically skewed, outlining solutions to remedy the situation. Neo-Nazi propagandists emphasize "white" problems and the threats posed by nonwhites and race traitors. Neo-Nazi propaganda emphasizes the need to neutralize "inner voices" that question the culpability of blacks, Jews, race traitors, or the federal government. All neo-Nazi propaganda in this sample follows the same format of emphasizing diagnostic frames over prognostic solutions. This finding is significant because it does not change over time, despite different external variables associated with current events, culture, and politics.

When compared to their neo-Nazi counterparts, violent jihadi propaganda is prognostically skewed across the sample. A possible explanation can be found in the difference between racial and religious in- and out-groups. Neo-Nazis must convince the white population that their race is the apex of natural selection and headed toward racial extinction. Although institutional racism is prevalent in the United States, linking race to natural selection, racial wars, and a white-based religion does not share the same degree of institutional memory for the current generation of whites. For that reason, neo-Nazis are attempting to *transform* a white population's view rather than trying to modify it. A neo-Nazi transformation method is to emphasize diagnostic frames that are intended to awaken whites to the "racial threat" they face.[16]

Violent jihadis, however, only need to *modify* a worldview over transforming it. Unlike racial wars, violent jihad is a legitimate concept within Islam. Violent jihadis (the in-group) are not engaged in trying to promote "violence as a solution" as a "new" concept separate from Islamic theological grounding, whereas neo-Nazi propagandists are trying to promote violence as a legitimate solution based on racial theological grounds as a response to "white racial extinction/pollution." Neo-Nazis attempt to legitimize violence by arguing that "ignorant" whites are engaged in shameful "racial treason" by being passive and letting their race become "muddied" or "extinct." Whites who are involved in race mixing and are actively polluting the white race are deemed equal to nonwhites and deserve violent retribution. In other words, neo-Nazis are trying to reframe problems and solutions where violent jihadis are focused on reframing the use of a violent solution. This point is illustrated when contrasting neo-Nazi racial wars with violent jihad.[17]

Violent jihadis are attempting to reframe *how* and *when* violence should be legitimized. Violent jihadis reframe the argument by claiming that it is only "true" Muslims who engage in violence. Findings reveal that "true" Muslims understand that violent jihad should be a sixth pillar of Islam and is a correct response to the threats, humiliation, or violence directed toward Muslims. Therefore, it becomes logical to reframe an existing violent solution in their propaganda and apply it to current problems experienced by Muslims across the globe. Unlike neo-Nazis, whose solidarity is based on skin color and who must convert whites to their problem/solution interpretations, violent jihadists must convert Muslims to a violent jihadi interpretation of a legitimate theological solution—jihad. This is quite different and offers a possible explanation to why violent jihadis are skewed prognostically, where neo-Nazis assert diagnostic frames.[18]

Violent jihadis are unified by a theological belief where different races and nationalities form a community—the ummah. Although this community is diverse, it is unnecessary to morph violence into a sacred notion. Jihad already exists as a religious concept on a personal and collective level. The focal point for the violent jihadi propagandists is not to transform the dominant Muslim worldview by creating "holy violence," but to modify how violent jihad is perceived by all Muslims. Neo-Nazi propagandists must equate violence as an individual and collective response to racial pollution in order to transform a "white worldview." Furthermore, neo-Nazi propagandists must morph racial war into racial *holy* war in order to connect violence to a religious precedent. Neo-Nazi propagandists are attempting to create and promote a similar religious concept in which race is a divine characteristic and violence becomes a sacred endeavor to protect it. Disproportionately embedding diagnostic frames in text is a method to accomplish this morphing process.[19]

A difference between neo-Nazi and violent jihadi propaganda is how violent prognostic frames are used as solutions for blame targets. Neo-Nazi prognostic frames that solicit violent behavior are less frequent when contrasted with violent responses by jihadi propagandists. Pierce is the only neo-Nazi propagandist whose use of violence in the text reflects a similar prevalence level to violent jihadis. When compared to violent jihadi targets, the targets associated with neo-Nazi violence are more uniform over time. Neo-Nazi propagandists also assert violence against the same blame targets over time as compared to violent jihadi propagandists who disperse violence across various types of blame targets.

Historically, neo-Nazi propagandists also differ from violent jihadi propagandists in that they use more types of frames and distribute them proportionately in their propaganda. Violent jihadis use fewer frames and distribute them more unevenly. Fewer frames and an uneven distribution results in highlighting a "central" or dominant theme, which is followed by a wider margin of tertiary frames.[20] Having more types of frames with a more proportionate distribution increases the complexity of neo-Nazis' grievances because they are more broadly dispersed. Having a higher number of frames also suggests that neo-Nazi propagandists are attempting to increase the "appeal" of neo-Nazism by tapping into a wider range of grievances held by an ideologically and religiously diverse white population.[21] However, with information warfare being conducted by ISIS, the number and types of frames used by violent jihadis may have increased, especially since they are targeting the Western Muslim population.

Despite various differences, neo-Nazis and violent jihadis share similarities in typology, strategy, and use of neutralization techniques. Regarding typology, the majority of the frames were identified in the first sample, Rockwell and Qutb, with little variation from these central themes over time. Although new frames were added as current events and political structures changed, the frames used by Rockwell and Qutb were also used by subsequent propagandists. Using the same types of diagnostic or prognostic techniques over time illustrates that neo-Nazi and violent jihadi propagandists are not creating new ideas but rather reordering and restricting themes used by previous or contemporary propagandists.

A consistent strategy of using violent solutions at different intervals is reflected by both sets of propagandists. Individual propagandists from both ideologies can be identified as being extremely violent, while others seem to promote a "softer" version with very little violence reflected in their text.

A precondition for violence can be defined as the aligning of attitudes by rationalizing the solutions or problems outlined by neo-Nazism and violent jihadism.[22]

Neo-Nazis and violent jihadi propagandists focus on neutralizing threats to their ideology while promoting criminogenic ideas and behavior as normative. All neo-Nazi and violent jihadi propagandists use both diagnostic and prognostics frames to promote subcultural ideas and behavior deemed criminal under the norms and laws of conventional culture. Both sets of propagandists endeavor to manipulate ideas and behavior into forms that are criminogenic. Whether the outcome is explicit violence outlined by violent prognostic frames or ideas that turn other races or religions into pollutants, the goal is to promote or reinforce attitudes that "rationalize" a permanent drift into neo-Nazism and violent jihadism over conventional culture. Rationalization must occur to permit a permanent drift into a subculture where segregation, deportation, war, terrorism, or elimination is perceived as a legitimate solution over any conventional methods of "restoring justice."

INNOVATIONS NEED TO BE COUNTERED VIA INFORMATION WARFARE

Information warfare is not new. Targeting the opponent's communications, deception of all sorts—propaganda in particular—has been practiced since the dawn of organized warfare. During the Revolutionary War, Benjamin Franklin wrote a number of letters and documents under fake names to set other nations against the British. George Washington also used the press to spread exaggerated reports of enemy casualties to boost morale and counter British disinformation. During the U.S. Civil War, General Sherman employed information warfare that included censorship and battlefield reporting to the press that he knew would be read by southern audiences. Throughout the First World War, President Wilson used informational officers domestically and internationally to bolster public opinion against the German propaganda. In World War II, two organizations were established specifically for information warfare—The Office of Strategic Services (used all forms of information warfare) and the Office of War Information (focused on the primacy of truth).[23]

From the Vietnam War to the War on Terror, information warfare has continued to evolve. During Vietnam, U.S. agencies did very little to influence public perception, and censorship was virtually nonexistent. However, during the invasion of Grenada, censorship was back in primary focus, and the press was excluded from any information on the conflict. In Panama, Operation Just Cause saw the reversal of Grenada policies and the establishment of a Washington-based press pool. The pool was designed as a compromise between the desire for media access and "truth in reporting." Operation Desert Shield/Desert Storm saw the emergence of the "CNN" effect where both sides witnessed the power of media, real-time warfare, and information dominance. The Global War on Terror began with the understanding that Al Qaeda had a "media wing," and policy makers debated the term "strategic communication." Governmental agencies became aware of information vulnerability, the flip side of the information dominance coin (i.e., the use of the term "crusade" by President George W. Bush), and how violence, recruitment, and radicalization were influenced by information. It was during U.S. military actions in Iraq and Afghanistan against the Al Qaeda that violent jihadi demagogues accelerated their use of propaganda in the digital domain.[24]

U.S. governmental officials have debated how to best engage in counter-propaganda campaigns against violent jihadis and neo-Nazis. For example, General Stanley McChrystal attempted to counter the Taliban spiritual leader Mullah Omar's "Hearts and Minds campaign" with his own. Even more recently, Executive Order 13584, entitled "Developing an Integrated Strategic Counterterrorism Communications Initiative," established a center specifically devoted to information warfare.[25] The Center for Strategic Counterterrorism Communications is housed in the State Department and is staffed by experts and analysts from the Defense Department, the intelligence community, and the Special Operations Forces. While the Center focuses primarily on violent jihadi propaganda, their focus could easily shift to domestic activities. For example, Stormfront, the largest neo-Nazi site in the world with some 240,000 registered members, was shut down by an internet hacking collective, Anonymous, in an operation declared "Operation Blitzkrieg." Anonymous disrupted Stormfront's activity for several days and subsequently published personal information of alleged members online in order to remove confidentiality and deter participation. Although the U.S. government was not responsible for shutting down Stormfront, policy makers may use similar tactics against neo-Nazis' propaganda repositories.

Policy makers have used three dominant approaches in response to information warfare. The first approach can be described as a passive approach. The passive approach emphasizes downplaying or ignoring conflicting propaganda. The objective is to minimize drawing attention to an opponent's propaganda and the media attention that any acknowledgment would bring. The passive approach is detached from counterpropaganda of any sort. The second approach upholds the "primacy of truth" in that correct information is used to counter an opponent's propaganda. When employed, it directs that governmental agencies be active and correct an opponent's incorrect reports and accounts; however, it stops short of deception and is limited to upholding the "truth" in reporting. Approach three incorporates all forms of information warfare, including deception and disinformation, and uses the media to deceive the enemy and their targeted population. Examples include targeting opponent's websites, publishing counter-narratives, generating fictitious news releases, and/or generating alternative frames of interpretation. It is the third approach that has gained traction over the past five years, but it not necessarily that effective. This approach will continue to advance as the violent extremists continue to wage information warfare campaigns. The U.S. State Department's Center for Strategic Counterterrorism Communications provides a recent and interesting example of this last approach.

In May 2012, the state department's new Center for Strategic Communications targeted websites run by Al Qaeda's Yemeni branch. Members of the Center successfully changed Al Qaeda's message to one that illustrated how Al Qaeda actions in Yemen are actually harmful for Yemeni citizenry. In an effort to recruit members, Al Qaeda's affiliate in Yemen began posting propaganda on killing Americans on tribal websites. In forty-eight hours, a team from the Center altered the propaganda of killing Americans to instead show Al Qaeda's toll on Yemeni citizenry. Secretary of State Hillary Clinton attributed the success to a number of specialists fluent in Urdu, Arabic, and Somali who worked to "pre-empt, discredit, and outmaneuver extremist propagandists."[26] Specialists in the Center are also actively patrolling the web using social media and other tools to contradict Al Qaeda propaganda and highlight Al Qaeda's use of violence against Muslim civilians. Again in December 2013, the state department launched an English "Think Again and Turn Away" campaign to combat ISIS and Al Qaeda radicalization through video production and Twitter. The U.S. State Department is not the only organization attempting to battle ideas in the digital domain.

In January 2015, the French government launched a 1:56 counterpropaganda video against the Islamic State terror group's online recruitment strategy for fighters and Muslim women interested in becoming jihadi brides. The video's objective was to dissuade French Muslims from joining ISIS under the hashtag #Stopjihadism. The video juxtaposes ISIS propaganda footage that glorifies jihad with images of death and brutality inside the self-styled caliphate.[27] Finally, in August 2015, the Quilliam Foundation, British counter-extremism think-tank, as part of their #NotAnotherBrother campaign, released an anti-radicalization video to challenge ISIS recruiters. The video depicts a young British fighter somewhere in Iraq or Syria, wounded and alone in a decrepit apartment taking cover from a firefight. As the sounds of gunfire and bombs echo outside the apartment, he bleeds from his wound. He reads a letter sent from his apologetic older brother in the United Kingdom, who contributed and encouraged him to join ISIS. The video agency, Verbalisation, took four months to produce the video with input from military experts, psychologists, and linguists. The video was in response to a Google request to counter the ISIS jihadi narrative by exposing the group's "inhuman and atrocious" actions and viewpoints.²⁸ The video ends with the following quote, "Don't let your words turn our brothers into weapons."

Finally, the question is how to be proactive in the evolving nature of information warfare and to develop effective counterpropaganda methods. There is considerable debate among the armed services and other government agencies about how to label and define this type of warfare. In the U.S. security sector, information warfare is often described as an asymmetric strategy employed by rogue states in regional conflicts or terrorist groups.²⁹ While the definitional debate remains complicated because of the fact that information embraces so many disparate activities, the U.S. Air Force's definition of information warfare as "any action to deny, exploit, corrupt, or destroy the enemy's information and its functions; protecting ourselves against those actions; and exploiting our own military information functions" is sufficient.³⁰ Information warfare under this definition encompasses six means: psychological operations, electronic warfare, military deception, physical destruction, security measures, and information attacks. These six means blur the relationship between ideas and actions.

If information warfare against violent extremists will ever be successful, it has to be generated from an "inside out" perspective. This means that culture, context, and ideas need to be understood from an adherent's perspective, not as irrational psychological babble. In regards to addressing ideas, *Dark Ideas* affords a way to isolate certain innovations, analyze them in context, and provide a conceptual path forward. It is the hope that this text will inform future discussions on the connection between ideas and incidents of violence, how these ideas are transmitted, and the relationship of the idea to the men or women who advance them.

NOTES

1. Bjørgo, Tore. *Root Causes of Terrorism: Myths, Reality, and Ways Forward.* London: Routledge, 2005.

2. Morf, Gustav. *Terror in Quebec: Case Studies of the FLQ.* Toronto: Clarke, Irwin, 1970.

3. Juergensmeyer, Mark. *Terror in the Mind of God: The Global Rise of Religious Violence.* Berkley: University of California Press, 2003.

4. Anthropologists have also identified cultural similarities that transcend national boundaries to include Middle East and North African nations or MENA societies.

5. Said, Edward W. *Orientalism.* New York: Vintage Books, 1979.

6. Victoroff, Jeff "The Mind of the Terrorist: A Review and Critique of Psychological Approaches," *The Journal of Conflict Resolution* 49, no. 1 (February 1, 2005): 3–42.

7. Blowback, the term is used here as it applies to politically unintended consequences.

8. Simi, Pete and Robert Futrell. *American Swastika: Inside the White Power Movement's Hidden Spaces of Hate.* Lanham, MD: Rowman & Littlefield Publishers, 2010.

9. But the same date historically had a different meaning for Tim McVeigh because it represented the 200th anniversary of the Battle of Lexington, 1775 and also the two-year anniversary of Waco that ended the Branch Davidian siege.

10. Blumer, Herbert. *Symbolic Interactionism: Perspective and Method.* Berkeley: University of California Press, 1986.

11. Poverty and education level are examples.

12. Sproule, Michael J. "The Propaganda Analysis Movement since World War I." (1984).

13. Jowett, Garth S. and Victoria O'Donnell. *Propaganda & Persuasion.* Sage Publications, 2014.

14. Ibid.

15. Norris, Pippa Montague Kern, and Marion R. Just. *Framing Terrorism: The News Media, the Government, and the Public.* Psychology Press, 2003.

16. Morris, Travis. "Networking Vehement Frames: Neo-Nazi and Violent Jihadi Demagoguery." *Behavioral Sciences of Terrorism and Political Aggression* 6, no. 3 (2014): 163–182.

17. Morris, W. T., & University of Nebraska at Omaha. School of Criminology and Criminal Justice. (2011). Breaking the criminogenic code: a frame analysis of neo-Nazi and violent jihadi propaganda. Retrieved from http://pqdtopen.proquest.com/pubnum/3465747.html?FMT=AI

18. Morris, T. (2014). Networking vehement frames: neo-Nazi and violent jihadi demagoguery. Behavioral Sciences of Terrorism and Political Aggression, 6(3), 163–182. http://doi.org/10.1080/19434472.2014.922602

19. William Travis Morris. "Breaking the Criminogenic Code: A Frame Analysis of Neo-Nazi and Violent Jihadi Propaganda." (2011). Retrieved from http://pqdtopen. proquest.com/pubnum/3465747.html?FMT=AI

20. Ibid.

21. Ibid.

22. Ibid.

23. Taylor, Philip M. *Munitions of the Mind: A History of Propaganda.* Manchester University Press, 2003.

24. Paul, Christopher. *Strategic Communication: Origins, Concepts, and Current Debates* (ABC-CLIO, 2011).

25. "Executive Order 13584—Developing an Integrated Strategic Counterterrorism Communications Initiative | Whitehouse.gov," accessed August 30, 2015, https://www.whitehouse.gov/the-press-office/2011/09/09/executive-order-13584-developing-integrated-strategic-counterterrorism-c.

26. "US Targeted Al Qaeda Sites to Undermine Propaganda: Clinton—World— DAWN.COM," accessed August 30, 2015, http://www.dawn.com/news/721018/us-targeted-al-qaeda-sites-to-undermine-propaganda-clinton.

27. "Isis: France Launches Propaganda War against Islamic State with #StopJihadism Video," International Business Times UK, accessed August 30, 2015,

http://www.ibtimes.co.uk/isis-france-launches-propaganda-war-against-islamic-state-stopjihadism-video-1485560.

28. "Think-Tank Releases Anti-Radicalisation Video to Counter ISIS Propaganda," Newsweek, August 5, 2015, http://europe.newsweek.com/think-tank-releases-anti-radicalisation-video-counter-isis-propaganda-331225.

29. Paul, *Strategic Communication*.

30. "Cornerstones-Iw.html," accessed August 30, 2015, http://www.csse.monash.edu.au/courseware/cse468/2006/cornerstones-iw.html.

Appendix

Table A.1 Violent Extremists and Their Awlaki Connection

Name	Action	Link to Awlaki
Umar Farouk Abdulmutallab[1]	Indicted on December 15, 2010, on six counts of attempted use of a weapon of mass destruction; attempted murder with special aircraft jurisdiction of the United States; willful attempt to destroy an aircraft; willfully placing a destructive device in, upon, and in proximity to an aircraft; possession of a firearm destructive in furtherance of a crime of violence	Awlaki's student in Yemen
Zachary Adam Chester[2]	Convicted on February 24, 2011, for providing material support to a foreign terrorist organization, use of the Internet to incite violence, and indicted the murder of a U.S. citizen indicating violence against the writers of the television show, "South Park"	Told the FBI that he was inspired by Awlaki's sermons and was in direct contact with him via email
Nidal Malik Hasan[3]	Charged in December 2, 2009 with 13 counts of premeditated murder and 32 counts of attempted murder under the Uniform Code of Military Justice	Personally knew Awlaki and was in direct contact with him before the Fort Hood Attack
Samir Khan[4]	Editor and producer of Al Qaeda's *Inspire Magazine*	Interacted with Awlaki directly

Table A.1   Violent Extremists and Their Awlaki Connection

Name	Action	Link to Awlaki
Rajib Karim[5]	Worked as a British staff member at British airways and was requested by Awlaki to plant a bomb on a plane and pass through crucial air support security measures. Sentenced to 30 years in prison on March 18, 2011, after being convicted of possessing and collecting a record of information likely to be useful to a person committing or preparing for an act of terrorism	Was in direct email contact with Awlaki
Farooque Ahmed[6]	Convicted on April 11, 2011, for attempting to provide material support to a designated terrorist organization; collecting information to assist in planning a terrorist attack on a transit facility; and attempting to provide material support to terrorists	Awlaki's sermons and speeches were found by law enforcement at his home.
Mohamed Mahmood Alessa & Carlos "Omar" Eduardo Almonte[7]	Sentenced on June 20, 2013, for conspiring to murder persons outside the United States on behalf of the designated foreign terrorist organization al-Shabaab	Watched al-Awlaki's audio and video lectures
Betim Kaziu[8]	Convicted in July 2011 for a number of terrorism offenses, one being conspiracy to commit murder after traveling to Egypt in 2009	Inspired by Awlaki's sermons
Collen LaRose "Jihad Jane"[9]	Plead guilty on January 28, 2011, to four counts of terrorism-related charges	Posted on al-Awlaki's blog
Abdulhakem Mujahid Muhammad[10]	Sentenced to life without parole in July 2011 for the fatal shooting of a U.S. Army recruiter in Little Rock, Arkansas, and the attempted murder of another Army recruiter	Refers to Awlaki as his Sheikh
Paul Rockwood Junior[11]	Convicted on August 24, 2010, for making false statements to the FBI in a domestic terrorism investigation	States that he devoted himself to Awlaki's teaching.
Faisal Shahzad[12]	Sentenced to life in prison on October 5, 2010, for an attempted truck bomb in Times Square, New York City.	Told investigators that he was influenced by Awlaki's sermons
Fort Dix Plotters[13]	Three out of four sentenced to life on April 28, 2009, for planning an attack on Fort Dix, New Jersey	Possessed Awlaki's sermons and was recorded to state their importance

Table A.1 Violent Extremists and Their Awlaki Connection

Name	Action	Link to Awlaki
Roshonara Choudry[14]	Sentenced to life on November 3, 2010, for attempted murder of Stephen Timms due to his support for the 2003 invasion of Iraq	Told police he was inspired by Awlaki's lectures
Aabid Hussain Khan[15]	Convicted and sentenced to 12 years for possession of terrorism documents	Awlaki's sermons were seized after his arrest
Toronto 18[16]	Planned to carry out a series of attacks on various targets in Toronto, Canada; four convicted, seven plead guilty, and seven were cleared of charges	Members of the group used Awlaki's sermons at their Canadian training camp
Tsarnaev Brothers[17]	Sentenced to death on June 24, 2015, for killing three and wounding over 264 at the April 2013 Boston Marathon	Told investigators that he and his older brother learned how to create pressure cooker bombs from *Inspire* magazine

NOTES

1. "Al-Awlaki Directed Christmas 'Underwear Bomber' Plot, Justice Department Memo Says—The Washington Post," accessed August 30, 2015, https://www.washingtonpost.com/world/national-security/al-awlaki-directed-christmas-underwear-bomber-plot-justice-department-memo-says/2012/02/10/gIQArDOt4Q_story.html.

2. "Zachary Adam Chesser, Linked to 'South Park' Threats, Pleads Guilty—CSMonitor.com," accessed August 30, 2015, http://www.csmonitor.com/USA/Justice/2010/1020/Zachary-Adam-Chesser-linked-to-South-Park-threats-pleads-guilty.

3. Johnston, David and Shane, Scott. "Fort Hood Suspect Communicated With Radical Cleric, Authorities Say," The New York Times, November 9, 2009, http://www.nytimes.com/2009/11/10/us/10inquire.html.

4. Ordoñez-McClatchy, Franco Washington Bureau, "Files Show FBI Closing in on Al Qaida Blogger Samir Khan before He Slipped Away," Mcclatchydc, accessed August 30, 2015, http://www.mcclatchydc.com/news/nation-world/national/article24779683.html.

5. "Rajib Karim: The Terrorist inside British Airways—BBC News," accessed August 30, 2015, http://www.bbc.com/news/uk-12573824.

6. Cratty, Carol. "Guilty Plea Entered in Thwarted Metro Station Bomb Plot." CNN. April 11, 2011. Accessed July 11, 2016. http://www.cnn.com/2011/CRIME/04/11/virginia.bomb.plot/index.html.

7. "New Jersey Men Arrested for Attempting to Join Somali Terrorist Group," ADL, accessed August 30, 2015, http://www.adl.org/combating-hate/international-extremism-terrorism/c/alessa-almonte-shabaab.html.

8. "Brooklyn Man Sentenced to 27 Years in Prison for Conspiring to Kill U.S. Soldiers Abroad and Attempting to Provide Material Support to Al Shabaab," FBI, accessed August 30, 2015, https://www.fbi.gov/newyork/press-releases/2012/brooklyn-man-sentenced-to-27-years-in-prison-for-conspiring-to-kill-u.s.-soldiers-abroad-and-attempting-to-provide-material-support-to-al-shabaab.

9. "Countering Individual Jihad: Perspectives on Nidal Hasan and Colleen LaRose—globalECCO," accessed August 30, 2015, https://globalecco.org/countering-individual-jihad-perspectives-on-nidal-hasan-and-colleen-larose.

10. Dao, James. "A Muslim Son, a Murder Trial, and Many Questions," The New York Times, February 16, 2010, http://www.nytimes.com/2010/02/17/us/17convert.html.

11. "In Alaska, A Domestic Terrorist with a Deadly Plan," FBI, accessed August 30, 2015, https://www.fbi.gov/news/stories/2012/november/in-alaska-a-domestic-terrorist-with-a-deadly-plan/in-alaska-a-domestic-terrorist-with-a-deadly-plan.

12. Esposito, Richard, Chris Vlasto, and Chris Cuomo. "Sources: Shahzad Had Contact With Awlaki, Taliban Chief, and Mumbai Massacre Mastermind." ABC News. May 06, 2010, accessed July 11, 2016. http://abcnews.go.com/Blotter/faisal-shahzad-contact-awlaki-taliban-mumbai-massacre-mastermind/story?id=10575061

13. Baden Copel et al., "Anwar Al-Awlaki's Suspected Ties to Terror Plots," accessed August 30, 2015, http://www.nytimes.com/interactive/2011/09/30/world/middleeast/the-killing-of-anwar-al-awlaki.html.

14. Vikram Dodd and crime correspondent, "Roshonara Choudhry: Police Interview Extracts," The Guardian, November 3, 2010, sec. UK news, http://www.theguardian.com/uk/2010/nov/03/roshonara-choudhry-police-interview.

15. "The Global Intelligence Files—Anwar Al-Awlaki: MI5 Warns of the Al-Qaeda Preacher Targeting Britain," accessed August 30, 2015, https://wikileaks.org/gifiles/docs/15/1594356_anwar-al-awlaki-mi5-warns-of-the-al-qaeda-preacher-targeting.html.

16. "Anwar Al Awlaki: The New Osama Bin Laden?—Telegraph," accessed August 30, 2015, http://www.telegraph.co.uk/news/uknews/terrorism-in-the-uk/8009819/Anwar-al-Awlaki-the-new-Osama-bin-Laden.html.

17. "Dzhokhar Tsarnaev Trial: The Radicalization of Jahar—CNN.com," accessed August 30, 2015, http://www.cnn.com/2015/03/27/us/tsarnaev-13th-juror-jahar-radicalization/.

Bibliography

Adnan, Musallam. *From Secularism to Jihad: Sayyid Qutb and the Foundations of Radical Islamism.* Westport, CT: Praeger, 2005.

"Al-Awlaki Directed Christmas 'Underwear Bomber' Plot, Justice Department Memo Says—The Washington Post," accessed August 30, 2015, https://www.washingtonpost.com/world/national-security/al-awlaki-directed-christmas-underwear-bomber-plot-justice-department-memo-says/2012/02/10/gIQArDOt4Q_story.html.

"Al-Aulaqi v. Panetta—Constitutional Challenge to Killing of Three U.S. Citizens," *American Civil Liberties Union.* accessed August 30, 2015, https://www.aclu.org/cases/al-aulaqi-v-panetta-constitutional-challenge-killing-three-us-citizens.

almuwahideenmedia, "Interview with Shaykh Abu Muhammad Al Maqdisi (English)," *Al Muwahideen Media.* accessed August 30, 2015, https://almuwahideenmedia.wordpress.com/2015/02/09/interview-with-shaykh-abu-muhammad-al-maqdisi-english/.

"Anwar Al Awlaki: The New Osama Bin Laden?—Telegraph," accessed August 30, 2015, http://www.telegraph.co.uk/news/uknews/terrorism-in-the-uk/8009819/Anwar-al-Awlaki-the-new-Osama-bin-Laden.html.

"Anwar Al-Awlaki Describes Post-9/11 Mood in U.S.: Watch the Interview," *PBS NewsHour.* accessed August 30, 2015, http://www.pbs.org/newshour/rundown/a-post-911-interview-with-anwar-al-awlaki/.

As American As Apple Pie: How Anwar al-Awlaki Became the Face of Western Jihad / ICSR. (September 11, 2011). accessed July 11, 2016, http://icsr.info/2011/09/as-american-as-apple-pie-how-anwar-al-awlaki-became-the-face-of-western-jihad/

"Asharq Al-Awsat Interviews Umm Mohammed: The Wife of Bin Laden's Spiritual Mentor," *ASHARQ AL-AWSAT.* accessed August 30, 2015, http://english.aawsat.com/2006/04/article55266896/asharq-al-awsat-interviews-umm-mohammed-the-wife-of-bin-ladens-spiritual-mentor.

Atkins, Stephen E. *Holocaust Denial as an International Movement* (ABCCLIO,2009).

Atwan, Abdel Bari. *After Bin Laden: Al Qaeda, the Next Generation.* New York, NY: The New Press, 2013.

Azzām, Abdullah. *Defence of the Muslim Lands.* London: (Azzam Publications, 2002).

Azzām, Abdullah. *Join the Caravan*, Second Revised Edition (Azzam Publications, 2001).

Baden Copel et al., "Anwar Al-Awlaki's Suspected Ties to Terror Plots," accessed August 30, 2015, http://www.nytimes.com/interactive/2011/09/30/world/ middlee-ast/the-killing-of-anwar-al-awlaki.html.

Bergen, Peter L. *Manhunt: The Ten-year Search for Bin Laden from 9/11 to Abbot-tabad.* New York: Crown Publishers, 2012.

Bergen, Peter L. *The Osama Bin Laden I Know: An Oral History of Al-Qaeda's Leader.* New York: Free Press, 2006

Bergen, Peter L. *Holy War, Inc.: Inside the Secret World of Osama bin Laden.* New York: Free Press, 2001.

Berner, Brad K. *Jihad: Bin Laden in His Own Words : Declarations, Interviews, and Speeches.* Adelaide, SA: Peacock Books, 2007.

Bernstein, Lenny, Sari Horwitz, and Peter Holley. "Dylann Roof's Racist Manifesto: 'I Have No Choice'" Washington Post. (June 20, 2015). accessed July 11, 2016, http://www.washingtonpost.com/national/health-science/authorities-investigate-whether-racist-manifesto-was-written-by-sc-gunman/2015/06/20/f0bd3052–1762–11e5–9ddc-e3353542100c_story.html

Bjørgo, Tore. *Root Causes of Terrorism: Myths, Reality, and Ways Forward.* London: Routledge, 2005.

Blumer, Herbert. *Symbolic Interactionism: Perspective and Method.* Berkeley: University of California Press, 1986.

"'Breivik Manifesto' Details Chilling Attack Preparation," *BBC News.* accessed August 30, 2015, http://www.bbc.com/news/world-europe-14267007.

Braithwaite, Rodric. *Afgantsy: The Russians in Afghanistan, 1979–89.* New York: Oxford University Press, 2011.

"Brooklyn Man Sentenced to 27 Years in Prison for Conspiring to Kill U.S. Sol-diers Abroad and Attempting to Provide Material Support to Al Shabaab," FBI. accessed August 30, 2015, https://www.fbi.gov/newyork/press-releases/2012/brooklyn-man-sentenced-to-27-years-in-prison-for-conspiring-to-kill-u.s.-soldiers-abroad-and-attempting-to-provide-material-support-to-al-shabaab.

Brown, Adrian. "Osama Bin Laden's Death: How It Happened," *BBC News.* accessed August 30, 2015, http://www.bbc.com/news/ world-south-asia-13257330.

Burke, Jason. *Al-Qaeda: The True Story of Radical Islam.* London: Penguin, 2004.

Burns, John F. "Yemen Links to Bin Laden Gnaw at F.B.I. in Cole Inquiry," *The New York Times*, November 26, 2000, sec. World, http://www.nytimes. com/2000/11/26/world/yemen-links-to-bin-laden-gnaw-at-fbi-in-cole-inquiry.html.

"Cageprisoners.com—Serving the Caged Prisoners in Guantanamo Bay," accessed August 30, 2015, http://old.cageprisoners.com/articles.php?id=22926.

Callimachi, Rukmini. "Before Killing James Foley, ISIS Demanded Ransom From U.S.," *The New York Times*, August 20, 2014, accessed September 30, 2015, http://

www.nytimes.com/2014/08/21/world/middleeast/isis-pressed-for-ransom-before-killing-james-foley.html.

Calvert, John. *Sayyid Qutb and the Origins of Radical Islamism.* New York: Columbia University Press, 2010.

Calvert, John C. M. *The Striving* Shaykh: Abdullah Azzam and the Revival of Jihad. *Journal of Religion and Society.* Supplement Series 2, 2007.

Carroll, James. "The Bush Crusade. Sacred violence, again unleashed in 2001, could prove as destructive as in 1096." *The Nation.* September 20, 2004, accessed July 30, 2016, https://www.thenation.com/article/bush-crusade/

Caspi, David J., Joshua D. Freilich, and Steven M. Chermak. "Worst of the Bad: Violent White Supremacist Groups and Lethality," *Dynamics of Asymmetric Conflict* 5, no. 1 (March 1, 2012): 1–17, doi:10.1080/17467586.2012.679664.

"CF2R—Analysis of the Influence of Sayed Qutb's Islamist Ideology on the Development of Jihadism," accessed August 29, 2015, http://www.cf2r.org/fr/foreign-analyzes/analysis-of-the-influence-of-sayed-qutbs-islamist-ideology-on-the-development-of-djiha.prh.

"Charleston Shooting," *NPR.org.* accessed August 29, 2015, http://www.npr.org/tags/415878235/charleston-shooting.

Chesney, Robert. "Who May Be Killed? Anwar Al-Awlaki as a Case Study in the International Legal Regulation of Lethal Force," in *Yearbook of International Humanitarian Law—2010*, ed. M. N. Schmitt, Louise Arimatsu, and T. McCormack, Yearbook of International Humanitarian Law 13 (T. M. C. Asser Press, 2011), 3–60, http://link.springer.com/chapter/10.1007/978–90–6704–811–8_1.

"CNN—'Turner Diaries' Introduced in McVeigh Trial—Apr. 28, 1997," accessed August 30, 2015, http://www.cnn.com/US/9704/28/okc/.

"Conclave is talking about negotiations with Daesh." . المقدسي يتحدث عن مفاوضات مع داعش حول الكاسبة. accessed June 30, 2016, http://assabeel.net/local/item/90290-

"Cornerstones-Iw.html," accessed August 30, 2015, http://www.csse.monash.edu.au/courseware/cse468/2006/cornerstones-iw.html.

"Countering Individual Jihad: Perspectives on Nidal Hasan and Colleen LaRose—globalECCO," accessed August 30, 2015, https://globalecco.org/countering-individual-jihad-perspectives-on-nidal-hasan-and-colleen-larose.

Cratty, Carol. "Guilty Plea Entered in Thwarted Metro Station Bomb Plot." CNN. April 11, 2011. accessed July 11, 2016, http://www.cnn.com/2011/ CRIME/04/11/virginia.bomb.plot/index.html.

"Creativity Alliance—Sixteen Commandments," accessed August 29, 2015, http://creativityalliance.com/16commandments.htm.

"Creativity Movement," *Southern Poverty Law Center.* accessed August 29, 2015, https://www.splcenter.org/fighting-hate/extremist-files/group/creativity-movement-0.

Dao, James. "A Muslim Son, a Murder Trial, and Many Questions," The New York Times, February 16, 2010, http://www.nytimes.com/2010/02/17/us/17convert.html.

"David Duke.com," *David Duke.com.* accessed August 30, 2015, http://davidduke.com.

"David Duke vs. Thom Hartmann: The Confederate Flag | Thom Hartmann," accessed August 30, 2015, http://www.thomhartmann.com/bigpicture/ david-duke-vs-thom-hartmann-confederate-flag.

"David Duke," *Southern Poverty Law Center.* accessed August 30, 2015, https://www.splcenter.org/fighting-hate/extremist-files/individual/david-duke.

"Declaration of War by Osama Bin Laden, 1996," *Council on Foreign Relations.* accessed August 30, 2015, http://www.cfr.org/terrorist-leaders/declaration-war-osama-bin-laden-1996/p13174.

Dobratz, Betty A. "The Role of Religion in the Collective Identity of the White Racialist Movement," *Journal for the Scientific Study of Religion* 40, no. 2 (June 1, 2001): 287–301.

Duke, David Ernest. *My Awakening: A Path to Racial Understanding.* Covington, LW: Free Speech Press, 1998.

Duke, David. "David Duke Achieves Doctorate in Ukraine." September 09, 2005. accessed November 16, 2006, http://www.davidduke.com/index.php?p=394.

Dylan Storm Roof Manifesto." Daily Stormer. accessed July 11, 2016, http://www.dailystormer.com/dylann-storm-roof-manifesto/comment-page-1/.

"Dzhokhar Tsarnaev Trial: The Radicalization of Jahar—CNN.com," accessed August 30, 2015, http://www.cnn.com/2015/03/27/us/tsarnaev-13th-juror-jahar-radicalization/.

"Emerson, Steven. *American Jihad: The Terrorists Living Among Us.* New York: Free Press, 2002.

Esposito, Richard, Chris Vlasto, and Chris Cuomo. "Sources: Shahzad Had Contact With Awlaki, Taliban Chief, and Mumbai Massacre Mastermind." ABC News. May 06, 2010. accessed July 11, 2016, http://abcnews.go.com/ Blotter/faisal-shahzad-contact-awlaki-taliban-mumbai-massacre-mastermind/ story?id=10575061.

"Essays by Louis Beam on History, Government, Politics, Vietnam, Police State," accessed August 30, 2015, http://www.louisbeam.com/.

"Exclusive: Who Is Anwar Al-Awlaki? (Hasan's Va. Imam)." accessed July 11, 2016, http://www.freerepublic.com/focus/f-news/2383383/posts.

"Executive Order 13584—Developing an Integrated Strategic Counterterrorism Communications Initiative | Whitehouse.gov," accessed August 30, 2015, https://www.whitehouse.gov/the-press-office/2011/09/09/executive-order-13584-developing-integrated-strategic-counterterrorism-c.

Figueira, Daurius. *"Salafi Jihadi Discourse of Sunni Islam in the 21st Century": "The Discourse of Abu Muhammad Al-Maqdisi and Anwar Al-Awlaki."* Bloomington, IN: iUniverse, 2011.

Firestone, Reuven. *Jihād: The Origin of Holy War in Islam.* New York: Oxford University Press, 1999.

"Former Hate Music Promoter George Burdi Discusses His Experiences with Racism and the White Power Music Industry," *Southern Poverty Law Center.* accessed August 29, 2015, https://www.splcenter.org/fighting-hate/intelligence-report/2001/former-hate-music-promoter-george-burdi-discusses-his-experiences-racism-and-white-power

Gerges, Fawaz A. *The Far Enemy: Why Jihad Went Global.* Cambridge; Cambridge University Press, 2005.

Gessen, Masha. *The Brothers: The Road to an American Tragedy.* New York, NY: Riverhead Books, 2015.

Goodrick-Clarke, Nicholas. *Black Sun: Aryan Cults, Esoteric Nazism, and the Politics of Identity.* New York: New York University Press, 2002.

Griffin, Robert S. *The Fame of a Dead Man's Deeds: An Up-Close Portrait of White Nationalist William Pierce.* Bloomington, IN: AuthorHouse, 2001.

Haley, Alex. "George Lincoln Rockwell: A Candid Conversation with the Fanatical Führer of the American Nazi Party." *Playboy* 13 (1966): 71–74.

Haroro J. Ingram. *The Charismatic Leadership Phenomenon in Radical and Militant Islamism.* New York, NY: Routledge, 2016.

Hassan, Muhammad Haniff. *The Father of Jihad:'Abd Allāh "Azzām"s Jihad Ideas and Implications to National Security:* 2. ICP, 2014.

Hitler, Adolf and Dietrich Eckart. *Bolshevism from Moses to Lenin: A Dialogue between Adolf Hitler and Me.* Hillsboro, WV: National Vanguard Books, 1999.

Holton, Christopher. "'Lone Wolf' or Jihadi?," *Center for Security Policy,* (July 31, 2015) accessed August 30, 2015, https://www.centerforsecuritypolicy.org/2015/07/31/lone-wolf-or-jihadi/.

Honigsheim, Paul K., Peter Etzkorn, and Paul Hongisheim. *Sociologists and Music: An Introduction to the Study of Music and Society.* New Brunswick: Transaction Publishers, 1989.

"House of Commons Hansard Debates for 18 Dec 2003 (pt 18)," accessed August 30, 2015, http://www.parliament.the-stationery-office.co.uk/pa/cm200304/cmhansrd/vo031218/debtext/31218–18.htm.

"In Alaska, A Domestic Terrorist with a Deadly Plan," FBI. accessed August 30, 2015, https://www.fbi.gov/news/stories/2012/november/in-alaska-a-domestic-terrorist-with-a-deadly-plan/in-alaska-a-domestic-terrorist-with-a-deadly-plan.

"Inspire Magazine | JIHADOLOGY," accessed August 30, 2015, http://jihadology.net/category/inspire-magazine/.

"Inspire Magazine—Make a Bomb in the Kitchen of Your Mom," accessed August 30, 2015, https://whitehouse.gov1.info/cyber-warfare/inspire-magazine.html.

"ISIS, Abu Bakr Naji, And Applied Qutb | The American Conservative," accessed August 29, 2015, http://www.theamericanconservative.com/dreher/isis-abu-bakr-naji-sayyid-qutb-jihad-islam/.

"ISIS Burns Hostage Alive," MovingImage, *Fox News,* (February 3, 2015), http://video.foxnews.com/v/4030583977001/warning-extremely-graphic-video-isis-burns-hostage-alive/.

"Isis: France Launches Propaganda War against Islamic State with #StopJihadism Video," *International Business Times UK.* accessed August 30, 2015, http://www.ibtimes.co.uk/isis-france-launches-propaganda-war-against-islamic-state-stopjihadism-video-1485560.

Johnston, David Cay. "William Pierce, 69, Neo-Nazi Leader, Dies," *The New York Times,* July 24, 2002, sec. U.S., http://www.nytimes.com/2002/07/24/us/william-pierce-69-neo-nazi-leader-dies.html.

Johnston, David and Shane, Scott. "Fort Hood Suspect Communicated With Radical Cleric, Authorities Say," *The New York Times,* November 9, 2009, accessed June 17, 2015, http:// www.nytimes.com/2009/11/10/us/10inquire.html.

"Jordanian Pilot Kaseasbeh Burned Alive by Islamic State; Jordan Executes IS Requested Prisoner Rishawi in Response," *LeakSource*. accessed August 29, 2015, http://leaksource.info/2015/02/04/jordanian-pilot-kaseasbeh-burned-alive-by-islamic-state-jordan-executes-is-requested-prisoner-rishawi-in-response/.

Jowett, Garth S. and Victoria O'Donnell. *Propaganda & Persuasion*. Thousand Oaks, CA: Sage Publications, 2014.

Juergensmeyer, Mark. *Terror in the Mind of God: The Global Rise of Religious Violence*. Berkley: University of California Press, 2003.

Kazimi, Nibras. "A Virulent Ideology in Mutation: Zarqawi Upstages Maqdisi." *Current Trends in Islamist Ideology* 2 (2005): 59.

Kepel, Gilles. *Muslim Extremism in Egypt: The Prophet and Pharaoh*. Berkley: University of California Press, 1985.

Kepel, Gilles, Jean-Pierre Milelli, and Pascale Ghazaleh. *Al Qaeda in Its Own Words*. Cambridge, MA: Belknap Press of Harvard University, 2008.

Griffin, Robert S. *The Fame of a Dead Man's Deeds: An Up-Close Portrait of White Nationalist William Pierce*. Bloomington, IN: 1st Book Library, 2001.

Khan, Azmat. "The Magazine That 'Inspired' the Boston Bombers—Al Qaeda In Yemen," *FRONTLINE*. accessed August 30, 2015, http://www.pbs.org/wgbh/pages/frontline/iraq-war-on-terror/topsecretamerica/the-magazine-that-inspired-the-boston-bombers/.

Klassen, Ben. *Nature's Eternal Religion*. Milwaukee, WI: Church of the Creator, 1992.

Klassen, Ben P.M. *The White Man's Bible*. CreateSpace Independent Publishing Platform, 2011.

Klassen, Ben. P.M. *Trials, Tribulations, Triumphs: A History of the Church of the Creator During Its 10 Year Domicile in the State of North Carolina, Coordinated with Biographical Details During the Same Period*. Niceville, FL: Church of the Creator, 1993.

Kleg, Milton. *Hate, Prejudice, and Racism*. Albany: State University of New York Press, 1993.

Kramer, Martin. "Fundamentalist Islam at Large: The Drive for Power." *Middle East Quarterly*, June 1, 1996, accessed May 29, 2016, http://www.meforum.org/304/fundamentalist-islam-at-large-the-drive-for-power.

Kubizek, August. *The Young Hitler I Knew*. London: Greenhill Books, 2006.

Lane, David and Lane, Katja. *Deceived, Damned & Defiant: The Revolutionary Writings of David Lane*. St. Maries, Idaho. HC 01 Box 268K, St. Maries 83861: 14 Word Press, 1999.

Lock, Helen. "Isis vs Isil vs Islamic State: What Do They Mean—and Why Does It Matter?" *The Independent*. accessed August 29, 2015, http://www.independent.co.uk/news/world/middle-east/isis-vs-isil-vs-islamic-state—what-is-in-a-name-9731894.html.

"Louis Beam," accessed August 30, 2015, http://archive.adl.org/learn/ext_us/beam.html; "Leadership vs. Leaderless Resistance: The Militant White Separatist Movement's Operating Model | Foundation for Defense of Democracies," accessed August 30, 2015, http://www.defenddemocracy.org/media-hit/leadership-vs-leaderless-resistance-the-militant-white-separatist-movement/.

"Louis Beam," *Southern Poverty Law Center*. accessed August 30, 2015, https://
www.splcenter.org/fighting-hate/extremist-files/individual/louis-beam.

Macdonald, Andrew. *The Turner Diaries*. Fort Lee, NJ: Barricade Books, 1996.

MacEion, Denis. "Anwar Al-Awlaki: 'I Pray That Allah Destroys America,'" *Middle
East Quarterly*, Spring 17, no. 2 (March 1, 2010): 13–19. http://www.meforum.
org/2649/anwar-al-awlaki-pray-allah-destroys-america.

Maher, Shiraz. November 25, 2011 at 4:30 Am http://www.gatestoneinstitute.
org/2609/Inspire-Magazine-Open-Source-Jihad, "'Inspire' Magazine: Open Source
Jihad," *Gatestone Institute*. accessed August 30, 2015, http://www.gatestoneinsti-
tute.org/2609/inspire-magazine-open-source-jihad.

Mastors, Elena and Alyssa Deffenbaugh. *The Lesser Jihad: Recruits and the Al-
Qaida Network*. Lanham, MD: Rowman & Littlefield, 200).

"Matt Hale," *Southern Poverty Law Center*. accessed August 29, 2015, https://www.
splcenter.org/fighting-hate/extremist-files/individual/matt-hale.

McCants, William and Jarret Brachman, *Militant Ideology Atlas: Research Compendium*. West Point, NY: Combating Terrorism Center, 2006.

McGregor, Andrew. "'Jihad and the Rifle Alone': 'Abdullah 'Azzam and the Islamist
Revolution," *Journal of Conflict Studies* 23, no. 2 (February 21, 2006), accessed
October 21, 2016 https://journals.lib.unb.ca/index.php/JCS/article/view/219;
Azzam, Join the Caravan.

Michael, George. *Lone Wolf Terror and the Rise of Leaderless Resistance*. Nashville:
Vanderbilt University Press, 2012

Michel, Lou and Dan Herbeck. *American Terrorist: Timothy McVeigh and the
Oklahoma City Bombing*. New York: Regan Books, 2001.

Mitchell, Richard P. *The Society of the Muslim Brothers*. London: Oxford University
Press, 1969.

Morf, Gustav. *Terror in Quebec: Case Studies of the FLQ*. Toronto: Clarke, Irwin, 1970.

Morris, Travis. "Networking Vehement Frames: Neo-Nazi and Violent Jihadi Demagoguery," *Behavioral Sciences of Terrorism and Political Aggression* 6, no. 3
(September 2, 2014): 163–82, doi:10.1080/19434472.2014.922602.

Morris, W. T. and University of Nebraska at Omaha. School of Criminology and
Criminal Justice. (2011). *Breaking the criminogenic code: a frame analysis of neo-
Nazi and violent jihadi propaganda*. accessed September 21, 2015, http://pqdtopen.
proquest.com/pubnum/3465747.html?FMT=AI.

Musallam, Adnan. *From Secularism to Jihad: Sayyid Qutb and the Foundations of
Radical Islamism*, First Edition. Santa Barbara, CA: Praeger, 2005. 70.

"Music and the Holocaust: Music amongst the Hitler Youth," accessed August
29, 2015, http://holocaustmusic.ort.org/politics-and-propaganda/third-reich/
music-hitler-youth/.

"National Alliance," *Southern Poverty Law Center*. accessed August 30, 2015,
https://www.splcenter.org/fighting-hate/extremist-files/group/national-alliance.

"New Jersey Men Arrested for Attempting to Join Somali Terrorist Group,"
ADL. accessed August 30, 2015, http://www.adl.org/combating-hate/international-
extremism-terrorism/c/alessa-almonte-shabaab.html.

Nietzsche, Friedrich, Thomas Common, and H. James. Birx. *Thus Spake Zarathustra*.
Buffalo, NY: Prometheus Books, 1993.

Norris, Pippa Montague Kern, and Marion R. Just. *Framing Terrorism: The News Media, the Government, and the Public*. New York, NY: Psychology Press, 2003.

Obermayer, Herman. *American Nazi Party: Northern Virginia Sun, Arlington, Virginia, 1958–1984*. Cambridge, MA: Nieman Foundation, Harvard University, 1997.

"Obituary: Anwar Al-Awlaki," *BBC News*. accessed August 30, 2015, http://www.bbc.com/news/world-middle-east-11658920.

"Open Source Jihad On America | SOFREP." SOFREP. May 12, 2014. accessed July 11, 2016, https://sofrep.com/35355/open-source-jihad-americans/.

Ordoñez-McClatchy, Franco Washington Bureau, "Files Show FBI Closing in on Al Qaida Blogger Samir Khan before He Slipped Away," Mcclatchydc. accessed August 30, 2015, http://www.mcclatchydc.com/news/nation-world/national/article24779683.html.

"Osama Bin Laden—Fatwa—Background and Declaration of War against the Americans Ocupying the Two Holy Places," accessed August 30, 2015, http://www.mideastweb.org/osamabinladen1.htm.

"Osama Bin Laden's Jihad." Osama Bin Laden. accessed July 11, 2016, http://mideastweb.org/osamabinladen1.htm.

"Osama Bin Laden: Famous Quotes—Telegraph," accessed August 30, 2015, http://www.telegraph.co.uk/news/worldnews/asia/afghanistan/8487347/Osama-bin-Laden-famous-quotes.html.

Pantucci, Raffaello. "What Have We Learned about Lone Wolves from Anders Behring Breivik?," *Perspectives on Terrorism* 5, no. 5–6 (July 12, 2011).

Paul, Christopher. *Strategic Communication: Origins, Concepts, and Current Debates* (ABC-CLIO, 2011).

Pierce, William. "Rockwell: A National Socialist Life" | Counter-Currents Publishing. CounterCurrents Publishing. accessed July 11, 2016, http://www.counter-currents.com/2012/03/rockwella-national-socialist-life/.

"Profile: IS-Held Jordanian Pilot Moaz Al-Kasasbeh," *BBC News*. accessed August 29, 2015, http://www.bbc.com/news/world-middle-east-31021927.

Qutb, Sayyid. *Milestones*. Islamic Book Service, 2006. Print. Pp. 20

Qutb, Sayyid. *Milestones*, April 12, 2013, http://gemsofislamism.tripod.com/milestones.html.

Qutb, Sayyid. *The Political Thought of Sayyid Qutb: The Theory of Jahiliyyah*. London: Routledge, 2006.

Qutb, Sayyid, M.A. Salahi and A.A. Shamis, *In the Shade of the Qur'ān*. London: MWH, 1979.

"RAHOWA LYRICS," accessed August 29, 2015, http://www.metallyrica.com/r/rahowa_us.html.

"Rajib Karim: The Terrorist inside British Airways—BBC News," accessed August 30, 2015, http://www.bbc.com/news/uk-12573824.

Riedel, Bruce O. *The Search for Al Qaeda: Its Leadership, Ideology, and Future*, Washington, D.C.: Brookings Institution Press, 2010.

"Remarks by the President at the 'Change of Office' Chairman of the Joint Chiefs of Staff Ceremony," *Whitehouse.gov*. accessed August 31, 2015, https://www.whitehouse.gov/the-press-office/2011/09/30/remarks-president-change-office-chairman-joint-chiefs-staff-ceremony.

Rockwell, George Lincoln. *White Power*. Dallas: Ragnarok Press, 1967.

Rockwell, George Lincoln. *This Time the* World. New York: Parliament House, 1963.

Roggio, Bill. "The Arrest of Abu Musab Al-Suri?" *The Long War Journal*. November, 3, 2005. accessed August 30, 2015, http://www.longwarjournal.org/archives/2005/11/the_arrest_of_a.php.

Rose, David D. *The Emergence of David Duke and the Politics of Race*. Chapel Hill: University of North Carolina Press, 1992.

Roy, Olivier. *Globalized Islam: The Search for a New Ummah*. New York: Columbia University Press, 2004, 289.

Sageman, Marc. *Leaderless Jihad: Terror Networks in the Twenty-First Century*. Philadelphia: University of Pennsylvania Press, 2008.

Said, Edward W. *Orientalism*. New York: Vintage Books, 1979.

Sakolsky, Ronald B. and Fred Wei-han. Ho. *Sounding Off!: Music as Subversion/resistance/revolution*. Brooklyn, NY: Autonomedia, 1995.

Samuels, David. "The New Mastermind of Jihad," *Wall Street Journal*, April 7, 2012, sec. Life and Style. accessed September 2, 2016. http://www.wsj.com/articles/SB10001424052702303299604577323750859163544.

Sandler, Todd and Harvey E. Lapan, "The Calculus of Dissent: An Analysis of Terrorists' Choice of Targets," *Synthese* 76, no. 2 (August 1988): 245–61, doi:10.1007/BF00869591; Philip Keefer and Norman Loayza, *Terrorism, Economic Development, and Political Openness*. New York: Cambridge University Press, 2008.

Savitri, Devi. *The Lightning and the Sun*. Buffalo, NY: Samisdat, 1958.

Scheuer, Michael. *Osama Bin Laden*. Oxford: Oxford University Press, 2011.

Schmaltz, William H. *Hate: George Lincoln Rockwell and the American Nazi Party*. Washington, D.C.: Brassey's, 1999.

"SEDITIONIST." Leaderless Resistance. accessed July 11, 2016, http://www.louis-beam.com/leaderless.htm.

Selections from 'The Lone Wolf Creed.' Anonymous. (2000, May). Advice for the Lone Wolf. *White Aryan Resistance Magazine*, 5. Often attributed to Tom Metzger.

Shane, Scott. "The Lessons of Anwar Al-Awlaki," *The New York Times*, August 27, 2015, accessed July 30, 2015, http://www.nytimes.com/2015/08/30/magazine/the-lessons-of-anwar-al-awlaki.html.

Shane, Scott. "U.S. Approves Targeted Killing of American Cleric—The New York Times," accessed August 30, 2015, http://www.nytimes.com/2010/04/07/world/middleeast/07yemen.html.

Sheikh Terra feat Soul Salah Crew Dirty Kuffar—YouTube. (n.d.). accessed June 8, 2016, from https://www.youtube.com/watch?v=SWP_95eSLBI.

Shepard, William E. "Sayyid Qutb's Doctrine of Jāhiliyya," *International Journal of Middle East Studies* 35, no. 4 (November 1, 2003): 521–45.

Simi, Pete and Robert Futrell. *American Swastika: Inside the White Power Movement's Hidden Spaces of Hate*. Lanham, MD: Rowman & Littlefield Publishers, 2010.

Simi, Pete and Robert Futrell, "Neo-Nazi Movements in Europe and the United States," in *The Wiley-Blackwell Encyclopedia of Social and Political Movements*. Lanham, MD: Blackwell Publishing Ltd, 2013.

Simmonelli, Frederick J. *American Fuehrer: George Lincoln Rockwell and the American Nazi Party*. Urbana: University of Illinois Press, 1999.

Sivan, Emmanuel. *Radical Islam: Medieval Theology and Modern Politics*. New Haven: Yale University Press, 1985.

Smith, Brent L. *Terrorism in America: Pipe Bombs and Pipe Dreams*. Albany: SUNY Press, 1994.

Solomon, Ariel Ben. "Al-Qaida Faction Calls Its New English Magazine 'Palestine'" (August, 20, 2014) The Jerusalem Post. accessed July 11, 2016, http://www.jpost.com/Middle-East/Al-Qaida-faction-calls-its-new-English-magazine-Palestine-371579.

Sproule, J. Michael. (1984). "The Propaganda Analysis Movement since World War I." Paper presented at the 70th Annual Meeting of the Speech Communication Association, Chicago, IL, 1–4 November

"Statement by the President," *Whitehouse.gov*. accessed August 29, 2015, https://www.whitehouse.gov/the-press-office/2014/08/20/statement-president.

"Statement by the President on the Shooting in Charleston, South Carolina," *Whitehouse.gov*. accessed August 29, 2015, https://www.whitehouse.gov/the-press-office/2015/06/18/statement-president-shooting-charleston-south-carolina.

"START.umd.edu," accessed August 29, 2015, http://www.start.umd.edu/.

Suellentrop, Chris. "Abdullah Azzam," *Slate*, April 16, 2002, http://www.slate.com/articles/news_and_politics/assessment/2002/04/abdullah_azzam.html.

Sullivan, Cheryl. "Why Yemen Claims Role in US Drone Strike on Cleric Anwar Al-Awlaki," *Christian Science Monitor*, May 7, 2011, http://www.csmonitor.com/USA/2011/0507/Why-Yemen-claims-role-in-US-drone-strike-on-cleric-Anwar-al-Awlaki.

Tal, Nahman. *Radical Islam in Egypt and Jordan*. Sussex Academic Press, 2005.

Tally, Stephan. "The Method of a Neo-Nazi Mogul," *The New York Times*, February 25, 1996, sec. Magazine, http://www.nytimes.com/1996/02/25/magazine/the-method-of-a-neo-nazi-mogul.html.

"Targeting Anwar Al-Awlaki Was Legal, Justice Department Said—The New York Times," accessed August 30, 2015, http://www.nytimes.com/2014/06/24/us/justice-department-found-it-lawful-to-target-anwar-al-awlaki.html.

Taylor, Philip M. *Munitions of the Mind: A History of Propaganda*. (Manchester University Press, 2003).

"The Awlaki Effect," *The Investigative Project on Terrorism*. accessed August 30, 2015, http://www.investigativeproject.org/2323/the-awlaki-effect.

"The Global Intelligence Files—Anwar Al-Awlaki: MI5 Warns of the Al-Qaeda Preacher Targeting Britain," accessed August 30, 2015, https://wikileaks.org/gifiles/docs/15/1594356_anwar-al-awlaki-mi5-warns-of-the-al-qaeda-preacher-targeting.html.

"The ISIS Murder of Jordanian Pilot Moaz Al-Kasasbeh: 'Healing the Believer's Chests' (Complete Uncensored Video) | Sharia Unveiled," accessed August 29, 2015, https://shariaunveiled.wordpress.com/2015/02/08/the-isis-murder-of-jordanian-pilot-moaz-al-kasasbeh-healing-the-believers-chests-complete-uncensored-video/.

"The Islamic State's (ISIS, ISIL) Magazine | Clarion Project." ClarionProject.org. accessed July 11, 2016, http://www.clarionproject.org/news/islamic-state-isis-isil-propaganda-magazine-dabiq.

"Think-Tank Releases Anti-Radicalisation Video to Counter ISIS Propaganda," *Newsweek*, August 5, 2015, http://europe.newsweek.com/think-tank-releases-anti-radicalisation-video-counter-isis-propaganda-331225.

"Timeline: How Norway's Terror Attacks Unfolded," *BBC News*. accessed August 30, 2015, http://www.bbc.com/news/world-europe-14260297.

Toth James. *Sayyid Qutb: The Life and Legacy of a Radical Islamic Intellectual.* Oxford: Oxford University Press, 2013.

"US Targeted Al Qaeda Sites to Undermine Propaganda: Clinton—World—DAWN.COM," accessed August 30, 2015, http://www.dawn.com/news/721018/us-targeted-al-qaeda-sites-to-undermine-propaganda-clinton.

Victoroff, Jeff. "The Mind of the Terrorist: A Review and Critique of Psychological Approaches," *The Journal of Conflict Resolution* 49, no. 1 (February 1, 2005): 3–42.

Vikram Dodd and crime correspondent, "Roshonara Choudhry: Police Interview Extracts," *The Guardian*, November 3, 2010, sec. UK news, accessed June 30, 2016, http://www.theguardian.com/uk/2010/nov/03/roshonara-choudhry-police-interview.

Wagemakers, Joas. "Maqdisi in the Middle: An inside Account of the Secret Negotiations to Free a Jordanian Pilot « Jihadica," (February, 11, 2015). accessed August 30, 2015, http://www.jihadica.com/maqdisi-in-the-middle-an-inside-account-of-the-secret-negotiations-to-free-a-jordanian-pilot/.

Weaver, Mary Anne. "The Short, Violent Life of Abu Musab Al-Zarqawi—The Atlantic," (June 8, 2006). accessed August 30, 2015, http://www.theatlantic.com/

"What We Have Learned Since ISIS Declared a Caliphate One Year Ago | TIME," accessed August 29, 2015, http://time.com/3933568/isis-caliphate-one-year/.

White, Jonathan. R. "Political Eschatology A Theology of Antigovernment Extremism," *American Behavioral Scientist* 44, no. 6 (February 1, 2001): 937–56, doi:10.1177/00027640121956601.

Whitsel, Brad. "The Turner Diaries and Cosmotheism: William Pierce's Theology," *Nova Religio: The Journal of Alternative and Emergent Religions* 1, no. 2 (April 1, 1998): 183–97, doi:10.1525/nr.1998.1.2.183.

"William Pierce," *Southern Poverty Law Center*. accessed August 30, 2015, https://www.splcenter.org/fighting-hate/extremist-files/individual/william-pierce.

Wright, Lawrence. *The Looming Tower: Al-Qaeda and the Road to 9/11*. New York: Vintage Books, 2006.

"You Can't Kill an Idea," *The Huffington Post*. accessed August 29, 2015, http://www.huffingtonpost.com/robert-koehler/you-cant-kill-an-idea_b_830881.html.

"Zachary Adam Chesser, Linked to 'South Park' Threats, Pleads Guilty—CSMonitor.com," accessed August 30, 2015, http://www.csmonitor.com/USA/Justice/2010/1020/Zachary-Adam-Chesser-linked-to-South-Park-threats-pleads-guilty.

"Zarqawi Mentor Maqdisi Free Again via @intelwire," accessed August 30, 2015, http://news.intelwire.com/2008/03/zarqawi-mentor-maqdisi-free-again.html.

Zimmerman, John C. Zimmerman. "Sayyid Qutb's Influence on the 11 September Attacks," *Terrorism and Political Violence* 16, no. 2 (January 1, 2004): 222–52, doi: 10.1080/09546550480993.

Index

Note: Page references for figures are *italicized*.

About the Author

Travis Morris, assistant professor of criminology and criminal justice, is currently the director of Norwich University's Peace and War Center. The mission of the Center is to promote discussions and understanding of war and its effects; to convey that there is always a relationship between peace and war; to advance interdisciplinary knowledge for students, scholars, and practitioners on the relationship between peace and war at local, national, and global levels. Dr. Morris holds a PhD from the University of Nebraska, an MS in criminal justice from Eastern Kentucky University, and a BA in criminology from Northern Illinois University. He was a Ranger-qualified infantry officer with the 10th Mountain Division, U.S. Army, and a police officer in Lexington, KY. His research interests include violent extremist propaganda analysis, information warfare, and comparative justice systems. He has published on the relationship between policing, peacekeeping, counterterrorism, and counterinsurgency and has conducted ethnographic research in Yemen and published on how crime intersects with formal and informal justice systems in a sociocultural context.

Lightning Source UK Ltd.
Milton Keynes UK
UKHW01f2155130918
328755UK00001B/27/P